BIBLIO

THE INTIMATE CONFESSIONS OF A USED-BOOK DEALER

"The author in his bookshop work area February 1997"

BIBLIO

THE INTIMATE CONFESSIONS
OF A USED-BOOK DEALER

BY RALPH A. CASPERSON

RALPH A. CASPERSON BOOKS

1997

Printed and bound by
JOHNSON GRAPHICS
DECATUR, MICHIGAN

Published for

RALPH A. CASPERSON BOOKS
1303 Buchanan Road, Box 634
Niles, Michigan 49120-0634

BY

INVICTUS
P.O. BOX 317
DECATUR, MICHIGAN 49045

ISBN - 1-883228-15-8

First Edition March 1997

DEDICATION

This work must be dedicated to Harriette Barnette and Don Allen, bookmen who taught me their trade. To Victoria Brehm, scholar, teacher, author, editor, and friend who stimulated me to sharpen my pencils and taught me how to use them.

Lastly, though she's really first, to Doris my life mate, who, among many other things transcribed the scratching of those pencils into readable type.

Beauty, it is said, is in the eye of the beholder.
The most beautiful thing ever beheld by a
book collector is an empty shelf.

R.A.C. - MT

The following introduction by Victoria Brehm was written after she, and her dogs, had spent a weekend with Ralph and Doris Casperson in their home and bookshop. While there she read the unfinished manuscript of this book.

Vicky never gave a thought to the fact that her letter would be adopted for this book's introduction. Her letter is a "bread and butter" letter yes, but it also captures the spirit of the message on the following pages far better than if it had been written as an introduction on purpose.

Victoria Brehm is a published author having written several books and many articles mostly about women's roles on the Great Lakes. She holds a PHD from the University of Iowa where she was employed in their writing school.

Sunday night

Dear Doris and Ralph:

The more I think about The Book the happier I am. And I keep remembering things you've both talked about: interior designers buying pretty bindings that will then be chopped up to fit a shelf, for example. I think you have so many, many stories to tell together that this should be a wonderful book. Other book dealers who've written tell about famous deals and famous books, but you can tell about the people who buy and sell them, and perhaps I'm prejudiced, but the people seem far more interesting. But that is my view, and finally, I'm not a book collector--or dealer for that matter. I am finally less interested in the book itself than what it says.

I've also thought about why I keep coming to your shop and buying more than I can afford, since I don't ever do that in other bookshops. Why with Ralph? (And no, it's not because you're cute. Sorry.) But I think that you've created mystery and intelligence. There's always a feeling that around the next pile of books or overloaded shelf, I'll find a wonderful book that will teach me something. And, in fact, usually I do. In other words, you have created a bookshop as treasure chest and we all get to look through it. Yeah, it's small, it's cramped, and it seems old, even though it's not. But there is the great sense of some treasure buried there, and the wonder is, I usually find it. Part of that is the small space, part of that is the stock (which is really good), part of that, as you well know, is personality. Ralph is, finally, an expert marketer, a superb salesman, since he's been selling things all his life. I thought today on the way home that Ralph started selling things at about the age when I started seriously writing: which is why Ralph can sell anything and I can look at anything and make it work as prose. It's all we've ever done and eventually you do learn your trade. (Doris, of course, appears to have always made things function and still does. Thank God.)

Lord knows I've been in wonderful used book shops all over the country, but yours is special. It appears to promise little, yet it gives so much. It appears disorganized, yet I always find things. It almost appears nonchalant. It's always as if you sort of did this on the back stroke and it just seemed to work. That's crazy, of course, you both worked like hell--but it doesn't show. And that is how we finally describe grace. And talent. To do what others try to do but with less effort and more success and enjoy yourselves in the bargain. In a world that is hard-edged, sharp, clean, and brightly lighted--harsh, in a word--you've created a place that is messy, small, comfortable, and interesting: all values that have been lost. Walking into your bookshop is like walking into the home many of us never knew: warm, inviting, messy enough to be comfortable, and always interesting. If you cleaned up all the piles of stuff on the floor, and made neat shelf labels, etc., etc., and dressed right, the ambiance would be gone. (God knows, I expect Doris has tried, but it's OK.)

Then, of course, there's both of you. When you eventually sell the shop, it will never be the same, since there won't be bean soup and conversation and love. You have just made all of us lone, wandering scholars and book people the kids you never had and drawn us into your world of good food, good books, and good conversation. What an incredible gift! That's finally the story you have to tell, and what a story it will be. How you make a place that could be like so many other places but because of the people involved, becomes incredibly special. You can't sell that. You can't even pass it on. Because it finally doesn't have much to do with books. To be blunt, most used-bookshop people are wierd as hell and don't really like other people. They like books. They don't even like what's in the books; they just like books. They don't appear to understand that books are life, and life doesn't stop at the bookshop door. That finally a first edition is wonderful, but the whole point of any first edition is that it's wonderful because of what it says. There are lots of first editions that are worthless because they say nothing. There are lots of truly beautiful books that are worthless because they say nothing. Books, finally, are about people: what they thought, what they did, what mattered. And so by adopting all of us you have made the transition from the dead text to the living thought--you've brought the bookshop into the living room where it can live. Where it belongs. And that is a special gift.

So celebrate that gift. Tell us that finally the books don't really matter. What matters is who reads them, buys them, loves them. Without this, book dealing just becomes another business and books become just another Yuppie collectible. And why should we care about that? We of this generation think we can buy anything and will so possess what we buy. In fact, we never do. That explains why the great book shop I used to go to in Washington, D.C., was finally cold and I never bought many books there: the lighting was harsh, the shelves were too high, the staff didn't give a damn, and books were simply another commodity in a city that thrived on commodities. Neat bookshops, like neat desks, are a sign of small minds. Or minds that have never been tested or had experiences. That believe everything can be categorized--and of course, little can ever be satisfactorily categoried truthfully.

How do I say that what you've created is magical? And how do you get that down in prose? *Ach du leiber Gott*, I have no idea. Better you should try to describe the butterfly's wing. You might have more success. You may find that to truly write about what you've done the past 25 years-or however long you've done it--becomes impossible.

It is not so many books sold, or bought, or resold, or so many people in and out. It probably has more to do with bean soup and adopted dogs and wierd scholars and love. That's what you've created, like it or not. How many of us have you adopted and in so doing given us the courage to go on in impossible situations, whether you knew it or not?

Finally you have done what the older generation (how you must hate that. Sorry) can do for the younger: given us a model for how to live. You teach us we can do what we dream. You can take risks if we're willing to work hard enough. We can do OK leaving the computerized, industrialized, officized world of the late twentieth century and be OK. And that is a powerful lesson. God knows, Thoreau would have understood exactly and applauded you. Reread *Walden* if you don't believe me. But you have both done it. Granted, it must not have been easy. You have worked far, far harder than either of you admit. But you did do it. You simply stepped out of "normal life" and made a life of your own. You, were lucky in that your marriage worked with it. You, Doris, were lucky in that Ralph was a good businessman. You were lucky, Ralph, in that Doris can entertain anyone, including, I am convinced, the Russian Parliment, and make them feel wonderful about themselves, including well fed. You don't often judge. You accept wierd academics and their equally odd dogs, perhaps believing that someday we may repay you. I don't know if we ever do, but we certainly appreciate what you've given us. And for that we are thankful.

Like Robert Frost used to say, "somewhere ages and ages hence," I will look for a bookshop and a home like you have both provided and it will be gone because you are not there and then I will know what it means to be old and therefore to have lost things that are irreplaceable. One of the lessons of middle age, or age--what you will-- is that some things come only once, and when they are gone, life is less. When the day comes that the bookshop is no longer there, when both of you are no longer there, I will know again what it means to be old and to have lost some things that are irreplaceable. I will still buy first editions to chew up in my office, I will still have

impossible dogs that no one else will tolerate, but the place where I
can bring these two things and be accepted and loved will be gone.
And then, again, I will understand that growing old means looking
forward to meeting once again those best people one knew in life,
and if Christianity is right, may know again. Well, I hope so, at
least. But I'm not much of a Lutheran unless Ralph bawls me out,
and he seldom does. What, finally, does life amount to, after all?
Why do we do what we do? Why do you create a book shop? Why
do I teach? What do we really think we're doing here? And what
does it all mean? Bean soup, I expect.

(Signed) Love, Vicky

FOREWORD

To the many folks who have been exerting mild heat on your author to finish his second book, he says, "Here it is at last." He hopes your four year wait is amply rewarded by his efforts between these covers. The first book, *A NORTHERN BOYHOOD* published in March 1993 is a record of his growing up in Northern Wisconsin in the 1920's and 1930's.

This second effort is biographical to some extent also, but more than that it is an account of a lifestyle. A way of life put together around a book shop by two people completely devoted to each other. The book you hold tells about the book shop and things that transpire there. You will also learn about some of the people who are attracted to the place. The author writes about his relationship with D.C. Allen, one of his great teachers. Lastly you will find reminiscences by the author and some of his ideas flavored with his philosophy.

For a number of years the patrons of the book shop have been getting monthly essays called, *"BIBLIO"* written by the book shop proprietor, your author. These *BIBLIOS* are the core around which this book has been constructed, but it contains much new writings as well. Some of these pieces have been published in various local periodicals.

Most of the observations about book shop proprietorship are based on the author's experience in putting together and operating a used-book shop with a general inventory. His aim from the beginning has been to create a shop containing books in every field of human knowledge. This focus colors many subsequent chapters.

Vicky Brehm, who has also written the introduction, furnished the idea for the scope of the book. She also edited a good part of the work.

Mrs. James (Josephine) Clark edited the entire manuscript. A superb English language technician, she has prevented the author from falling into many traps common to those who scribble.

Edith Allen read, corrected, and wrote additions to the manuscript about her husband, D.C. Allen. Her additions to the Allen essay are touching and valuable.

Years ago James Rose wrote the spoof obituary, located it among his papers and kindly gave permission to publish it here for the first time. He also contributed helpful marketing information.

Though we didn't use the title he suggested, Larry Massie was consulted in this regard. He and his wife Priscilla, who operate "The Priscilla Press" in Allegan, Michigan are always supportive.

We are fortunate in having met Karl R. Crisler at the Cassopolis, Michigan VFW post where we are members. Karl is handy with a camera. He took the Frontispiece and a number of pictures in the photo section.

Another friend we can always count on also took some of the pictures. Lou Mumford whom we have known for over twenty-five years is always there when he is needed.

It is one thing to have a daughter-in-law. Lots of people have one of those. But to have one with computer skills when they are sorely needed is unique. Our Linda Casperson bailed out the expediter around here more than once when the computer failed to behave.

An author can't continue writing and publishing books for long if these objects of his hot pencil can't be sold. In order to get this glittering dissertation into the hands of the paying public Mary Miars came to the fore with her computer generated marketing skills.

Usually the printer of a tome gets scant attention when credits are written. We would be derelict not to mention George and Velma Johnson, however. Sure he printed the book, but his wife's input in making this effort happen cannot go unmentioned.

Everyone coming through the front door of the book shop contributed to the flavor of this writing. Without their financial support the author would have had to go out and find honest work too and the book would not have been born.

My gratitude is deep and endless to all who have contributed to filling these pages. To use a modern colloquialism - thanks bunch you guys!

Okay, so I wrote the thing. This writing is only part of the story about making a book. The other partner in this enterprise has spent endless hours pounding on an ailing word processor. Graduating to a new computer, she had to master its electronic intricacies as well. She is well schooled in tackling insurmountable obstacles 'cause she has become expert at deciphering my hand writing. The only person . in the world able to do so.

Keeping track of all the paper involved in book production is no small task either. She managed that on top of her household work. When I take a minute to ponder what Doris has had to do to get this work into print I come to the conclusion that merely writing the thing is like a soft early summer breeze. Her name should go on the front cover and mine, though the author, should adorn a footnote buried deep in the text.

A note on the author's background here may be helpful in making some chapters easier to understand.

His boyhood was spent in Ashland, Wisconsin. After high school he reached the limits of his capabilities quickly being employed in the warehouse of the local power company. During World War Two after five years in the army the power company, in 1949, sent him to manage their gas utility in Niles, Michigan. After twenty-one years of this managing he had had quite enough of corporate security. In 1970 he quit the company and struck out on his own.

He and Doris then became more of a team than ever working together in a gas yard lamp and barbecue grill business and other efforts to keep their spaghetti pot filled.

Their last endeavor is the book shop they opened in 1973. Your author, a book collector and omnivorous reader all of his life actually began to sell books in 1971. The rest, as it's said, is history.

BEAN SOUP

I get a glow when I recall the times many years ago when our house was a haven for budding book dealers and other book lovers twenty years my junior. These youthful friends didn't eat regularly. Poverty and their lack of a stable martial status contributed to their unsatisfactory mealtimes. Because she is a good sport, and a superb and innovative cook, Doris did well in providing a haven in a choppy sea for these undernourished souls.

A place at our table, and sometimes a bed, were always available to these youngsters; they were our extended family. Impending disaster stalked one and all from time to time. Though it was unnatural for us to do so, we played the role as banker, financing some of their book-buying adventures. If their circumstances really disintegrated, we played the role of government too, with outright grants from our own shallow pockets.

Considering it a compliment, not a burden, Doris and I were happy to have these young people converging on us. During these years it was unusual for us to sit down to a meal by ourselves. It was a mixed group that homed in on our beacon of hospitality. Young men and women both tied up at our dock. They sometimes came for support when a personal storm was about to break over their heads. Our help was needed and expected; it was provided.

Today some of these kids (middle-aged now) own flourishing antiquarian book shops. One, a hapless soul then. has found himself and is now a successful artist. It is with pride that we see his name on the title page of a book, "Illustrated by .....". With more than a dozen books to his credit, another is not only an author but has become a leading historian in his home state. Consulting for government and industry is the life work of another. One of the fellows went east and became a specialist book dealer; military and Civil War are his specialties. Psychiatry is the chosen field of one of the girls. I always envied one of the young men; he was so extremely well read. Now he is a controller for a large Chrysler dealership. None have failed. Doris and I harbor the hope that we furnished some of the cement for the foundation of their professional lives.

The following episode will dramatize a happening during those wonderful years.

It was an ordinary Saturday morning. I am going out the door to open the book shop. I notice that Doris is putting navy beans in the crock pot for soup. All day long I will look forward to bean soup for supper.

Two of our hungry friends arrive at ten to spend the day. I trot to the house to inform Doris that there will be four of us at the supper table. Unflustered, she adds more beans to the pot and I return to the shop.

The usual comings and goings mark my day. I sell a few books and buy few books and enjoy good conversation hour after pleasant hour. Along about mid-afternoon three more budding bibliophiles show up; Doris enters the shop at the same time. I was not surprised, after the helloes were exchanged, to hear Doris say, "You'll stay for bean soup, won't you?" An affirmative answer is a foregone conclusion.

Doris is showing no sign of panic, but I am. Shepherding her into a secluded corner, I whisper, "For God's sake, Kid, what are you going to do? There's not enough time for more beans to cook." She is giving me her ignorant school boy look. As she starts for the door, she whispers, "I'll add water, Stupid."

Before supper time Doris "added more water, Stupid" two more times. Late arrivals shot the total to nine. Our cozy candle-lit supper for two turned into something quite different when the nine perennial famished bibliomanics tucked themselves around our old oak table, never realizing that they were eating Doris's "stretched" bean soup. Her golden cornbread, spread with Amish butter, filled the crevices the soup couldn't reach.

ONIONS

Doris and I were working at the gas company in Niles in 1954. Our home was a one bedroom apartment in the complex located in the 1700 block of Broadway. Newly married but ambitious, we yearned for more. A house of our own seemed beyond our reach. Both recently divorced, we found ourselves broke, busted, absolutely devoid of funds. Had we wanted to rub one dime against another, we would have had to find a partner.

We plugged along, paying for dead horses, until an expandable house on a large lot and several people who trusted us without qualification finally surfaced. A deal was made.

After paying our borrowed down payment on the place, we moved into our very own house on Buchanan Road in the fall of 1954. A land contract at six-percent interest financed the seemingly impossible $9000 balance. At last we lived the American dream; we, like so many World War II veterans, had a debt-ridden house in the suburbs.

The place boasted a kitchen, living-dining room, bathroom, floor furnace, and two bedrooms. One bedroom became our "Stamp Room," a place for our budding postage stamp business. We acquired a $9000 debt and still had a one bedroom dwelling place.

On the day we carted our meager possessions into our dream house I performed a seemingly despicable act. One of our neighbors needed visiting. Walking next door and finding our neighbors at home, I hastened to tell them that our reason for buying the house next door did not include the fact that they were our neighbors. In a nice manner I reminded them that years ago neighbors helped each other, like, I said, when one was building a barn. I added that building a barn was not in our plans. Historically, I went on, neighbors took care of each other when illness struck; without a telephone, perhaps, someone had to fetch the doctor. I explained that we had a telephone, a family doctor, and hospitalization insurance. Their help in this area? Not needed. Friendships, I went on, are built on common ground. We had no common ground so I could see no hope for sustained friendly communication between us. As practicing Baptists, they had little in common with people who subscribed to the Episcopal persuasion. Hearing all of these things, shocked my neighbors. I counted on the shock to achieve my purpose.

My aim was not to start a war but to establish a basis for living in close proximity. I stated quite bluntly the basis I wanted to prevail. The accident of living in adjacent houses was not enough for establishing an intimate friendship and constant communication. My statement made, I returned to our mortgaged premises and continued to help Doris arrange furniture.

Such deportment! Why would anyone do what I had just done? What a way, in a new neighborhood, to win friends and influence people. My mission was not to win friends but I did want to influence people. Advised by the people we purchased the house from that our neighbor had an insatiable curiosity, it made good sense, I thought, to dampen his ardor at the outset. On one occasion, we were told, the man next door had walked into the house and into the bathroom where he spied the lady of the house in the bathtub. We were told, "If you let him, he will live with you." Having been apprised of similar acts on his part, I decided to stop things before they got started, to prevent my new neighbor from having a role in our lives. His name would not appear on our program.

It worked. For fifteen years we got along splendidly. We were friendly, waved at each other across the boundary, and passed the time of day. Our relationship never blossomed beyond that. Even after our swimming pool was built and bathing beauties adorned the deck around it in various stages of undress, our neighbor stayed on his side of the property line.

We told the holders of our land contract about my neighborly visit. They admitted that the ten years they spent in the house would have been more pleasant had they summoned the fortitude to do what I had done. Usually it pays to call a spade a spade. If more people did this, Ann Landers would have considerably less to write about.

Before filling our three-quarters of an acre lot with a swimming pool and book shop buildings, we used a lot of it for gardening. In my book A <u>NORTHERN BOYHOOD</u> I write about my upbringing in an environment that includes gardens. Before the ink dried on the land contract, Ralph began to agitate the soil behind the house.

Spring onions came first. Calling around I found a store in South Bend, Indiana with a handy supply. The price of twenty cents a pound sounded reasonable, so off we went to pick up a couple of pounds. The store located, we walked in and asked that the twenty cent price be confirmed. The little man in charge told us they were thirty cents a pound. "But," I said, "in our 'phone conversation you said they would be twenty cents." The clerk replied, "Yes, they are twenty cents if you buy forty pounds."

In those days, sporting a short fuse, I lost my cool and said, "O.K., give me forty pounds."

I can still see Doris and me staggering out of the store with forty pounds of onion sets. (Close to a bushel basket full.) What do two people do with forty pounds of onion sets? I don't know what someone else might do, but I broke my back in three places planting every blessed one. Kind to those little tan bulbs, nature saw to it that they all pushed their green heads through the earth. The long green rows looked like an Irish regiment marching in review. Assuredly beautiful, but what to do with the damned things?

One evening while shopping at the neighborhood grocery, Doris spied their display of sickly looking onions. She plied the major domo of the produce section with a couple of well-thought-out inquiries: "Why do you put such junk in the display case?" and, "Certainly you can find better than that, can't you?" My faithful partner heard the man in charge say that what she saw was all that was available; this was a bad year for spring onions, etc. Entrepreneurial genes went to work and Doris made a deal for our crop on the spot.

We got busy. In marshaling our resources, we discovered that the plastic used by the laundry to pack my white shirts made ideal wrapping material for spring onions. After all, we had to protect our little babies from fresh air in such a way that they could be seen. The plastic was transparent, so our packaging problem was solved and the shirt covers were recycled at the same time. Recycling hadn't been invented yet, but then, being children of the Great Depression, we had been recycling all of our lives. Sometimes I felt that our motto should be, "Make do, use what you have at hand, and don't cry about it."

But, back to the onions. We toted them in a borrowed wheelbarrow (remember, we had little more than each other, love, ambition, energy, and a new $9000 mortgage) from the garden to the outside water spigot for their initial washing. Cold, wrinkled, chapped hands scrubbed the gumbo off our precious crop. Bleeding fingers, wet feet, and a re-broken back were the price we paid. The city girl became an agrarian field hand and food processing slave overnight. We created our own sweatshop. Bowed, but not beaten, we stood back, looked at ourselves, and had many a good laugh as the torture went on.

Our little kitchen looked like the washroom of a highway construction project. Over a period of a couple of weeks we sold every single onion. In the process we acquired new names: the onion king and queen of Buchanan Road.

Our records show that we made less than twenty-five cents an hour and a new sponge mop for Doris's kitchen. Our real pay was in the humor of the whole thing and the fun we had working and laughing together.

RECONCILING THE CHECK BOOK

Doris is in perennial charge of mechanical and material things around this place that boasts an inventory of 100,000 books, more or less. She also maintains the infrastructure. When a light bulb goes grey from bright she changes it. In an effort to be helpful I tried to do it once. It did no good to enlist the aid of two philosophers that happened to be bending my ear in the book shop at the time. We three couldn't get it done, but Doris did.

When there is building to be done I never even interrupt my reading or writing. There's no need to hinder my major occupation for mere lumber and nails. Doris either does the building or supervises its doing. My intrusion in these matters would only be just that - an unwanted and unneeded intrusion.

I feel as Henry David Thoreau felt when he wrote to the effect that a man should take care not to be thrown off the track by every nutshell and mosquito's wing that falls on the rails. How he managed without a Doris around is something I have yet to fathom.

Nails to pound, VCR's to program, clocks to reset, drapes to put up, pictures to hang, book shelves to build - Doris does it. Usually there are six or seven ways of accomplishing any given task. The eighth way is Doris's way and that's the way she does it. Running off (she actually chased them out of the house) two big burly plumbers, one day years ago, she installed the shower they were here to do. These pros made the mistake of disagreeing with her modus operandi. Really, the only reason she needed the plumbers was because she needed their tools. When they effected their departure (in haste) they left their tools behind long enough for Doris to exploit them in getting the shower installed by her lonesome.

It's fun to see the old hands scamper and pretend to hide when my wife walks into her favorite hardware store. They look like frightened woodchucks peering out from behind stacked cans of paint or other merchandise. Because she speaks their language, they are very happy to work with her. Doris Elaine doesn't ask for a thing-a-ma-jig on a whatcha-ma-callit. She knows the moniker's proper name in technical terms. For instance, a miter box is just that, a miter box, not a "slanted saw between two boards, you know." No one has ever sent her looking for a left-handed screw driver either. Me, maybe, but Doris - never.

My wife is not a masculine strong-man type with a large body and big biceps. She is very feminine and her stature might be termed petite. So why her unnatural orientation? Her father, Harold, was a man of all trades: carpenter, electrician, mason, heating specialist, plumber, and more. It was always apparent to me that Harold invented the building trades. Little Doris, Harold's first born, became his go-fer. Old enough to toddle about found her underfoot when Harold was building and fixing things. After awhile Harold didn't have to ask for a crescent wrench or a crow bar. Little Doris anticipated her father's needs and placed the needed tool within his grasp; she performed more or less like a good surgical nurse.

Our automobiles have a way of speaking to Doris in a tongue unintelligible to me. Riding down the road in a car that never sounded better to me, Doris will say something like, "There's something amiss with this car." This sixth sense about cars is infallible. When we get the vehicle that has injured her sensibilities back from the repair shop the sizable invoice always proves she knows what she's talking about.

My bailiwick is books, writing, and most importantly running a book shop. After she finished building the book shop buildings, the girl I live with leaves their operation to me. However, it is embarrassing sometimes, at a sale, when she does exercise her "book sense" by handing me a desirable volume I have passed by.

Doris does two things with books that no one can do as well. The design engineers at Chrysler couldn't pack more books in our mini-van than she can. The car springs love to have me load the vehicle. They groan and complain when she does it. Packing books into a bag or a box? She defies the laws of physics. Why she is endowed with these super-human packing skills has never been revealed to me. I have learned to stand clear however when she is loading the van or packing a box.

Usually when we are on a book buying trip we have to stop to buy a tooth brush or something else I have forgotten to pack. Doris does all of the packing except my toilet articles. Allowing me this simple task is one of the very few mistakes she ever makes. During the course of our sojourn, I can ask her for anything under the sun. Digging around in the baggage, she always comes up with it, be it a fingernail clipper or a hunting knife. Doris puts the Army Quartermaster to shame.

They want to know the best route to Yonkers or Sarasota? Book shop customers often ask these questions. Doris tells them. Our friends call wanting to know where to buy some obscure item or where they can go to find out about something. Doris knows.

I wouldn't attempt to buy clothing for myself. Even a handkerchief would pose a problem. I wouldn't know where to find it and if I did find the place, I wouldn't know the size. Doris buys most of my stuff on approval. I wouldn't know how to operate a dressing room in a men's clothing store. Anyway, I'm shy. And I'm particular where I take off my trousers. I certainly wouldn't do it in a place as public as a clothing store.

Reconciling the checkbooks, banking business funds, handling accounts receivable and payable, answering the 'phone, getting the cars serviced on time, keeping our appointment calendar, sending people greeting cards, or nagging someone about washing the windows? Doris does it all and more. What is left for Ralph to do? What it all amounts to is that Doris handles the overhead leaving me unfettered to concentrate on the business end of things - particularly the book business. Doris does little in the day-to-day operation of the book shop, but if she didn't do all of the things she does do, the shop wouldn't amount to much. Not being preoccupied and diverted by the "nutshells and mosquito wings" of living allows me to concentrate on trying to be an author and operator of a fairly large book selling business.

Doris does the typing, leaving me free to produce manuscripts for her to type. If I had to do both the writing and the typing, frustration would take charge of my life and my creative capacity and production would surely grind to a rusty halt.

Beginning when she was my secretary at the gas company, Doris and I have become a team. We have figured out, over the years, who does what best. Early on we two learned that mechanics was not my strong suit. I passed manual training in high school with a "conditional" grade. The "condition" was that I finish constructing a footstool I had started to build in class. I last saw this thing in a bag of parts hanging in our old shed when I left for the Army nine years after the "condition" was to be fulfilled. Doris, on the other hand, was the first girl to receive an Industrial Arts degree from Niles High School.

Even with our over forty years of cutting and trying, we occasionally get off the track. Either I attempt to do something that she does better or she starts to mess in my bailiwick. Things resemble a train wreck around here then until we realize that the wrong people are running the train and we get it back on the track.

Hey, you youngsters out there who are trying to live together, don't worry about the gender of the tasks that need doing. Whoever does it best should do it. If you're both good at it, do it together. But be sure that one of the partners is responsible for each task. No need to write it all down - it comes naturally over time.

The only time we ever bounced a check in our forty years of married life was during our first year. Neither of us bothered to reconcile the checkbook. Naturally Doris, also a trained bookkeeper, does it now.

STAMP COLLECTING

In late grade school and early high school, I was an avid stamp collector. This was during the deep dark days of the Great Depression, the days when hamburger was ten cents a pound and nobody had a dime. I pestered everyone I knew to save stamps for me (the preacher, my Sunday School teacher, neighbors, and my parent's friends).

There was a stamp dealer who occupied a small office upstairs over a drug store on the main street of the town where I grew up. In spite of the Depression, I did have some small change to spend for the products of Roy Hogan's little store. I managed to keep myself in spending money by selling the weekly newspaper, GRIT, and peddling eggs in our neighborhood for a few cents a dozen more than they cost. Then, too, I bought new United States stamps at the post office. I could fund this expense by cutting grass, baby-sitting, piling wood, and doing other things for people that they couldn't or didn't want to do for themselves.

I spent much of my spare time during the winter of 1935-36 making an album for U.S. stamps. This was a good time to be drawing squares on white paper at a table near the heating stove, because for one thirty day period that winter in northern Wisconsin, where I lived, the temperature never got above zero for thirty straight days.

During my early high school days I started my own postage stamp business. I met with some success because I had a lot of friends who collected stamps.

The collecting frenzy continued through high school. I also collected cigar bands, Indian head pennies, and match-book covers. After finishing high school, with the ink on my diploma barely dry, I got a full time job in the warehouse with the power company. I drew $27.50 every two weeks and during the summer of 1937 I worked ten to twelve hours a day, seven days a week. This rigorous schedule left no time for stamp collecting. The albums, tools, and little boxes full of my philatelic treasures were put in the bottom drawer of my father's roll-top desk. When I stowed them away I said to myself, "When I'm forty, and not so busy, I will collect stamps again." I gave the stamp company to my younger brother.

Years passed, a war was fought and won, a marriage failed, promotions were mine in my job, and a transfer as manager of the gas company found me in Niles, Michigan in 1949. In 1953 I married Doris Short and though I wasn't forty, I thought I would like to take up my stamps again.

Something strange had happened. One stamp of a kind didn't satisfy anymore. When I got one, I wanted ten. When I had ten, I wanted a hundred. I was on my way toward bankrupting the fragile newlyweds' budget with a hazy idea that "someday" I would start a stamp business. Doris went along with my more or less haphazard expenditures. I could feel that she was somewhat less than enthusiastic because we had no definite goal.

One day, because they were cheap, I bought 6000 packets of foreign stamps. This made quite a stack in the middle of our small living room. Actually, there was no room in our small living quarters for this hoard. I can still hear my loving partner exclaim, "Ralph, I know that stamps can be sold 'cause people sure as hell sell them to you - but can you sell them?" Of course I didn't know. We decided to find out. "The Casperson Stamp Company" was born. Together, Doris and I built a thriving mail-order stamp business selling stamps to collectors all over the world.

We were newly married, and working together in this enterprise brought out our various strengths and weaknesses. By trial and error, each began to do what he did best. For instance, Doris was mechanically inclined, so she did the mechanical things. My imagination was well-honed, so I was the idea person. Also, I knew the product and had an affinity for it, so pricing, ordering, and selling were my bailiwick.

That was the beginning. Since those early days we have had two more successful enterprises. In fact, the stamp company was sold in the mid 1960's to finance our gas lamp and grill business. In the early 1970's when I wanted a book shop, Doris had the building built. She insulated, wired, and paneled it herself and did much of the work building the shelves. This left me free to deal with the books themselves.

Without the 6000 foreign packets and Doris's embarrassing question about the ability to sell them, would we have ever worked out our methods of working together in a successful enterprise?

The preceding chapter told a tale about how my stamp collecting activities sprouted into a stamp company. That experience revealed to Doris and me that we were a team in a commercial enterprise. We found each other's strengths and weaknesses. We learned what each did well and in what endeavor one or the other would most likely bomb out. This knowledge has made us unafraid to tackle new activities. What we would never attempt alone, we attempt together with confidence. This is one key to our success in the book business and other enterprises.

Another key is Doris's tolerance and positive attitude toward my ideas, some of which must sound impossible to her at the outset. Justifiably negative at first, she, in time, throws her constructive criticism into the pot. We stir it a bit and the project is launched. Certainly some schemes fail. One of my more notable flops was our investment in Michigan and Ohio oil wells. We also had a debacle in the commodities market when I bet the price of pork would go down. This was terrifying. A live pig couldn't be found in the whole state of Ohio (we looked). The price of pork went through the roof and we tottered on the verge of bankruptcy.

Another fiasco was the commercial paint venture. We were able to sell only about twenty gallons out of a truckload we invested in.

My point is that failure doesn't keep us from trying again. Anything but funny when they happen, these flops provide raw material for lots of laughs when they become ancient history. The free enterprise system (we are dues paying members) gives people the right to fail. Because we prevailed more times than we stumbled, we are able to eat quite regularly.

All of the above is an important preface to the book shop. With negative attitudes the business would still be in the "someday" stage. The first nail would still be in the nail keg if Doris and I had not discovered each other's strengths and weaknesses.

If you're staying with me this far, you are entitled to hear the story about how the book shop got its start. Being born into a world of books was not a detriment to my becoming a bookman. My mother was a school teacher and my father was self-educated.

Neither parent ever quit learning. During my childhood our home was full of books and reading material. This is one of the factors that made it a home. When I was old enough to read, my aunts gave me books for Christmas and for birthdays. My first earnings were spent for books (these earnings started with a paper route when I was nine). Book fines at the public library ate up some small change; I didn't want to return the books I had checked out.

The seed that germinated and grew into our book shop was planted in 1936; I was a junior in high school. Two brothers opened a used-book shop in my hometown that year. The Browser Book Shop was the most interesting place I had ever experienced. I haunted the place during my spare hours. Surplus coins didn't wear holes in my pockets. I spent them at the Browser Book Shop. Poverty limited my acquisitions, but I was on my way. More important than the books I acquired, was the idea that the little shop implanted in my fertile brain. I wanted a shop like the Browser some day. The Army and career changes put off that day.

I only felt comfortable in the service when I had books at my fingertips. Even in the mountains of Italy, where I was babysitting a machine gun during the winter of 1944-45, I read books by candlelight in a sandbag bunker. G.I. paperbacks (Armed Service editions - collectors items now) were my fare and I devoured my share.

Buying books became an obsession after the war. I was a frequent visitor in the Chicago area book shops. To me, the Edgewater on Broadway was especially attractive. Locally, I drove Don Allen and Harriette Barnette nuts just hanging around. I was a good customer though and a good listener. Those two, both excellent bookmen, were not stingy when it came to sharing information on book lore. Don and Harriette are the professors in my master's program in bookmanship. Endless hours were spent "at their feet" soaking up an education. They buttered the bread of knowledge with the secrets of the book trade. I ate ravenously. Both of these venerable souls have gone to the great book shop in the sky. To them I owe a debt of gratitude that can never be discharged. Later in this book you will find an account of my relationship with Don Allen.

Books continued to accumulate in our home. Doris, my ever

tolerant mate, lived with it. I bought bookcases. She made room for them. More bookshelves were needed. She found places for them, then she built more. She got dirt stained hands and smashed fingers trying to keep up with the flood. Cardboard boxes full of books accumulated. Her dwelling was cluttered. She somehow accommodated them. Books were tucked in every nook and cranny of our house, even under the bed. I continued to buy books.

Her relief was palpable on that day in 1973 when I said, "Doris, I think we can fund a building for the books." I continued, "Would you get some plans and figures together so we can see where we might be going?"

Later, after we had looked at her plans and numbers, I said, "O.K., go ahead and build it." She did. Our first building was erected. Supervising its building, she then insulated and paneled it herself.

I didn't ask Doris to build a book shop. I only asked for a building to house the books. It never really occurred to me that we had created a book shop until after the building was completed.

I continued to buy books. In two years Doris built another building, hitching it to the first one. First it became a warehouse, then an extension of the original shop. Another two years went by. Doris was at it again. She put up two more buildings. One became a warehouse and what is now called "The Annex." The other is used for general storage (translated - more books). This little structure is called "The Stuga." A "Stuga" is a small storage building found in backyards in Norway. One happy day, when the last of these structures was finished, my chief engineer, and life mate, told me that she had just retired from the contracting business. That was OK because we don't have anymore land to build on anyway. Currently book buying and selling is in rough balance; more room is not needed. Thank heaven for the builder in residence when her skills are needed.

When the accomplishments of over twenty years in the book business are viewed in our backyard, it all looks pretty easy. Ask Doris. Our house is still full of books.

GRIT

At this late date I still have a vivid recurring dream, or more appropriately a nightmare. I am a little boy again, it's Sunday and I haven't sold any of my GRIT newspapers. In the dream my unsold papers haunt me. Dropped off at our house by the post office delivery man in the grey-blue uniform the previous Thursday, the two fat bundles, sealed in their heavy brown wrapping paper, rest ominously unsold and undelivered in the back shed just outside the kitchen door.

In 1928 reading an ad in "Boy's Life", "Liberty", or some such publication extolling the virtues and outlining the benefits of being a boy entrepreneur, I decided to become one.

I was nine years old, an age when pocket cash was becoming quite necessary, but my supply of it wasn't wearing holes in the pockets of my bib overalls. In response to my initial order, the GRIT Publishing Company of Williamsport, Pennsylvania sent me five copies of its paper, GRIT. In business for myself with a debt to the publisher of fifteen cents and a potential of twenty-five cents in gross sales, I was the proudest kid in the neighborhood; my potential profit was ten cents.

Getting hooked up with this weekly publication produced a fabulous income and attractive prizes too. I won a flashlight, a pocket watch and fob, and a Boy Scout knife for efforts above and beyond the ordinary. In addition to the prizes and income, I was learning some valuable business principles too. The coins gleaned from the difference between the cost and selling price of an article could be spent for school supplies, clothes, movies, five cent candy bars, ten cent hamburgers, and fifteen cent malted milks. I was learning the game - sell something for more than its cost. The GRIT sold for five cents. I owed the publisher three cents, and the remaining two cents were mine. The drawback here was that the publisher wanted his cut even if the papers were not sold. That last part is the stuff from which nightmares are fabricated.

GRIT, the greatest five-cent value going, billed itself as "America's Greatest Family Newspaper", but nickels were scarce during my nine year stint. From a cold start though, after considerable selling, I developed regular customers. Part of every Thursday, Friday, and Saturday were spent peddling and selling the GRIT, delivering the paper to my repeat customers, banging on doors, and giving my sales pitch trying to create additional regulars.

"Do you want to buy a paper?" Sometimes this boyish inquiry was answered with a violently slammed door. Such harsh treatment further lowered my never too-healthy self-esteem. But given the chance, I went into my sales pitch. "It's the GRIT, 'America's Greatest Family Newspaper'. Each week it carries news of the day, 150 pictures, a twenty-seven page story section, a women's page, children's page, and a sermon for the people. You get all of this for only a nickel." My experience wasn't all banged doors and negative responses. Enough people were positive so a route of seventy regular customers was built up by the time I graduated from high school and my younger brother took over the enterprise. I couldn't continue to run around with a newspaper bag over my shoulder after landing s regular job with the power company that paid real money, $27.50 every two weeks.

I had no trouble giving my sales pitch, but it embarrassed me to ask the customer his name. It never occurred to me to enter my customer's address in my account book. I either gave them fictitious names or relied on my memory (faulty) to keep track of my little accounts receivable (a bad system). Scrawled by a young boy's hand, in the yellowing account book, some of the names stare back at me today. "Oh, my good boy," (the woman called me that and that became her name) "Next to Halverson's Store, fat lady, with green eyes, etc." Some of my creditors who still owe me small sums are now at rest in Mount Hope Cemetery - I could never summon up the courage to ask them to pay up; luckily most of them did so without prompting. These losses were light and sustainable. My business was prosperous. After all, my profit was over a dollar a week.

One Saturday morning a girl a couple of years younger than I answered my knock as I canvassed for new customers. Rather boldly, I thought, she said, "My mother told me to tell you she isn't home."

"Go tell your mother I heard what she told you to tell me." Having unburdened myself of that remark I vacated the premises promptly.

Robert Hatch, a good friend, decided to make his fortune at my expense. He proposed that we go into business together. He would deliver half of my papers to my customers and we would split the profits from the whole enterprise 50-50. Sorry Robert, but my problem wasn't getting papers delivered; acquiring new customers was the problem.

I did hire a kid to get new customers for me. He got a penny for each paper he sold. After suffering under my lash for about six weeks and selling papers to all of his acquaintances, he quit. His efforts put about thirty cents in his pocket. The GRIT was habit-forming if you could get people to read it once; I continued to serve the customers my little friend had acquired.

I was developing into a true little entrepreneur. My GRIT customers became my market for other wares too. I sold them eggs, honey, cleaning fluid, dressed chickens, strawberries, blueberries, and butter. From the time I added groceries to my line at about age twelve until I gave it up at age eighteen, I was a walking grocery story and news-stand.

Recently a young couple from Williamsport, Pennsylvania, GRIT's home town, visited our book shop. I told them about my experiences with GRIT. These folks told me that the publishing company was moving to Kansas City. About a month later I received from my new friends a brand new GRIT paper-sack with GRIT emblazoned on it in big red letters. It's just like the one I carried all those years when I was a kid in Ashland, Wisconsin. This one hangs on the wall in our den; I'm proud of that bright paper-sack. It's a diploma from the only business school I ever attended.

THE JUMPSUIT

Some people, mostly wives, have the strange notion that if their husband doesn't bisect his middle with a leather belt, he is in low fashion. I wear jumpsuits.

The jumpsuit is my uniform, my badge of identity. Rarely will I be found in the book shop dressed in anything else. When the shop was being established, I wore jumpsuits exclusively. I didn't conform. At receptions, weddings, fine restaurants, meetings, and occasional church services, Ralph stuck out like a bandaged finger. Dressed in my best jumpsuit, on one occasion, I delivered a funeral eulogy for a fellow bookseller. (See the chapter, "New Kid On The Block.)

If this was not a fetish, then why this strange behavior? I began to wear a jumpsuit for two reasons: Comfort and identity. Before the book shop was built, I attended many book sales -around the country. Sales events such as these resembled "free-for-all" fights. Competition for the choice books was intense. Crawling on the floor under tables was the modus operandi. The whole procedure was highly physical. By the time the fracas was over, I was a complete mess. My shirt was dangling from my trousers. Being slightly heavy in the middle, my belt had slipped down below my protruding abdomen. Its sharp leather cut into my tender flesh. Who said this bookselling thing was sedentary? There had to be a better way.

One day I went into one of these battles wearing a jumpsuit, a garment given to me by an erstwhile friend as a joke. I fought the fight in comfort with my efficiency enhanced. The first reason for wearing a jumpsuit had become apparent.

When the book shop was first established, it was necessary that its proprietor stand out in a crowd. We couldn't afford expensive advertising, but the book shop had to be put on the map. I grew a beard and wore a jumpsuit to all functions. I was making the effort to change myself from the smooth-shaven, white-collared man in a business suit, who had managed the gas company for over twenty years, into the fellow who had a used-book shop on Buchanan Road.

Inquiries were made about the identity of the bearded guy in the jumpsuit. The interrogator got the answer I wanted him to hear. "Oh, that's Ralph Casperson. He has a used-book shop on Buchanan Road."

Currently this non-comforming apparel is worn exclusively in the book shop. When I frequent other places now I dress like other people - not as comfortable maybe, but there is no substitute for a happy wife. Book sales are not as rough as they once were. Now that our shop contains 100,000 volumes, I don't go to as many sales either. My identity is established. Even when I wear uncomfortable attire like everyone else, folks know that "He has that used-book shop on Buchanan Road."

═══════════════════════════

CLOTHES MAKE THE MAN

═══════════════════════════

For so many years I don't remember them all, I have been writing to amuse myself, bore my close friends, and entertain the public. Lots of this stuff has never seen the light of day but reposes silently, aging, in dark files where many hope the darkness will prevail forever. Most of the prose could possibly survive a faint ray of sunshine, but the poetry (and I dignify it by calling it poetry), should never be given the chance of life; consigned to the darkness, it rests in its proper place.

Published over four years ago, my book, *A NORTHERN BOYHOOD*, enjoyed general acclaim. At least those who didn't like it kept - that sordid fact to themselves. *BIBLIO*, a well-known publication emanating from my pen, is published monthly by our book shop. Essays escaping from my dull pencil are carried by several newspapers on a regular basis.

The perfectionist dynamo I live with answers to the name Doris. On those occasions when I need her and can't recall her simple given name, she will respond when I shout, "Hey."

Recently this bundle of energy sat me at attention in a straight-backed chair and, without wasting time on preliminaries, informed me that I must improve my writing. She quickly added, smothering my unuttered negative protest, that she knew how this could easily be accomplished.

It seemed she had been pondering my problem for a long time, ever since our local haberdasher got his last shipment of men's garb.

"How in the name of whatever," she said, launching her propaganda attack, "can you expect to put one word after another, sounding like an author, when you don't look like one?"

At first her pointed inquiry was driftless until I recalled seeing her perusing the pictures in some of my biographies of literary figures. She knew, from her recent inspection, what authors looked like. Her opener required an answer. I replied softly, "So?" I said no more and could hardly say less - I just said, "So?"

This word has a way of igniting Doris's slow burning fuse. She keeps all of her many different fuses in her big fat billfold with her credit cards; a fast fuse, an explosive one, one that is perpetually wet, and one that takes two weeks to light add up to a well-rounded supply that keeps our married life from getting impossibly dull. My intelligent sounding, "So?" had provided a good light to her slow-burning fuse and we were launched.

With her fuse sparkling brightly, Doris continued with what I recognized as the slow pitch. "All authors wear tweeds and corduroys. Even Faulkner, in the heat of Oxford, Mississippi, was faithful to this something less than cool uniform." Continuing she drove on, "It is what men of letters wear. You will never be a Hemingway, a Stevenson, or a Steinbeck, but you can at least make an effort to get into the anteroom of their fraternity. If you knock on the door in a jump-suit, your favorite garb, you'll surely be turned away."

She had my attention. Her point was driven home. She closed the sale by using one of my favorite arguments against me, an unforgivable but much-used and effective tactic. "E.B. White, your hero, couldn't write his essays wearing a jump-suit and you should quit flouting convention and dress appropriately if you expect to fill the shoes of the great."

As she left to go to the men's store for my new uniform, I was left mercifully alone with my thoughts. I didn't know I aspired to fill anyone's shoes but my own.

Within twenty-four hours I was positioned behind my desk in my new writing outfit. Doris viewed me with satisfaction and left me alone, fully expecting the metamorphosis to transpire. Nothing seemed to happen. I wrote ten pages and compared it to Hemingway. My writing still sounded like me - not him. I wrote five sheets more and then read some Steinbeck. I still sounded like me.

I tore the fifteen pages to shreds. If Doris thinks this new costume thing will work, I have to think otherwise. I'm waiting for the elbows on the tweed jacket to bulge and the pants to get baggy. Maybe that will do the trick.

This essay was written upon completion of our first book

Some years ago we published *BIBLIO*, a news letter. It was distributed from the book shop and through the mail during the formative years of the shop. It became, after five issues, a project the young enterprise could no longer support. (Translation - a dearth of time and money.) Its production was fun. We missed writing the sheet and at least a few of our customers mourned its demise.

In 1991 our friend James Pomeroy suggested that I write a column for *VISTAS*, a publication of his. The July issue of the *VISTAS* began to carry my scribbling. Many customers' hands clutched this little treasure as they left the book shop. Wielding my pencil, I was again enjoying myself and at least some of my readers indicated that they, too, were happy with my efforts.

Time passes and situations change. Now, *VISTAS* will be published quarterly instead of eight times a year. To fill the gaps, *BIBLIO* is being resurrected. *BIBLIO* will be published in those months when *VISTAS* is sleeping. Each *BIBLIO* will have an essay on "books and other thoughts."

It is probably appropriate that the essay in this first issue be devoted to the production of our book, *A NORTHERN BOYHOOD.* Finally, after four years work, the book is finished. This is the story of my life in Northern Wisconsin from birth until I left for the army in 1942. It is finally off our backs and on the market. My wife, Doris, has typed every word at least sixty times. When we handed the bulky manuscript to the printer Doris said, "I feel that I have just given birth to triplets after four years of labor." I felt I had just dropped my full field pack after a thirty-mile hike.

How many times have you heard someone say, "I'm going to write a book. I even have a title for it." Almost everyone has been told at one time or another, "You should write a book," or, "he should write a book," or, "one of these days I'm going to write a book."

It all sounds so easy. Relying on your memory, it seems that all you have to do some evening when the TV is slow, is grab a pad of scratch paper, or a used envelope and a pencil, sit down at the kitchen table, open a beer, and dash off your memoirs.

I am a living witness to the fact that writing and getting a book ready for the printer requires more than a few short hours of missed TV time. While massaging her near-numb fingers, Doris gives the above a resounding second.

My mother was a "string saver." She maintained that if an object was put away, a use would be found for it within seven years. She was probably right, but could the thing be found when needed? An elderly company treasurer once told me not to throw anything away until I had made two copies of it. I am sure I carried my mother's "squirrel away" genes and I tended to follow the advice of the company treasurer.

I may be short on formal academic training, but I acquired a master's degree in "string saving" long years ago. Letters, pictures, scraps of paper and other mementos that are generated on our journey down life's path have stuck to my fingers. I have many boxes full of this stuff. Also, on occasion, I have written diaries. A dream of mine has been to put these papers in chronological order. After annotating them, I felt that they would have some value in an historical museum, a research library, or a military archive. A researcher could interpret my paper hoard after my bones were dust. He would have a picture of an ordinary life during the World War II period of history.

I have had a long-standing desire to leave a record of my life for posterity; to paint a picture of one unimportant mortal who occupied eternal time prior to, during, and after World War II. Such a sketch would, I thought, exemplify the lives of many during this period of history - a time of great prosperity, dismal economic depression, and war. My desire to leave this testimonial was prompted by my lifelong interest in reading about the past. I have been drinking from the well of history for many years. I wanted to replenish the reservoir in a small way with this record of my life. My debt to recorded history would then be, at least partially, repaid. But I never intended to write a book.

This concept was abruptly changed in 1989. At that time a friend of ours, who is a professional writer herself, inspected the paper hoard and read parts of the diaries. One evening while sitting in a small area surrounded by the countless boxes of paper, she said, "You should be the interpreter of your life." She fixed me with her earnest eyes and continued, "You are going to pull two or three books out of this junk." Later that night she agreed to be my editor and the first book was launched.

The process of "pulling books out of this junk" has changed our lifestyle. We have demonstrated, after forty years of marriage, that a couple can cooperate on something more joyful than going out for lunch. At any time in life it would be satisfying to face, and successfully complete, such a challenge as writing this book. It becomes even more gratifying, though, when you are old enough to cash your own social security check.

Early in our effort we had worked endlessly on a chapter entitled, "The Powerful Penny." The writing and rewriting seemed to be interminable and the typing continued apace. At one point I weighed the paper we had generated for this one chapter. (Remember, I am a "string saver", and had saved all of the working copies.) We couldn't believe that this bundle of paper, for a chapter that became twenty-seven pages in the book, weighed one pound.

I did the writing. Doris did the word processing and she designed the book. We owe a debt of gratitude to many others who became involved. Our requests for information and materials were answered. An artist was engaged to paint a picture for the cover and dust jacket. At least four people did yeoman service editing the manuscript, all of this before the printer put it through the press.

Now, after spending over $6000 on it, the job is done. Doris's word processor is cooling off my big cup full of pencils - only half as long as when I started to scribble - are at rest.

BIBLIO - OUR DOG

There have been two Biblios in our lives. One is the one mentioned in the previous chapter. The other was our dog. This short essay is about the dog. A friend had acquired this little tan bundle for his wife who thought she wanted a dog. She changed her mind. She didn't want the lovable puppy. Worse than the rejection, she demanded that her spouse either take the little thing to the dog pound, or remove himself from the premises. Her premises were not a pleasant place to reside, but he had no other. The embattled guy had to comply with the tyrant in residence's edict. The little dog had to go. His fate was certain and undesirable. It awaited him at the dog pound.

When I found out about my friend's and the dog's plight, I decided to pay them a visit. I would look, only look, at the object of the woman's scorn.

Our dog of thirteen years, Dessie, had been gone for a year and Doris and I had decided she would not be replaced. No more dogs for us. Dessie had been wonderful. We had made a good home for her and had enjoyed her a lot, but the responsibility was too much and the parting too wrenching. Our first dog would be our last dog.

I drove off to look. Doris said, "Ralph, just look, don't touch-" This small cross between a cocker and blond Labrador was in a chicken wire pen. When the little fellow saw me, he instantly recognized a soft hearted meal ticket. The tiny fellow didn't protest when I picked him up. The little guy licked and wriggled with enthusiasm. What is a man to do? I couldn't let go of this soft warm bundle. To put him back down was to seal his fate. If I didn't rescue him, he would face the exterminators. He stayed in my arms and snuggled. Like an automaton, I slowly walked to the car. I wasn't thinking because my brain wouldn't function. Love is like that.

As I drove down the road toward home, the realization of my plight began to sink in. I had acquired a puppy. Though she had never been adamant about it, Doris had made it plain that she didn't want a puppy. I couldn't return it. Such an action would reflect on my integrity. It would also guarantee the little fellow's extinction, but if I took my baby home, I risked getting killed. I opted for the lesser of the two evils and went home

On the way I tried to think of a name for my little bundle of joy. He would be, I was sure, more acceptable if he had a name. The name should have some connection with books. After all, this was going to be a bookman's dog. How would it be to call him Preface or Index? I tried it aloud, "Here, Preface; come, Index." No way. Could I call him Chapter, Spine, Fore-edge, Page, Sheet, or Print?

Nothing fit.

When I drove into our yard, Doris was in the kitchen. I scooped up my handful of warm fur, screwed up my courage, and went into the house. Confronting my mate, I said, "Meet my friend, Biblio."

Biblio remained a fixture around our home and yard for 11 years. I'm sure many of you remember and miss him as much as we do. But it's for sure this time, no more dogs. Doris is getting too old for it.

WOODCHUCKS

I could say that this is a lazy day, but that would be a misnomer. The day itself isn't lazy. Because it is an overcast rainy day, and business is slow, the darkness and gloom make it seem like a lazy day. Actually the day is similar to any other day; it's a typical Sunday. This day, like all days, started early this morning before I got out of bed. The dismal day has continued to unfold until it is now three-thirty in the afternoon.

Last night I slept badly and very little. Even though I know better, I drank a can of caffeinated soda pop before going to bed. Now I'm sleepy. Nature is trying to redress the balance. My body pines for repose. The sunless day suggests sleep. And the rain softly pattering on the book-shop roof lulls me in the direction of oblivion.

But I can't just drop off, for gosh sakes. There is a customer here with me in the shop. What would the lone browser think if he caught me napping? It is not enough to have droopy eyes, but my ambition is on vacation too. It stayed in bed this morning when my body got up. I'm in sorry shape. I tried to read a book awhile ago but it hit the floor and I woke up with a sudden jolt.

Doris is waiting to type the *BIBLIO* I haven't written. It's past due, so sleepy or not, I have to get at that task posthaste. But first of all, I have to invent something to write about. Don't you know these essays are fashioned out of whole cloth? I don't pick them out of the ether.

The world is full of bright ideas that need exploring in a literary way. These notions, not hard to come by when I am well-slept, today are as scarce as bird spit; nothing jumps into my exhausted consciousness. In my subdued condition, I could not recognize a dynamite explosion, much less the gentle tapping of a story that wants to get born. The lead in my pencil throbs with anticipation but nothing drifts into my tired head. My eyelids droop as I think about that little caffeine in that can of Dr. Pepper I drank last evening.

Think about it. If I had had the good sense to bend the stopper on a can of de-caffeinated stuff, I'd have gotten my usual eight hours of slumber and today my mind would be as alert as a Boy Scout in his first Memorial Day parade.

Oh, my mind is sifting out some ideas, but none are worth writing about. I could spew out a paragraph or two about the customer who once tried to purloin books out of the Indian section. After filling his huge briefcase with books he planned to steal, he came to the check out-desk with the one book he intended to pay for. Using my military voice, I ordered him to open the briefcase. Reluctantly he opened the briefcase, revealing a stack of choice books about Indians. Rather sternly, I said, "Put them on my desk." (The check out desk.) He did. Adding them to the tab for the one book I said, "That will be $126.50." He paid up. I could tell you that until he left the area he was a good customer. Never again did he try to "rip me off". Sometime I will write about that episode, not now. The story has no glitter today. I'll scribble it out sometime, after a good night's sleep.

Well, the browser just paid for his stack of books and left me alone with my sleepiness. The rain stopped too, so I'll sneak a wink or two. Before that indulgence though I'll take a peek out the back window to see if maybe a woodchuck is wandering around in the yard. If I weren't so lazy, I could tell the story about those critters and the nuisance they have become during the last four summers. One of them decided to gain some book learnin', one evening before we had the shop covered with vinyl siding. Just a little additional chewing on the composition wood siding, and the woodchuck would have taken up residence in the book-shop itself. Far be it from me, one who promotes learning, to prevent anyone from gaining access to the knowledge of these shelves, but the line must be drawn with woodchucks.

My battle with the varmints began after patching the hole with flattened tin coffee cans. Spring steel traps were the first weapons employed in my campaign. Much too hazardous for me to handle, these devices were set for me by a friend, reducing our adversaries' population by six the first summer.

The next year, judging traps to be inhumane and too hazardous to the trapper, I employed a twelve gauge shotgun and a twenty-two caliber rifle in the continuing conflict. By this time, the groundhogs are tunneling under two buildings, and have built a first class hotel in a pile of dirt back of the book-shop. Fifteen critters went to their reward in 1992.

Anyway, I've done away with a dozen in 1993. No woodchucks have been seen around here for a month. Have we won the war? Who knows. I do know there is more to this bookselling business than just handling books.

My inspection trip to the back window just now was unproductive, no woodchucks. Come on, Ralph, pick up a pencil and write something. But this would be an ideal time for that nap. Fear keeps me from implementing the latter idea. My image will be badly fractured if a customer catches me sleeping. Such an eventuality pales into insignificance when compared to a much greater calamity. What if Doris breezes in on one of her inspection trips, and catches me slumbering? She visits the shop quite often when she's been sitting by an empty word processor for three days waiting for me to write an essay. No, in spite of my eyes being at half mast, I'd better think of something and start composing.

It would require more energy than I have today to write about the reception we scheduled on March 5, 1993 for the debut of our book, *A NORTHERN BOYHOOD*. With 150 RSVP's on hand we had no book thirty-six hours before the scheduled event. The meeting room at the Holiday Inn was reserved and their preparations were going forward. That experience would make quite an article, but in my weakened condition, remembering that disaster is too unnerving to think about.

If I had the strength, I could tell you about our printer who was having trouble producing the book's colored dust jacket. The clock was ticking. The deadline was almost upon us. I was sweating, Doris was going bonkers, and the printer, our friend George

Johnson, working around the fast-diminishing clock, had already lost his mind. Twenty-four hours before the party the guest of honor, our book, refused to make its appearance.

It would be nice to tell you that all ended well, because it did. Our treasures arrived just in time to make the reception a smashing success.

It's raining again. A soft soothing patter on the book-shop roof makes wakefulness next to impossible. My leaded eyelids are about to close. Oh, boy, as I thought she might, Doris is coming through the front door. She accidentally sprinkles me with cold raindrops from her dainty pink umbrella. What a fortunate happening! The cold drops shock me awake. Lucky for me she didn't realize I was half asleep. Satisfied with the little lie I told her, she pitter-pats out into the rainy early evening and I am alone once again.

What am I going to do? Nothing has been written and now she thinks the damned thing is about finished, and I don't even have a subject, much less a near-done manuscript.

I'll go and check on the woodchucks again. Maybe gazing out the back window will gain me strength and inspiration. Of course, I see no woodchucks and I'm as devoid of inspiration as before. I am also out of time. The clock says the book shop must be closed for the day. That's a plus, but the downside is that I'll have to confess my dereliction to Doris. Nothing has been written. Do you think she'll understand? I wouldn't bet on it. Woe is me.

I'll bet caffeinated Dr. Pepper will be hard to find around this place from now on.

THE BOOK SHOP

There are antiquarian book shops, used-book shops, and just plain book shops. The term book shop, or more properly book store, would generally be applied to stores vending new books. The waters of definition become quite murky when we begin to deal with the words Used and Antiquarian. An antiquarian book is always a used book, but a used book is not always antiquarian. For the uninitiated, this should be as clear as brown mud.

Most second-hand book shops carry a mixture of recently printed used books and books with some age. Age is, of course, relevant. To the teenagers a book that came off the press in 1940 is ancient history. But the book trade would consider a book old only if it was printed a hundred years or more ago.

Some few shops offer only old or very old books. Such shops are generally found in the large cities. Quite properly, antiquarian may appear on their shingle We who run used-book shops sometimes refer to our places as antiquarian shops. Using the word is not a glaring error because we do carry a number of antiquarian books along with our more recently printed merchandise. Our older, more expensive tomes are sometimes hidden away or they may rest on restricted and protected shelves. A book doesn't have to be old to be good. Conversely, age alone does not guarantee excellence.

This essay deals with used-book shops. Again I hasten to remind the reader that the type of shop addressed here also stocks old books. What then is a used-book shop?

Used-book shops range from a hole in the wall with a few nondescript books on makeshift shelves, supported by paint spattered cement blocks, to super emporiums in multi-floored buildings containing thousand of books in a pristine environment. A used-book shop can be a mish-mash of musty, water-stained paperbacks rescued from a hundred garage sales, hiding between the hardback residue of three library sales, all housed in a onestall garage with a leaky roof. Don't fault it. Such a horror may be someone's accomplished dream Non-descript houses, recent escapees from the wrecking ball, complete with shaggy smelly pets, where stale cooking odors permeate the dank air and where dirty sweat socks lie moldering in a dark corner, may also be book shops stocked with unfamiliar treasures.

A highly specialized stock can be carried in the back of a neatly shelved truck. Mobile shops could do well traveling to shows dealing with their specialty: Civil War, guns, military. Used-book shops are located in houses, barns, castles, store fronts, garages, antique malls, and buildings built specifically for the purpose; you'll find them anyplace that fits the bookman's dream and pocketbook.

Some shops are cold and dreary, some hot and humid. I like shops that are a little dusty and much cluttered. Seldom seen under-priced gems like to hide in clutter. Dirty, musty, smelly shops extinguish my always robust enthusiasm. Shops can be well-ordered with comfortable appointments such as chairs, tables, coffee pots, carpeted floors, and good lighting. Flashlights should be given out at the front door of others.

The location of a shop or its physical condition mean little to the true bibliophile. A glittering hoard may lurk in shops on the wrong side of urban renewal as well as on the seventh floor of Chicago's Wrigley Building. Sleepers, important books that are under-priced, may dwell in the substandard shop by accident and in the well-appointed place by design. What the shelves contain is the book lover's main concern.

Mixtures of hardback and paperback books with comic books or baseball cards as a sideline will be found in many shops. If it's made of paper, anything paper, it may be found where used books are sold. Postcards, letters, calendars, pamphlets, paintings, prints, snapshots, maps, sheet music, magazines, newspapers, posters, ads and advertising cards are all of interest to the bookman and are offered for sale in his shop.

Most used-book shops are general shops, others specialize. A specialist shop will do best in a large city. Ours is a general shop. We aim to stock books in every field of human knowledge; these categories are endless and continue to proliferate as long as the shop is vibrant. Once, trying to stump me, a party asked for books about weather; we have a weather section.

The stock of a general shop quite often reflects the interests of the proprietor. Most general categories will be found in our shop with a strong bent toward Americana. The shop is a mirror of my interest in the history of our country. The Erasmus, a used-book shop in South Bend, Indiana, because its owner is a retired theology professor, has extra strong sections in religion and philosophy.

Specialist bookmen have generally planted their shops in large population centers or they conduct their business by mail. A small population can sustain a general shop well enough, but a shop with a specialized stock must have a larger mass of population from which to draw its clientele. Americana is the specialty of choice today along with the American Civil War, hunting, fishing, firearms, and the military. Two categories, not often looked on as specialties, that do well when located in small towns are comic book stores and paperback exchanges. Specialties are legion. Think of a subject and there is probably someone, someplace, dealing with books in that specialty, either in a small shop or by mail.

Presiding over a collection of books is not the only function of our book shop person. Some shops offer search services. Attempting to locate specific titles for their customers is a time-consuming task filled with lots of detail work and small remuneration, a labor of love. Other shopkeepers send postcard quotes to the people operating the search services. The computer is beginning to play a part in this process. Another non-book shop activity of book dealers is the exhibition of their wares at book fairs. Dealers also issue book lists and catalogues. Some of these catalogues are works of art and will be collectors' items in time. A wonder of the used-book business is that there are so many ways to do it.

Most good book shops are the tangible result of their owner's long-standing love affair with the book, dreams finally realized. In many cases the desire for financial remuneration is secondary. These people thought the long years spent reading and studying the book itself the prerequisite for dealership. A shop born of such a parent is the reflected image of the effort expended learning about the book.

A good used-book shop has an atmosphere like no other place on earth. The knowledge of the ages permeates the very air of the place. The odor of aging paper, ink, glue, leather, and dye drives the true bibliophile into goose bumps and cold sweats; the proprietor's love and knowledge of his product is palpable. The muses dwell there in a place where the ancients linger and kindred spirits come to mingle.

PATIENCE

The used-book business teaches patience. The novice may not possess this virtue when he launches his enterprise, but if he sticks with the bookselling business, patience will certainly be added to his other meritorious attributes over time. We have a general used-book operation so this chapter concerns itself primarily with that type of book selling endeavor.

The front door to our book shop opened to the public in October 1973 after we realized that the time had come to do something with the rather vast book inventory that continued to accumulate Not being a particularly patient individual, I was prone to shoot from the hip; rapid judgment and the following action were my forte. My habit of acting impulsively was a part of my character To illustrate this point I relate the following incident.

It was the first winter after I had left my steady employment at the gas company It took place on a snowy Sunday night in 1971. Being a free agent, then, I no longer "punched a clock", so to speak. Doris and I had had a good summer selling and servicing gas yard lamps and gas barbecue grills. No structured activity existed to tie us down. It was on this particular snowy night in the middle of January that Doris and I had put her sister on the Chicago-bound South Shore train in South Bend, Indiana. Large snow flakes were pelting us as we trundled back to the car, whereupon I character-istically "shot from the hip". When we reached our vehicle. I said to my mate, "Let's get the hell out of here." By mid-week we were on our way south where we spent a month or more roaming around New Orleans and Natchez, Mississippi.

On another occasion, when I was still employed at the gas utility company, I acted on the spur of the moment after talking to Doris, who was visiting my army buddy, Elliott Byron and his wife Minnie in Dallas, Texas. Doris and I were going together but were not married Late one Sunday night in a 'phone conversation, she suggested that I should join the trio in Dallas. After hanging up the 'phone I called my boss, getting him out of bed, receiving permission to take some vacation time, threw a few things into a suitcase and took off for the airport. I had no air reservation and little money in my pocket, but I did have a big bulge in my heart for Doris Short and the capacity to act fast if circumstances so dictated.

On this occasion we returned together after a wonderful week with our friends. I can't recall when my instant decisions. like the two mentioned above, have turned out badly.

As our possessions begin to possess us as we travel down life's road, I am unable to indulge my impulsive nature to the extent I could in the past, but I don't regret having this feature as a part of my psyche.

These character attributes are not bad ones to have in the book game. Often snap judgments must be made when buying books. Sometimes no time exists in which to ponder and delay a decision. This is true mostly when the bookman is buying books. Patience, however, becomes a factor in the book shop proprietor's life as he builds his stock section by section and category by category and then waits for the buyers to darken the front door of his shop.

In our shop all of the money we took in during the first six years of the shop's existence, plus a seemingly never-ending stream of new money, went back into additional inventory. This went on from 1973 until we took the first money out for our own use in 1979; this is incubation in the extreme, but it contributed to making the shop what it is today.

Because no one knew the shop existed, business at the outset was terrible. Now after twenty-five years of operation there are still individuals right here in our neighborhood who are surprised when they walk through the front door for the first time and "discover" us.

Molasses flowing uphill on a very cold day is faster than word-of-mouth advertising. It's effective, but slow. The book shop is, and has been, open on Wednesday, Saturday, and Sunday, or by appointment, every week for twenty-five years. We don't believe in confusing people by constantly changing our hours. On many days years ago I was "skunked." The "no sale" tab on our cash register would have been badly worn out if we had a cash register. This is another device I abhor in a used-book shop - too noisy, too grasping, and too harsh, like a grocery store transaction. A quiet cash drawer seems more fitting for this, the Antiquarian World. I'd like to retire the adding machine too, but I at least settle for one that is about forty years old. Back again to the subject at hand. On many days I had solitude aplenty in the shop. No one disturbed my reading.

Sitting in the lonely shop I passed the time by toting up the number of potential customers in our shopping area. Further, I wondered why they didn't come to find me. My figuring went something like this: The population of the City of Niles is 15,000. Surrounding the town on three sides, the Niles Township contains another 15,000 people who were ignorant of my existence. South Bend, Mishawaka, Elkhart, Roseland, and all the area in between these places in Indiana plus the cities of Buchanan, Galien, Three Oaks, Dowagiac, New Buffalo, St. Joseph, Benton Harbor, and other nearby places in Michigan must shelter another quarter of a million folks. Thinking of the people in towns just a little further away like Kalamazoo, brought me to the conclusion that there were at least half a million people within spitting distance of my new enterprise who didn't know about me and seemingly didn't care either.

In those early days I had plenty of time to toss those figures around in my head. At the very least there must be 100,000 out of my potential 500,000 souls who could read; I was more than conservative in my figuring. Of the 100,000, I thought that maybe one in ten bought a book once in awhile. Where, then, are those 10,000 people? They were certainly not breaking my door down.

Slowly, ever so slowly, over the years this all began to change and those readers and book buyers began to find us. But at the present time, after twenty-five years, and innumerable write-ups about us in the local newspapers, I am amazed at the number of people who are finding our shop for the first time. Maybe this is not so strange after all when we consider that many of our present customers were either not born yet or were babes in arms when the shop first opened; yes, some who come to visit us regularly were but a gleam in their father's eye in October 1973 when we first put out our shingle.

Now, of course, the worm has turned. Sometimes even now though I believe we are better known in far away places than we are here at home. Some years ago a township trustee told me he was just then returning from a business trip to Boston. Someone there remarked about Casperson's Book Shop in the trustee's home town. The trustee, a lifelong resident of Niles, Michigan said, "I had to go to Boston to find out that we have an outstanding used-book store in Niles."

I replied, "Yup, we are Niles's best-kept secret."

One would think that after that experience and our conversation the trustee would be curious enough to come out and take a look.

It's been five years and I'm still waiting. In some people the curiosity gene is dead, dead, dead.

The slow growth of our book business is not something that was unexpected. Don Allen, my friend, mentor, and fellow bookman warned me about the length of time it would take to become known. Once, during casual conversation Don remarked that his book business provided for about half of his livelihood. I asked how he funded the other half and he replied, "We don't."

It takes years and years to build a respectable general stock unless one is, un-typically, a wealthy person, and is able to raid other well-stocked shops. The categories from Art to Zoology are endless. Some don't, unlike us, aspire to put together an inventory containing books in every field of human knowledge. I feel that unless the entrepreneur has some other focus in mind, his long-term success is dependent on this type of all inclusive stock building. Any book stock, if it is worked with and added to, is like fine wine. It becomes seasoned and improves with age over the years. This is especially true of a general stock. At first the stock is predictable, but after awhile it begins to harbor a host of secrets. To the browsing customer the surprises are legion and serendipity is the rule. But, again, it takes time.

A good book that has rested on my shelves for years without being sold is not something that I lose sleep over. Such a book is like an aging girl still waiting patiently for the right suitor to walk into her life. In time the person who has been searching for a particular title for years will materialize. The fact that you have the title he has been seeking for such a long time will be remembered, as will the day he found it in your shop. Real bibliophiles tell many stories about the day they located that elusive volume. Generally these events make a deep impression. When I was studying the American Civil War I looked for Jefferson Davis's work, *THE RISE AND FALL OF THE CONFEDERACY*. The book seemed to have gone out of existence. I will never forget the day I found the two volume set in a dingy shop in New Orleans. Since that memorable day many copies have passed through my hands, but I remember their genesis not at all. The first set I found is stamped indelibly in my memory.

My customers worry more than I about the fine volumes that
have seemingly become permanent fixtures on my shelves. Knowing
my philosophy in this regard, it rankles me some when they say,
"That book has been there for five years. Why don't you reduce the
price, and then maybe you'd sell it." My answer is always the same,
"That book is fairly priced. It is waiting patiently for the right
person to come along and liberate it and the right person will come,
but it takes time." Sometimes I will add to my rejoinder, "Look, if
that tome bothers you why don't you buy it yourself and get it the
hell out of here?"

One afternoon in January 1996, during a blizzard, I was in the
book shop ignoring the weather and feeling sorry for friends
sweating in the torrid eighty degree heat in the southland. While
working to straighten out some cluttered shelves in the back room of
the shop I spied two small unopened boxes from the Kansas
Historical Society. Their labels were postmarked May 10, 1973 -
five months before the book shop opened for business. Having
kicked around the shop now for over twenty years, I haven't gotten
around to opening them yet. I have long forgotten what the boxes
contain and I don't really care. Patience in my long association with
the book business has become such an ingrained virtue by now that
perhaps it is at last turning into a vice.

Back to the boxes. What's in them? Historical pamphlets I
presume. Highly salable stuff I'd venture. Shall I open them? Maybe
I will and then maybe I'll let them sit a bit longer. Like fine wine or
other spirits, and unlike the groceryman's stuff, a good book
inventory doesn't spoil; it gets better with age. If I had opened those
boxes twenty-three years ago their contents would undoubtedly be
long gone. I still have them. Somehow this gives me a bit of
satisfaction. I wonder where that large box from the Illinois
Historical Society is. Some of the pamphlets in the box were 100
year old when I got them twenty-five years ago. I know they're
around here someplace. Someday I'll find them. It's a good thing the
roof on my warehouse doesn't leak.

I decided, in February 1994, to pay some attention to decorated
and illustrated covers. These beautiful books with colorful designs
and pictures on their covers were published in the early years of the

twentieth century. My search took me to the attic of the shop. A battered old notebook indicated that in 1981 I had wrestled a bunch of boxes to this unlikely place. A treasure trove awaited me there. Here were twenty boxes of books containing decorated covers. This cache was made thirteen years ago when this type of book was easy to come by. Now these little works of art are not plentiful. Before sticking these books away thirteen years ago I had priced them. The prices averaged from four to eight dollars each. I repriced them at their fair market value in 1994; now the prices average from eight to twenty dollars each, and where can you find any from original sources? They are even uncommon in book stores.

Covering these old books with transparent protective covers, I arranged them into an attractive display; it's quite impressive. Now my friends and customers, synonymous terms, ask where I got so many books of this type. My reply is, "I found them in the attic."

I'm then looked at as though my auditors are saying, "Yes, he's got the books all right, but he's lost his marbles."

I'll not belabor the subject further. Suffice it to say that if you choose to walk in the book world wearing my moccasins, be prepared to add patience to your quiver of virtues.

MISCONCEPTIONS

Probably the greatest misconception about used-book shops is that their inventory contains ancient tomes exclusively. This is untrue. Some books that are still on best seller lists can be found on our shelves.

The word "used" is a misapplication of terms. "Used" implies that the book has been read. Many books on our shelves have never had their pages turned. They are pre-owned, but have not been used. Our shops could correctly be called "pre-owned book shops" instead of "used-book shops." Semantics aside, most shops have recently published titles in stock along with those that were owned by someone's ancestors.

Many readers have a mental image of a used book store being located in the inner city where the rent is low and the environment is bad; a location shunned by more successful entrepreneurs. Years ago this was the case. Urban renewal changed that Today only a few shops are located in areas that escaped the urban renewal wrecking ball. Their business suffers because people are reluctant to frequent them without an armed guard. These places are the exception today. Now most shops are located in desirable downtown shopping areas. Some are found in malls, some are in suburbia.

Most modern shops are not the dingy, unattractive, badly lit storehouses of the past. Invention of the fluorescent tube light changed that. The idea that it is difficult to see in a used-book shop died with the naked light bulb hanging from the ceiling. There are exceptions, but it is no longer necessary to have a flashlight along when browsing.

Modern shops are not the dust bins of yesterday. Also, the unwashed proprietor no longer inhabits a hovel in the back of the shop where he lives on cold cereal and cheap whiskey. Most of the time the shelves and books of the modern shop are not covered with an inch of dust. The bookseller can be a nonconformist without living in filth. An unclean body and dirty clothing contribute nothing to the independence that yesterday's dealers so successfully portrayed.

Modern bookmen (not a sexist term, but a proper name for a profession as in mechanic, baker or tailor) tend to be people who do not conform. These days they don't telegraph their nonconformity as vividly as did their predecessors. The booksellers who have passed from the scene were nonconformist in their habits, dress, and life-styles, as well as in their thinking and beliefs Today we take as many showers as anybody else and, with minor exceptions, our dress conforms but our thinking and credos parallel those of the old-timers. We don't occupy space in mass America; and we don't act, talk, or think like most folks. We are not better than mass man. We're just different.

I am often asked if I am a librarian. The fact that I am surrounded by books promotes this question. Librarians are not bookmen because they have no need to be bookmen. Book dealers for the most part would make bad librarians. That is not to say that there are no former librarians who are now booksellers; there are. Curt and Lynn Bohling in Decatur, Michigan were both librarians and have become successful book dealers and bookmen.

The function of a librarian and a bookman differ by 180 degrees. A librarian presides over a process that consumes the book. The bookman's mission is to conserve the book. To illustrate this point I direct the reader's attention to the Library Sale. The bookman rescues that which the librarian discards. There are other disparities of function between the two professions Suffice it to say that librarians function in an environment that distances them from the main purpose of our being - the book.

I am also asked repeatedly if I have been a teacher. My total teaching experience is limited to instructing WWII Army recruits in machine gun culture.

The teachers I know who are now book dealers are not there because of what they learned as teachers. They were taught little in their formal teacher's training that fit them to be bookmen. These people were unable or unwilling to do what was required of them by modern school administrations. They revolted against endless, meaningless paperwork and the roadblocks that made it impossible for them to teach. They quit and have joined the book dealer fraternity. They have now found a home with us nonconformists in the book trade.

The first requirement for book dealership is the love, yes, the passion, for books. This must be followed by the absorption (as in sponge) of great amounts of knowledge about books and the book. Add to this an insatiable appetite for the acquisition of mountains of books and you are on your way to becoming one schooled in bookmanship.

BOOK EVALUATION

Book evaluation, or book pricing, cannot be done well unless the person doing the job has "book sense" and good judgment. Book sense is the ability to instinctively know at a glance, or after a hasty perusal, that a book is important or valuable.

I once thought that book sense was a faculty one was born with; you either had it or you didn't. Presently, I believe that book sense can be acquired by wide general reading, the study of the book itself, and long experience with books in the marketplace

A book dealer must evaluate a book twice, once when he buys it and again when he prices it for sale. On most occasions when buying books, our bookman must make snap decisions. He must decide right now if a book is worth buying at the asking price. At estate or other public sales, auctions, and even when buying from an individual or another dealer, our bookman does not enjoy the luxury of unlimited time. Book sense comes into play at these times. Without it the buyer may pay too much for common books, skip over desirable items, or aid his competition by taking too much time deciding what to buy.

Time is of no essence when books go through the pricing process in the book shop. This procedure should take place in a secluded area where the bookman has ready access to the tools of his trade. Some of the tools are bibliographies, price guides, auction records, biographical dictionaries, and the *Books In Print* volumes. When pricing books he can't price off the top of his head, the bookman consults his tools. The majority of books that pass through a bookseller's hands are priced without research. Book sense is essential when determining which items need to be investigated.

Bibliographies are used to find out more about the author, variations in editions, first edition points, and imprints. A bibliography can be about an author or subject. It is an authoritative work on the books and authors it deals with. Care and knowledge are essential when using bibliographies, too, because they do contain mistakes.

Biographical dictionaries are useful in determining who an obscure author might be; what is his claim to fame? After all, a book by the first person to see the Grand Canyon might have more value than one by the wife who wrote it at the big ditch, on her honeymoon.

Books In Print list the current selling prices of books that are still available from the publishers. These volumes are used constantly. All things being equal, a customer won't buy a used reprint of a book if he can get a new copy for less. It is also good to know that the old book being researched is important enough to still be in print.

Price guides are usually compilations of dealers' catalogs. These publications are what their name implies, guides. Their prices are not prices realized, but prices asked. The names of the persons who contributed the information are usually listed in the guides. It is important to know if these dealers have a reputation for pricing their books moderately, or high, or perhaps, low. As stated above, prices in guides are not biblical. The pricer must use good judgment in arriving at his price, using the guide as only one piece of the puzzle.

The preface to a price guide is important. Bradley plainly states in his guide that his prices are for fine copies in dust jackets. His listing of $600-800 for *"Gone With the Wind"* will not be valid for a dirty, shaken copy, or one without a dust jacket. Many folks' bubble is broken, and their treasure becomes trash, when I direct them to read the conditions, in the preface, that support the price in the guide they have used to inflate their balloon.

Book Prices Current are books that list prices actually realized at auction. "Oh, boy," you may say to yourself, "at last, unlike price guides, we are dealing with actual prices. We can throw judgment out the window." The first sentence above is true, but I must modify your enthusiasm by asking the following unanswerable questions: Were two bidders lusting after the same book, thus bidding up the price unrealistically? Was there a snowstorm in New York on the day of the auction causing it to be sparsely attended? How about the condition of the item being auctioned? *Book Prices Current* does not reveal this. Was the public preoccupied with a great news event, causing the auction to be held in a near empty room? How many people would attend an auction on Dec. 8, 1941? No, auction prices are not gospel either. Judgment must be applied here as well.

In pricing, many factors must be taken into consideration: condition, dust jacket, edition, binding, paper, imprint, typography, and illustrations, to name some.

Book evaluation is not a science or an art. It is a skill. One's effort in this area will be ineffective without book sense and judgment. Both are acquired by long years of general reading and exposure to the products of the commercial book world.

Charles E. Feinberg, a noted collector of Walt Whitman books, manuscripts and ephemera, had this to say about his collecting: "I was resolved to bring together as much as I possibly could, and this I have done, occasionally not being able to acquire what I wanted only because I lacked the money at the particular time the item was available and made the mistake of _not_ going into debt."

Charles lived to regret it when he didn't follow the great truism of the Antiquarian Book Trade: "The time to buy an out-of-print book is when you see it." The nature of this business being what it is, a book passed by may very well be a book that is gone forever.

The serious collector of books, records, art, bottles, or beer cans must be prepared to take on debt, at times, commensurate with his ability to repay, when a desirable item surfaces. The debt can be amortized over time, but the book or other collectible may never be available again. The item struggled for may be unique. In the case of manuscripts or ephemera, it may be one of a kind. Unlike a streetcar, a scarce book will not be along again in a few minutes.

Collectors' gems surface at very inappropriate times. A collection will never amount to very much unless the collector learns how to handle these unhandy times - money must be found and the desirable artifact brought home. Most dealers will bend over backwards with layaway plans and terms to make it possible for their customer to acquire a much wanted item.

If a book is scarce or rare, it may pass through a dealer's hands only once during his professional life. Many rare books are known but are never seen. These books materialize infrequently and are sold rapidly once they surface. Unlike the grocer, the used bookseller cannot call the wholesaler and have another copy of a work delivered posthaste. We don't have the luxury of that kind of warehouse behind our stock.

Book dealers who have been in the trade for any length of time agree there is an occult force working against those who procrastinate. A book that has rested undisturbed on a bookshop shelf for years is subjected to this force when someone removes it and says to the shopkeeper, "I have been looking for this book for years." In that case one would think that he would take it home, but no. He continues, "I will get it next time I'm in the shop." Invariably before "next time" comes, someone else has added the book to his library. This phenomenon takes place so frequently it has almost become a bookseller's law.

Recently two sets of Shelby Foote's volumes stood proudly on the shelves in our Civil War section. Their fate perfectly illustrates the weird occurrence mentioned above. These books had not been disturbed for a year. When the recent Civil War series, narrated by Shelby Foote, appeared on television, interest in these Civil War history books was stimulated. Two individuals spied the sets. Both said they wanted the books, but because there were two sets there, no one needed to act right now. I offered to put the books in layaway and was told there was no need for that.

As far as I know these two customers are still looking for Shelby Foote's *The Civil War-A Narrative*. Both sets sold within a week after my offer to lay them away was refused. When the procrastinators returned and saw the books were gone, they looked at me as though I was a star player in the Watergate cover-up. I'm not comfortable being the object of someone's misplaced wrath.

Repeatedly I tell customers about the mysterious force that goes to work when they, at long last, locate the book of their dreams. Quite often they still leave the book on the shelf. They then look at me as if to say, "Don't pull your salesmanship tricks on me." Invariably, when they come back in a month and the book is gone, I receive a different kind of look. "Why did you do this to me? You knew I wanted that book - you fink."

Some years ago, when studying the American Civil War, I needed the book *The Rise And Fall Of the Confederacy* by Jefferson Davis - it eluded me. I wrote to booksellers in New York and Boston but was unable to find a copy. During this period my wife, Doris, and I were in an out-of-print shop while vacationing in New Orleans. The proprietor of the New Orleans shop violated one of the major laws of book selling: "When a customer wants to browse leave him alone." He glued himself to my elbow where he delivered an endless stream of inconsequential verbiage. In spite of his interference I saw a copy of *The Rise And Fall* and clutched the two volume set to my chest. Because the verbose bookman confused me with his chatter, I returned the books to the shelf. We escaped without making a purchase. Doris knew what I had found, and when we returned to our motel room she asked why I left the tomes behind. She said that we could go back and pick them up the next morning and we did go back. The set was gone!

I made a firm resolve that sorry day. When I see an out-of-print book I want, or bump into a large desirable lot, I always find a way to fund the purchase - there is no hesitation.

I am often asked when I will be getting a copy of some specific title. It is not possible to answer this inquiry. Some people don't realize that the supply side of a used-book shop's equation is largely hit or miss. Sure, I keep my eyes open for someone's wants, but I would buy a good book anyway, even if no specific request had been made. Trying to tell when I will be getting another copy of a certain book is like predicting the date of the next big California earthquake. Actually predicting the earthquake would be less difficult because we know for sure it is coming someday, but I don't know if I will ever get another copy of a specific book.

Folks often ask me how I know what to buy. A partial answer to this inquiry is given in the preceding paragraph. Some booksellers see the face of a prospective customer when they see a book. If they don't see the face, they don't buy the book. In other words, if they don't have the chance of a ready sale for the book, they pass it by. I buy that way too, but if that were the only criteria used in book buying, the bookshop would soon become a very sterile place and the business would become stagnant. It couldn't grow. If the book is an important work, in reasonably good condition and I can buy it at a sensible price, I add it to my stock. My theory holds that there is a customer for every important book, and eventually that person will show up in my shop and will be matched up with the book. Sometimes years go by before this happens but I am amply rewarded when I see the expression on the person's face and hear him exclaim, "I've been looking for this book for years and here it is at last."

To sum up: Don't leave a wanted book on the shelf until "next time". The chances are good that the opportunity, missed today, will be as irrevocably lost as yesterday and "next time", like yesterday, will never come again.

BOOK SHOP CONVERSATION

A used-book store is a stage. There is no play bill and the actors recite the un-reherarsed parts prompted by the spirits of play directors who are no longer with us. The atmosphere of the place provides an environment conducive to good conversation, deep philosophical discussions and the give and take of political debate. It is also a natural place for artists and students of that discipline to toss about various artistic concepts.

The military minded verbally fight the battles of the past. The dress of their soldiers is a favorite subject. Men playing soldiers argue about the merits of weapons used in battles of yore-Railroad buffs meet and talk about their avocations. As they leaf through the picture books that show the old steam locomotives even I can hear the sharp hissing of the escaping steam.

Local history comes into its own. The exact location of Fort St. Joseph near Niles gets its share of attention. Was the Fort located on the east or west side of the St. Joseph River? Each side has its proponents. The proprietor of the shop shocks his listeners when he tells them they are both right. There was, he says, a fort used for trading on the east side of the stream and a military installation on the bluff overlooking the river on the west side. Should he be believed? Maybe he is playing the devil's advocate as he so often does to stimulate the discussion in progress.

The nautically minded individuals meet in The Ships and The Sea section. They have a fine time swapping stories from books about the sea. They exchange addresses. Strangers who have discovered common ground are strangers no longer. They arrange to meet again. A new friendship is born, fostered by the spirit of authors who have long since passed from the scene.

Being a gardener himself, the proprietor likes to eavesdrop on conversations emanating from the Gardening section. "But Rodale (also now gone) says ..." or, "Mrs. Stout (passed on) would certainly agree ...." Those who are no longer among us continue to speak through those who are still here.

Because I scribble a bit myself, I like to compare notes with anyone who is buying a stack of books on writing. In response to my inquiry I may be told, "No, I've not finished a book yet. I like political themes though and would like to emulate H.L. Mencken." Again, seeds planted by authors in the past are still sprouting today. When the shop is quiet I can sometimes hear customers talking to the authors. Or are they merely talking to themselves?

Many people are interested in finding out more about the book itself. What should they read in this area, they ask. I refer them to books by and about the great bookmen. Rosenbach, Targ, Newman, Everett, Randolph, and others have left for the great book shop on high. The spirits of all these great book figures haunt all good used-book shops. They help create the atmosphere where erudite conversation flourishes.

Writers of lasting stories have long vanished. They are brought back to life in book shop discussions. Their great works are alive and well between the covers of books on the shelves in the Literature section. Emerson, Thoreau, Twain, Hawthorne, Hemingway, Steinbeck, Louisa May Alcott, and James Fenimore Cooper to name a few Americans, are resting side by side with their foreign brothers and sisters. Their spirits mingle on my shelves. They too stimulate conversation and further reading.

We are especially proud that we have a place for Niles' own Ring Lardner. He, too, is alive and well in our shop. There is no metal marker here, planted by the Historical Society, to mark his place. But he lives on through his pen at the end of the Lit. bay.

Unlike a grocery store, bicycle shop, or haberdashery, the ghosts of the people who made the products we vend live on in their works. The authors have long since departed. The philosophers are gone. Biographers' subjects have left long ago for the ether regions. Soldiers who have fought their last battle are now at rest in the many "Arlingtons" where we see the white crosses row on immaculate row. Painters who now live only in their long stilled brush strokes have drifted away into the sunset. They are all gone but they are somehow still with us in the used-book shop.

"TREASURES" FOUND IN BOOKS

Many of the books I buy have presentation messages written on the flyleaf. Most of these messages are common, like, "To Emmy from Aunt Nellie, Christmas 1926", written in a copy of *ELSIE DINSMORE*. Some of these presentations are more complicated and are amply worthy of mention in this work. Books, too, have become depositories for letters and other literary efforts. Some of these are also worth publishing.

I do not know the people who wrote the messages that rest in books awaiting my inspection. The books I am working with today may have been in my warehouse for several years. By the time I get to them I have no idea where they came from. Here is a note written on pretty green note paper that I found in a philosophy book. "Since you have started studying religion you have become a divine lover." The author and recipient of this sweet missive shall remain forever anonymous.

I found the following essay lodged between pages 112 and 113 of Mitchener's *HAWAII*. "John held onto his life as tenaciously as the defenders of Bataan, but the end was as foreseeable as the dawn of a new day. He smouldered for several days but his life finally left him like the faint glow goes out of a pile of slowly burning leaves." Maybe today this budding author is writing romance novels.

This bit of advice appeared on the first free end paper of a copy of *INCREDIBLE JOURNEY*. "When driving, keep your neck tucked in." I would like to know the inside joke that prompted that inscription.

I can sometimes guess the age of a book when I read the messages and names written on the flyleafs. People's names were different years ago. The inscriptions that follow will illustrate my point. "To my dear Phoebe from your Aunt Emma, Christmas 1920."; or, "For your 12th birthday, to Gertrude from your mother with love, August 1933." Contrast these with the following modern inscriptions. "To Suzy from Mom, Xmas 1979." or "Happy Birthday Dad from Jennifer, 1982."

Inscriptions and notes are not the only things found in books. Here again a book can be dated by observing the objects concealed between its pages. Hair pins and common pins indicate that the tome was read between the late 1800's and 1930. Botanical items such as four-leaf clovers and flowers are found from the mid 1900's to the late 1930's. Bobby pins are found from the Depression years until just before the modern era.

Metal paper clips are still being used as bookmarks but lately their cousin, the plastic clip, has appeared. Both are bad, but at least the plastic variety doesn't stain the pages with unsightly rust.

Matchbook covers have been used as bookmarks for years. Serving the same purpose I have found rubber bands, wood matches, pencils, tooth-picks, gum and candy wrappers, toilet paper, Kleenex, and real bookmarks from defunct bookstores.

Tin-types and 'cartes de visite' show up from the American Civil War until the late 1800's. Since then we find business or personal calling cards and black and white snapshots. Present day books harbor color photos.

Obituaries of the author, and just about anyone else, fall out from between the pages regularly. Books are a handy repository for newspaper and magazine articles that have a relationship with the subject matter of the book.

Very large atlases are a convenient hiding place for larger, more substantial treasures. I recently found an envelope of charred leaves from an account book that had been through the Chicago Fire of 1871. I sold this frameable relic for ten dollars. Another atlas contained a newspaper map of the Civil War battlefields around Richmond, Virginia. The map, printed on the rag paper used in those days, was in mint condition. It had been stowed away when it was new in 1865 and had not been disturbed for 125 years. The atlas was dated 1860.

Atlases serve as family archives, too. Between maps showing countries that no longer exist, somebody's ancestors filed away military discharge certificates, marriage licenses, black-bordered funeral programs and other family documents. Frameable prints and engravings have also been found in atlases and other large books.

My greatest find in an old atlas was an engraved certificate from the World Columbian Exposition of 1892. This too had been tucked away when it was new and remained hidden and protected from foul air, sunlight, dust, and kids' sticky fingers for a hundred years. I found it just in time to sell it for fifty dollars to a person who started collecting Columbian Exposition material one-hundred years after the fact.

QUESTIONS ASKED

Isaac Asimov once wrote, "... self-education is, I firmly believe, the only kind of education there is. The only function of a school is to make self-education easier; failing that it does nothing."

Some people's common sense seem to take flight when they come through the front door of the book shop and view, for the first time, the floor to ceiling shelves filled with countless volumes of forgotten lore. Strange things seem to happen to them when they first smell the printer's ink, glue, and aging paper. Is it the atmosphere, unknown any other place in the world, that prompts the strange questions they ask?

There are 100,000 books in our collection. It is possible for me to read 100 books a year and I often attain this total. At this rate I would need 800 years to read all of the books on our shelves.

Quite often I am asked in all seriousness by one of those newcomers mentioned above, "Have you read all of these books?"

I believe a question like that merits the answer I give, "I've read all of them but six and will finish them this weekend."

"Do you buy books?", is another frequent inquiry that makes little sense. Is it not obvious that in order to build and maintain the stock that my interrogator is looking at it would be necessary to spend money? I explain that books are our stock in trade, just like the bicycle in a cycle shop. No one gives bicycles to the bike shop operator nor do they unload their books on me on a no-charge basis. I explain that I have laid out U.S. coin for every book on our shelves. In fact, I continue, "It is our policy not to accept books free of charge."

Owning and operating a used-book shop seems to appeal to many people. It never occurs to some of them that this business, like any enterprise, is fraught with trials and problems. Just find a bunch of books, put them on the shelves, and presto, we have instant success and a life of ease forever after A frequent question posed by these misguided souls is, "What book should I read that would teach me the book business?"

I answer that inquiry by saying, "There is no do-it-yourself monograph. No single treatise will teach you this business. I began to read about books and started to frequent book shops when I was in high school and I still know very little. Over fifty years of inquiry and I still have no sheepskin." I'm sure my questioner doubts my veracity.

At the risk of damaging your credibility I have to tell you that I am sometimes asked, "How much are your books?" Would anyone ask the Kroger Store Manager how much groceries are this week? The question must be answered and the answer goes something like this, "Our price range is rather wide. We have books priced from twenty-five cents to hundreds of dollars."

We get unusual requests, some of which are as easy to respond to as sliding down an icy hill, but some are as impossible as trying to climb the same slope. Variations of the following question are thrown at us with some frequency "When I was a kid I read a book about Uncle Amos and Johnny. Do you have it in stock?" The inquiry continues, "I've been looking for a copy for ten years; surely with all of the books you have here you must have a copy."

I'm sure that if the search continues for two times another ten years the tome will never surface to satisfy the nostalgic yearning. I wish kids would keep a record, by title and author, of the books they read. It would make booksellers' lives a lot easier fifty years hence.

Some folks are wrestling with the memory of a poem many years after they learned it "by heart" in elementary school. The poet's name has long been forgotten and so has the poem itself. I am expected to come up with a copy after my prospective customer gives me the following solid information: "You know, it's about a little red wagon and a dog named Spot and it sounds like this: La la, la la; sim bob to fa; la la, la la; we hom boo ba; you know, lots of rhythm."

My response to all of this is, "Oh sure, I know it well, but I sold my only copy last week."

On occasion we get requests through the mail in handwriting so bad that if the letter had been typed it would have been unreadable. We don't welcome mail requests anyway, so when I get one of these it burns my fingers as I consign it to the the waste-basket.

Over the years I have spent many hours putting together a shop for the enjoyment of browsers and I resent it when anyone tries to circumvent the browsing idea by writing letters or telephoning his requests. These make me as unhappy as a frog in a dry swamp. I don't care how absurd, non-sensible, or dumb a question or request might be, as long as it is delivered to me in person. We enjoy them all.

I am constantly questioned by folks who frequent my book shop. Many questions are next to impossible to answer, and some require lengthy complex answers. I don't have the inclination and the questioner wouldn't spare the time to listen to a full answer to some of his inquiries.

"What is the oldest book you have in stock?" The oldest book printed from moveable type would have been dated 1450 AD. Books printed from 1450 to 1500 AD are known as Incunabula. We get these on occasion. Books produced in the 1700's are not uncommon. I usually have some in stock from the seventeenth century as well. Books dated from 1450 to 1600 are not common.

I am asked to produce my most expensive book. Our books are not shelved according to price, so this is a difficult request. Books priced at fifty or one hundred dollars can be readily found in our stock. Some years ago I sold a book that carried a $2,500 price tag.

When I am asked what category of books sell best, I am at a loss to come up with an answer. Civil War books sell more readily than books about optics. But when I try to make a comparison of the activity between the Religion and the Art section I am unable to make a judgment. The truth is I don't really know what sells best.

One of the most often asked questions is what prompted my desire to become a bookseller. This inquiry is the easiest one for me to answer. I was born into a world of books. My mother was a school teacher and my father was self-educated. This meant that there were books in our home. At an early age I was exposed to a used-book shop in my home town. In that dusty old shop I fell in love with the idea of having such a place myself. It took about forty years to materialize, but the seed was planted in that shop

People want to know what I read. Outside of the hard sciences, I read in all fields of human knowledge. That's one of the reasons I have a general book shop. I'm interested in everything. My favorite subjects are books about books, history, economics, some philosophy, sociology, and literature.

"Where do you get your books?" is a question that is asked repeatedly. I buy household accumulations and private libraries. My customers and others bring books to me. Book scouts look for books for me. I buy from other dealers all over this country. I buy books anywhere I find them.

I am asked how I know what to buy. I buy what will sell in time. Experience and knowledge of books and the book market tell me what that is.

I am asked how I know what price to put on a book. Suffice it to say that book pricing is not an exact science but an imprecise skill. Various price theories are brought into play as well.

"How long have I been a book seller?" I began selling books by mail about twenty-five years ago. From these meager beginnings the shop was born in 1973.

People often call me wanting to know-what I buy because they have some books to sell. It is more productive to tell them what I don't buy: Reader's Digest Condensed, National Geographic Magazines, cheap out-dated encyclopedias. Some book club editions interest me not at all. I have to see everything else in order to determine if I want to buy it.

A question that is on a par with, "What is the price of your books?" is, "What do you pay for books?" The more valuable the book, the more I pay. This should be obvious.

Sometimes I think the questions are sort of dumb, but if someone is truly interested enough to pose the inquiry in good faith, who am I to pass judgment on the quality of the question? I answer as best I can.

At times people on the other end of telephone calls I receive are unable to express themselves; at other times the caller gives me joy by using the language as it was meant to be used--to communicate.

The good speakers' thoughts are well organized and they deliver complete sentences. Even paragraphs are apparent.

Fortunately, most of the people I come in contact with speak properly, so the ones whose language consists only of grunts and strange noises stick out like alligators in a small pond.

I have not kept pace with all the modern colloquialisms that have crept into the language. I know that our language is a living, growing, changing thing, so I accept the new expressions like, "cool," "get right," and "you know" as a part of this mutation. Some will survive and some will die like, "O yeah," "snafu," "fubar," and "GI" of a generation ago. Even when using the new expressions, however, some folks are unable to communicate.

Most of my bad conversational trips take place on the 'phone. The following example dramatizes a complete inability to convert thought into understandable language - an inability to communicate. One morning when I answered the 'phone the calling party said, "Hi, books ya know - um, uh, you know, m' grandma. Died, man, ya know - attic, wow, cool! You know, books - old house. Hey man, fantastic." Probing interrogation revealed that the fellow's grandmother had recently passed away, leaving a big house, with an attic full of old books which he wished to sell.

It was not difficult to find out that he thought most of the books were rare. The man had never seen such treasures (naturally) and he knew they were all priceless first editions. I made an appointment to view the bonanza and embarked on yet another bubble-bursting expedition.

On another occasion a girl called to inquire about the value of a book. Because some illustrated editions of this book were valuable, I asked if the book was illustrated. She left the 'phone and when she returned she said, "I can't tell if it's illustrated or not. It's printed in German." Could there be an art method around that escaped me too, like some of the new expressions that have crept into the language?

Illustrated or not, I would have had to see the volume in question before I could give a fair opinion of its worth. Most callers understand this requirement, but some don't and they are offended when I refuse to render an opinion concerning the worth of an item I have not been able to inspect.

Many points come into play in the evaluation of a book. It is not possible to assess all of them without holding the book in my hands. Is the book a first edition or a reprint? Are the binding and typography mundane or something special? What about the quality of the illustrations and is the illustrator collected? Who published the work? The printer might be important. Is there anything special about the paper? Many other points must be considered - lastly the condition.

My opinion of the condition of a book varies widely from the opinion of the person seeking the evaluation. When I mention to the 'phone caller that I must see the book to ascertain its condition, I am sometimes told, "Oh, the book is in fine condition. The front cover is missing, but the back one is here. The inside of the book is in excellent shape except for a few missing pages in front. Over all the book is fine." In this case I spell FINE - T-R-A-S-H.

A few questions about the book the person wants evaluated tells me if the book warrants a trip to the shop for a closer look. There is no reason to put someone to the trouble of toting the book to the shop when the answer to a question or two tells me that their treasure is valueless.

Any book, outside the scope of those that we know are valueless, must be seen to be evaluated. I am not being fair to the book owner or myself without a personal inspection.

My customers know about my passion for proper delivery of our language and they regale me, on occasion, with anecdotes about atrocious English usage. One of these tales had to do with a young man applying for admission to an English class at a junior college in one of our major cities. The prospective student carried a valid high school diploma. He, a product of twelve years in the American school system, asked, "Hey man, does youse needs to know readin' to do this here class?"

It looks like I will suffer for some time to come.

WHAT TO COLLECT

"What books should I collect?" Thank heaven, this question is not posed to me very often. When the question is asked I would like to reply by saying, "If you don't know what to collect, don't collect anything. Wait until the passion strikes you and then you will know. It's a little bit like choosing a wife or husband. When the right one comes along, you'll know."

A book collection should be dictated by that which appeals to us. A collection started because someone told us what to collect will soon pale. If spiders turn you on go ahead and form a collection of books about spiders. Just because your brother-in-law is a nice guy and you like him and he collects books on the six-sided square, don't feel obligated to do likewise.

I well remember when, twenty years ago, it was the thing to do to collect N.C. Wyeth, Arthur Rackham, Norman Rockwell, and other illustrators. Like the Kipling and Charles Dickens craze of the 1920's, the illustrator furor has started its demise. People collecting in this field today are there because they like the artist's work, not because the work is in vogue.

When "everyone" gets on the bandwagon and starts collecting books in any given area, prices skyrocket. This is a good reason to stay away from collecting that which is in favor. Today "everyone" is looking for hand-tinted botanical prints, Western Americana, and Lakeside Classics. (I collected them twenty-five years ago.) Five years ago the same "everyone" bid Gene Stratton-Porter's works to astronomical heights.

The ideal game is to form a collection of books that appeal to you, before others are doing the same thing. Have your collection well on the way before the demand becomes universal at which time you can sell out to the newcomers and go on to another sleepy field.

If a person likes to read books about fishing and accumulates a number of fishing books, he has just that - an accumulation. If, however, he seeks out and buys all of the books he can find about fly fishing, he is more likely to be putting together a collection. This is how collections are started. Let us say that the Civil War interests you greatly. Much reading is done and the books accumulate. Over time, maybe, a great interest in the Battle of Gettysburg develops. Because you can't buy everything available about the whole conflict, you specialize. Focus your resources on this one aspect of the war and in time you will have formed a respectable collection of books about this one battle A book collector is born.

Perhaps our mythical collector likes to read literature He develops a great love for John Steinbeck. At first reading copies of the great author's works will satisfy. Books with dust jackets will follow, after which the "keeper" will be a First Edition in dust jacket. If it is signed by the author, so much the better. Our collector will acquire magazine and newspaper appearances and introductions written by Steinbeck. Pamphlets by or about the author, promotional pieces, and photographs will be squirreled away. If his wallet is fat, his favorite author's manuscripts will be fair game, along with limited editions of the author's writings in fine bindings. Our collector won't stop there either. He will acquire books about his author. If he really gets carried away, he will add artifacts to his collection: Books annotated in the author's handwriting, his bookplate, his pen perhaps, or even his old hunting cap.

Central Michigan University has a collection of *The Compleat Angler* by Izaak Walton. This collection fills many, many shelves. A collection of just one title can be extensive I wonder how many feet of shelving would be filled by all of the editions of Thoreau's *Walden*.

Books with illustrated or decorated covers are being picked up and are going into budding collections at this time. The interest in these little works of art is quite new. Old books with artistic book jackets are another area of recent interest. Several of my customers have started putting together collections of Modern Library These areas of collecting interest are still do-able.

I collect books by Margaret Bourke-White, Edmund G. Love, Albert J. Nock, Hamlin Garland, Wm. Upson (*Earthworms Through The Ages*, et al), and books by and about General George Patton. My largest collection is a Modern Library hoard. There are many odds and ends of accumulations in my personal library as well.

Why do I possess these books? Why did I put these collections together? They exist because I like the subject matter. No one told me it was stylish to collect books by Wm. Upson. I collect his books because I like his books. Years ago a friend suggested that I might like to read Albert J. Nock. I did this and liked him enough to form a collection of his works, but forming the collection was my own idea.

And this is my message: Don't follow the crowd. Use your imagination.

Unexploited fields are legion. Collect what you like.

MY COLLECTING

Sifting the many offerings that pass through a bookseller's hands is like digging gold or potatoes, or finding rare archeological artifacts in the Arabian Desert. Much sand is shoveled between interesting finds. Would that I had time to read them all.

I keep a reading shelf in the shop, one in our living room library, and another in my upstairs study where I squirrel away tomes to be read "someday." These shelves don't contain my personal book collections; they only hold accumulations of things that looked interesting enough for me to read. When they were being processed for the shop they got waylaid and shunted aside against the day when I "have nothing to read." These shelves serve as pantries or little warehouses that I visit when I finish devouring my latest book.

Placing a book on one of these reading shelves is not tantamount to reading it. When these little store-houses become full to overflowing, housecleaning and weeding is necessary and books that looked interesting a year ago may have lost their appeal. These books are then returned to the world of commerce - the shelves of the book-shop.

Only my current files (that's what a friend calls his reading shelves) get pared down to size. The other books in my personal library only get dusted. This dusting business was always reserved to me alone. I never trusted anyone else to do it so it almost never got done. Lately I have found a young lady that I trust with the task, so my private hoard will be free of dust. Most of the books in my various collections rest behind glass doors in bookcases anyway, so they are practically dust free.

The above chatter might lead you to believe that I have some high-powered private collections of rare, valuable stuff that must be kept behind glass. This is not necessarily the case I like to store books behind glass - valuable or not. The condition of a book, stored in glassed-in bookcases, over a period of time, is markedly better than a similar book kept on an open shelf for the same period of time The glass enclosure protects the book from a hostile environment.

I am not, for the most part, a sophisticated book collector. My energy, time, and capital have been expended on our book shop instead of on extensive private collecting. My collecting activities, for my own pleasure, have been done on a hit-or-miss basis. My personal collections of local history, Patton, Thoreau, World War II, Italy, Margaret Bourke White, Edmund G. Love, and Hamlin Garland are nothing, more or less, than an accumulation of reading copies that never get returned to the book shop stock.

A collection of books by and about Albert Jay Nock, a most penetrating twentieth century social critic, has been put together more as a true collector of books would do it; first a reading copy, then a first edition, thirdly a first edition in a dust jacket, and finally a first edition in dust jacket signed by the author. Sometimes when Dame Fortune smiles, the first copy acquired is a first edition in dust jacket. The Nockian collection also contains magazine appearances of the author's works.

Our Modern Library Collection of some 600 volumes has been put together in a more scientific manner than any of my other collections, but I have not done the record-keeping or the research. I found the books all right, but a close friend did the organizing for me.

I have spent little time actively seeking books for these private collections like a true book collector must do. The collections have been built by short circuiting the books that come through my hands - shunted to the collection instead of the shop.

Some personal collections I accumulated over the years were returned to stock so the book-shop actually benefits from my collecting activity. Some of the collections returned to stock were: a collection of Henry David Thoreau, Lakeside Classics, Books About Books, and John King, to name a few.

One book in my library is a real treasure, but I didn't know it was valuable until thirty years after I purchased it. In 1936 when I was a junior in high school, the local used-book store in my home town of Ashland, Wisconsin, offered for fifty-five cents, a copy of *The Report Of The Secretary Of The Navy, 1865*. 1 lusted after the volume because it contained nautical charts. Our town is located on a bay of Lake Superior and since the lake played a big role in my life, the charts in the book fascinated me, but I didn't have fifty-five cents to squander on a book. Time passed and the book shop had a sale. The price of the volume was reduced to thirty-five cents and I bought it.

Many years later I discovered that the book was signed by Gideon Wells, the Secretary of the Navy in Lincoln's cabinet.

BARNS

I have put together a collection of books about barns. The collection contains Eric Sloane's precious book entitled, *An Age Of Barns*. With the others is a do-it-yourself book called *The Farmer His Own Builder*. It will guide Doris if she decides to build a barn for me someday. Anyway, the photographs in this book are good. The collection contains a book about the round barns of Iowa and one simply entitled *The Barn*. Its subtitle is, *A Vanishing Landmark In north America*. This subtitle outlines the reason for my collection of books on barns. I would like to collect the barns themselves; because that's impractical, I collect the books instead.

The red barn, once commonplace on the rural landscape, is disappearing. To me this simple expression of rural architecture is a symbol, a last vestige of a way of life. The barns are being allowed to fall to ruin because the way of life they supported is gone. It exists only in a small way. The Amish still practice this mode of living but for the most part, the family farm is finished.

The family farm flourished during my boyhood. On such a farm the land produced almost all of the farmer's needs, from the vegetables grown in the garden to the beef and pork butchered in the fall. The grain and hay fed to these cattle and pigs was raised on the farm. In the early years, baked goods and cereals were made from the home grown grain. In later years the farm wife traded eggs for flour and cereal at the village store Pulled from the udders of their cows twice a day, milk and cream were a staple used in abundance. Butter and cheese were once made on the farm, but in later days it made more sense to buy them in town - cottage cheese was the exception, thus its name.

In the summer hundreds of glass jars were filled with jams and jellies and fruit from the home orchard. Garden vegetables were canned as well. Apples and vegetables were stored away in the darkness under the dwelling or in a root cellar. The busy farm wife, with the help of her kids or a hired girl, also canned meat and made sausage. Meat was also preserved by smoking or storing it in salt brine. The woods provided nuts and berries free for the gathering. A mildly alcoholic wine was made from the wild choke cherries, pin cherries, and even dandelions. Home-made root beer was a summer delicacy.

Staples such as coffee, tea, sugar, salt, raisins, cocoa, molasses, and fabrics were beyond the farmer's magic to produce. These were bought in stores in the little market towns that sprang up at strategic places; they dotted the countryside Such small towns served the farmer, had vitality, and were very active places.

The general family farmer needed money producing products like milk, cream, and eggs to take care of his need for cash. He had to buy salt, sugar, molasses, tea, raisins, and fabrics with money. To keep the equation in balance, the farm produced nearly everything else the family needed. The farmer's kids provided for their cash needs by trapping animals and selling their pelts. Life went on like this until the family farm regrettably faded from the scene. When this way of life ended, we lost more than a method of producing food. A wholesome life style died as well.

Social life for these rural families centered principally around the church. The neighborhood school, the grange, and the county fair were also magnets that drew neighbors together for social fellowship. There was lots of social intercourse between farm neighbors and friends who lived in the city or market town nearby. With exceptions, the work ethic, high morality, and clean living were fostered by this way of life These farmers probably couldn't recite it, but they lived by the Golden Rule The Bible and the weekly newspaper were their principal reading materials. The Ten Commandments were all of the law they needed; obedience to this law was high.

The advent of the gasoline engine marked the start of the decline of the family farm. The tire track on the muddy road that ran past it was the handwriting on the wall that spelled the doom of this way of life. The internal combustion engine, married to advances in farm machinery, caused specialization; eventually these small farming operations became inefficient and economically untenable. Barns became superfluous. Not needed, they were not maintained. The roofs went first, allowing rain water to rot the supporting beams. They began to fall down. Some succumbed to the old barn-wood craze and their wood was used to decorate urban dwellings. These precious structures have all but disappeared along with the way of life that made them necessary in the first place.

General farming hung on until after World War II. Like a long slow-moving wave, it took technology several decades to destroy the family farm. Finally it has been done. Only a few faded red structures remain. Those of us who knew are reminded by them of the satisfactions of this bygone era. Soon the red barn will be no more. So I collect pictures and data on these monuments to a good way of life, now gone. My collection exemplifies a time and place where the spirit that once was America was born; would that we could recapture that spirit. At least the books help to recall the memory.

To close this chapter, I quote Eric Sloane: "We have finally come to realize the beauty and excellence of the homes built by the early Americans, but too often their barns are regarded as mere curiosities. They are, rather, the shrines of a good life and ought to be remembered."

This collection along with some of the author's diaries and papers now rest in the Historical Society Museum of Ashland, Wisconsin.

FOUR HUNDRED AND TWENTY-FIVE YEARS

A Fantasy written in 1969
A brief autobiography of a Bible
printed in 1545

I dedicate this, my life story, to bibliophiles and bibliomaniacs the world over. Without their care and thoughtfulness through the ages, I wouldn't have lived to this ripe old age. At age 424 I am still in good condition. While looking forward to many more years of existence, my life story thus far follows:

I saw the light of day in Germany in the year of our Lord 1545. Even if one does not understand the German language, he can readily see that I am the New Testament. I was born about one year before Martin Luther died and there is an admonition by that illustrious reformer on page 764, which page is marked by a red velvet ribbon. One will also find my birth date on the bottom of that very same page.

The quaint illustrations printed on some of my pages are actually woodcuts. That is one of the ways books were illustrated in those old days. Please notice the sixteenth century buildings with the Biblical people in the woodcuts on pages thirty-three and forty-three (grey and yellow ribbons). This practice was typical of the times. Note the woodcut which portrays the first Easter on page 162 (pink ribbon). The picture on page 213 (black ribbon) shows Christ casting out the devils. Note the devils in the upper right hand portion of the woodcut. (A magnifying glass is indicated to better view this phenomenon.) In this regard, it is also interesting to note that one of my earlier readers thought that page 213 was interesting also, as evidenced by the fact that the corner of the page is folded over. There is a small bookmark inserted there too. You will notice that one end of the tiny paper bookmark is discolored. My memory does not serve me well here. Is it possible that the early reader held one end of the bit of paper in his mouth? If so, his body acids left their mark on the paper. They have helped it deteriorate.

A winged devil can be seen on page eight (aqua ribbon). He looks not unlike the bearded devils I have seen in this year, 1969. The modern ones keep their horns well hidden and their wings are nonexistent. They are prone to burrow from within, not to fly about. My latest master told me these things. But now I digress. I must get on with my story.

My parents were Mennonites and because they dared to be different, they were persecuted.

My age can be dramatized by the fact that one of my earliest recollections is of the simple German folk whispering about the discovery of a New World, far to the west, by an Italian fellow who called himself Christopher Columbus. This discovery took place fifty-three years prior to my birth. Little did I think in those days, that when I was 150 years old, I, too, would be an emigre' to that new land.

Emigrate I did, however. Sometime after 1683 I went with my Mennonite family to the American colony of Pennsylvania where we settled near the village of Germantown. Some of the people among whom I lived were dedicated farmers. Today they are known as "Pennsylvania Dutch." They were, however, from Germany.

Some of the people with whom I made my home were those who followed the printer's trade. It is due to this fact that I attribute longevity. Being printers, the people with whom I lived valued the printed volume, and therefore preserved this type of possession.

I do not mean to say that I did not have to work hard during my long life. I did work hard as evidenced by the fact that my pretty silver clasps and leather closing straps are no longer extant. This is nothing for me to be ashamed of, however, because most volumes my age who have led an active existence have lost their appendages. Time takes its toll. My pages are in a good state of preservation because printers in those early days used paper with a high rag content. Books arriving on the scene today may live less than one hundred years.

Memory does not serve me too correctly or exactly because it has been so long ago, but I know that sometime after the War of 1812 was over, the people whom I was serving moved to the old Northwest Territory in the present State of Indiana. These people were Mennonite still. I am not sure, but it is entirely possible that these, my people, were of the Amish branch of that faith.

After some three-hundred years of working life I retired along about 1850, at which time the Mennonite Church adopted English in its publications and gave up the old German books of the past. So the generations continued on. There was much loving, playing, borning, marrying, baptizing, confirming, living, working, and dying. And from one generation to the other I was handed down. Always these hands were ones which embraced the Mennonite faith. The last pair of Mennonite hands that I knew belonged to a man whose grandfather was a printer. These last Mennonite hands delivered me to a kindly, bearded, book-seller named Don Allen, who resides in the Village of Three Oaks, Michigan. One day, a Ralph Casperson of Niles, Michigan saw me at Don's house. It was love at first sight, and I found myself being carried away by my new master, Casperson. For some days I led a very happy and comfortable existence in Ralph's library. I am not discontented about leaving him, however, because while I was with him he saw fit to give me a perusal that was not entirely perfunctory. His hands, though thorough, were the gentle hands of one who loves my kind. I have naturally known his kind before, but at my advanced age, I prefer repose to inspection.

I am now happily at rest in this velvet lined wooden chest in which I could exist for another century or more if I am given the proper care and affection.

BOOK DEALERS

There are as many ways to be a bookseller as there are people selling books. The options are manifold. Knowledge, capital, and energy are the primary ingredients needed to successfully conduct any business enterprise. Knowledge is the most important element for a bookseller. There are ways to conduct a book-selling enterprise without much money. On the other hand, dollars will paper over some deficiencies in knowledge, but not many.

It is possible to be in the book business without even having a place of business that is open to the public. A concept is important. You must have a plan in mind of what you want to do before the enterprise is launched. A limited number of book selling options should be selected to establish the modus operandi. Come hell or high water, these must then be pursued with vigor. A bookseller without a concept is like a ship adrift. There are successful book dealers who could not verbalize their plan of operation if their lives depended on it. They are, however, following a concept without knowing it, and they are doing it well.

The plan for my book-selling operation came to me naturally. I gave it little thought. I fell in love with the first shop I saw when I was a high school kid. It was a general shop. From that initial exposure, my concept was born. I wanted a general shop where customers could enjoy browsing. Catering to the person who walks through the front door has been my abiding wish. Let me work for the person who has time to spend along with his money.

My goal is to have a shop stocked with books in every field of human knowledge. Does our shop fall short of this concept? Of course it does, but we continue to strive to fulfill the original plan.

Most good general shops are capital intensive. Many years have gone into building them. But, it is possible to become a bookseller instantly without a large capital outlay. If a person has the knowledge of what to buy, where to buy, how much to pay, and where to sell, he can be a book scout. A budding book scout can spend his salad years buying at yard sales, library sales, AAUW type sales, thrift shops, estate sales, and auctions. His sales can be made to local book dealers who are chained to their shops.

Knowledge in this type of operation is essential. A book scout must recognize a good book when he sees it. He must know what his dealer clientele will buy. Because his capital is limited, the scout must turn his purchases into cash in a hurry. He can afford few mistakes. When buying at public sales he is often competing against knowledgeable book people and his decisions must be made instantaneously. Time spent in reflection at these sales is money and opportunities down the drain.

When the book scout has mastered these sales, he can graduate to buying underpriced books from one dealer and selling them to another dealer for more money. Believe it or not, good book scouts can make money paying retail prices and selling the same book at wholesale. Again, knowledge is king!

In a sparsely settled area where no store sells new books, a business can be created ordering new books for people from the publisher. In addition to this service, a book search service for out-of-print books could be an interesting adjunct. Neither of these book selling methods requires any capital to speak of.

Books can be sold at book fairs and flea markets. You need only spend weekends with your stock-in-trade. Books merchandised at a book fair should be high quality. At a flea market almost anything can be shown, including paperbacks.

Let us say that you have a book inventory but have no way to display it. Because of other commitments and lack of capital you cannot open a shop. A small investment in shelving and an initial rent payment will put you in business in an antique mall. This could be an ideal sideline to a regular job. The mall rent entitles you to have someone else sit with your books. The spare hours from your regular occupation allows you time to maintain your stock.

Lots of people are working out of their homes quoting individual titles by mail to prospective customers. Does this require a book inventory? Most of the time, yes, but there are folks around who are quoting books they don't even own. Books are quoted off another dealer's shelves on a "subject to prior sale" basis. When their quote results in them receiving a check, they buy the book and send it off in the mail.

Some very successful dealers, operating out of their homes or store, sell most of their wares by issuing book catalogues. Book lists are less sophisticated, but they too can be successful. Catalogues and book list merchandising require mailing lists. Good customer lists are valuable assets, built over many years, and dealers guard them religiously.

If you become knowledgeable in a specialty (hunting, fishing, Civil War, local history, etc.) a small specialty shop may be your bag. These shops can be operated out of a home or small building. Shops that specialize, unless their customer base is enlarged by catalogue sales, must be located in large population or high tourist areas.

There is no business that I know of that looks so much easier that it actually is. Some of the many ways to do it have been outlined above; but don't be fooled by appearances - it is not as easy as it looks.

THE NEW KID ON THE BLOCK

Harriette Barnette, a bookseller extraordinaire, staked out her specialty many years before I was privileged to make her acquaintance. With a book shop in South Bend, Indiana, she was a specialist in books about America (Americana). My interest in American History led me to her name, but her person eluded me for several years. My negligence in not meeting her sooner contributes only to the negative side of my ledger.

In the early 1970's Harriette and her husband Lew (Lewis Frederick) moved into a house on Adams Road north of South Bend. The place boasted an apple orchard on the back acreage. I made Harriette's acquaintance one day when she accompanied Don Allen, and me to a book sale. Through the years we three ranged far and wide together buying books. Many of our forays were to Evanston, Illinois where another book-selling friend held annual half-price book sales in his shop. We also went to library and AAUW sales in the days when it was almost guaranteed that several high-powered treasures would fill the grasping hands of any aggressively alert bookseller on the prowl. As a part of my learning process, I had to compete with two experts, Don and Harriette. What I lacked in knowledge was partially compensated for by my unparalleled aggression.

Born in 1912, Harriette was seven years old when I came onto the stage of life. Her book stock was well established long before I met her. Just beginning to sell books, my meager accumulation and small knowledge of the book and the trade put me in the deep shade in comparison to my new found friend. I became the new kid on the block, soaking up book lore while figuratively sitting at the feet of my mentor. The very favorable discounts she allowed me on books I bought from her large stock helped to build my stock.

What had been the dining room and living room of the Barnette's house when it was occupied by more conventional folk became

<u>Barnette's Books</u> Drinking excellent tea, I was spending many a long afternoon in Harriette's kitchen talking about books Harriette's little desk in the spare bedroom was not really her office The front room, filled with books, could have served as a conversation area too, but it didn't Her kitchen was both an office and visiting place A clutter of catalogs, letters, pamphlets, and books covered the electric range and counter tops in this small room Only the sink was free of paper things dear to the heart of a bibliophile The kitchen table supported our tea-cups and those tomes under current discussion The first time Harriette visited me in my book shop, I felt ill at ease because it was so squeakily uncluttered Now time has helped to transform my office into one that closely resembles Harriette's kitchen

In those days I wore nothing but jumpsuits The reasons for this strange attire have been covered in an earlier chapter I'll not go into the rationale here for wearing this costume Because it has a bearing on this story later on, suffice it to say that Harriette Barnette never saw me attired in anything but a jumpsuit

Conversations over the tea cups, going to book sales Lew Barnette's apple harvests, and my education at the hands of the bookseller on Adams Road continued over ten years The talk was the best part Whereas Don Allen, my other teacher, was consciously shaping me into a book merchant, Harriette unloaded information with no particular aim in mind She just liked to talk about books and I was her prime auditor

As it must to us all, death came to my friend in 1984 She was seventy-two The cancer that was alive and well in her small body finally arrived at her liver and after a twenty-four hours vigil at St Joseph's Medical Center, in South Bend, Indiana, she passed away

Near the end she was comatose, not recognizing anyone When I walked into her hospital room, she looked at me, her face seemed to brighten a little, and she said, "Ralph." Twenty-four hours later she was gone That word, "Ralph" was her last word

The Barnettes were not big about things of the spirit Lew's philosophy pretty much began and ended in the apple orchard Proud of the time he spent with the 45th Division in World War II, he often talked about his experiences on Anzio in the Italian Campaign I served with the 34th Division on the Italian Peninsula, too, but did not expose my tender flesh to German steel in the Anzio battle. Lew enjoys reminding me of this dereliction in my military career. His good-byes to me are always followed by splendid advice to any infantryman. He always shouts, "Keep your head down."

Harriette had neither the time nor the desire to burden her life with church activities. Her life was books. Her church was her book-shop and her Bible was Wright Howe's *Bibliography Of Usiana*, (a reference book about books about the USA). Harriette's church was open seven days each week and to those who came, she preached everyday.

Without ecclesiastical ties, coming up with a clergyman to preach a funeral oration poses a problem. But leave it to good wife Doris to come up with a solution. Helping Lew with the funeral arrangements, when they found themselves facing a blank wall created by the lack of a man of the cloth, Doris volunteered my services. She also suggested that Jim Rose (Andrews and Rose, Booksellers) do the words at the grave side, which he did.

Preaching funeral sermons is not something that I do a lot of. Being virginal in this area didn't seem to be a good reason for not doing it so I agreed to give it my best shot.

Of course, I wore my jumpsuit for the occasion because that's the only type of clothes I owned. Harriette's funeral was well attended. Standing in front of this group, my opening statement went something like this, "You probably think it strange that I am wearing a jumpsuit on an occasion such as this." Going on, I said, "I have to wear a jumpsuit. If I wore anything else Harriette wouldn't know me."

The casket was open and close at hand so it was not unnatural to direct some of my remarks to Harriette. The jumpsuit crack brought an uncharacteristic laugh, but before I was done, there were also tears.

I said nothing about, "In my Father's house are many mansions." My theme, after reviewing our relationship through the years, was that Harriette was going away to inhabit a new place where she would establish her book-shop This, I said, would again put her far ahead of me in the bookselling game.

Talking to the open casket, I thanked Harriette for being so nice and helpful to the new kid on the block. After she got her own shop established I asked that she find an old store-front for me so that when I got there I would have a place for my book-shop too and could be "THE NEW KID ON THE BLOCK" all over again."

BOOK SHOP PEOPLE

Meeting the many diverse people who frequent such places is one of the joys of operating our book shop. Folks with a variety of interests visit all places of business, but it's difficult to plumb the depths of these interests in most commercial environments. Can you imagine a meaningful philosophical discussion between the checker and shopper in a Kroger check out lane? A serious talk with store personnel in a clothing store, predisposing you could find a suitable place to conduct your discourse, could result in disciplinary action against the clerk for loitering. Long winded chit-chat and verbal congress frowned upon in mall stores might be quite permissible in those main street stores operated by the owner, but in most cases, a suitable place to converse is not available.

Some book shops, particularly used-book shops, are different. Batting around ideas that need to be explored is not a part of the agenda of all book stores. Most likely in shops where interminable discourse is not encouraged, a computer will be found in the back room.

Years ago in most book shops, conversation with his kind was as important to the owner as the merchandise on his shelves or his cash flow. Don Allen's shop in Three Oaks, Michigan was a "Let's go there and talk," kind of place. Don sat behind his desk like a king on his throne, where he held forth for hours. All the novice or others had to do to learn was to listen. Harriette Barnette, held talk-fests in her cluttered kitchen. Both Don and Harriette are gone now, hopefully holding their conversations in the big book shop in the sky, but when they were in business here on earth, it made no difference if you parted with five dollars or five-hundred, they were always good for a sizable hunk of conversation.

The more famous shops of old were also havens for those who

hungered to mingle with other philosophers and verbalists. The old Abraham Lincoln Book Shop in Chicago, Illinois played host to Carl Sandburg and his peers; it was their hangout. Shakespeare and Co., a bookstore owned by Sylvia Beach in Paris of the 1920's, provided a table around which Ernest Hemingway, James Joyce, Adrienne Monnier, Scott Fitzgerald, and other literati exchanged ideas on writing problems and topics of current interest. Sure, Sylvia had to sell books to keep her shop door open, but she exercised other priorities as well. Sylvia Beach's place is written about today, not because of its glittering inventory, outstanding appointments, or for any other reason except that she encouraged kindred souls to use her shop as a place to gather and converse. The people who met there in the 1920's became famous in their own time. When Ernest Hemingway needed a short term loan, he didn't go to a bank. A banker would have laughed him out the door. No, Ernest went to Sylvia Beach at Shakespeare and Co. to satisfy his pressing financial needs. When things like that transpire there, a bookstore becomes an institution, not just another commercial enterprise.

Browsing a used-book store was once an end in itself, an activity to be prolonged, not an errand to be run in a hurry. Yesterday's used-book shops didn't pretend to be efficient; therein lay their charm. The pleasure of browsing wasn't to be denied the customer of yore. Serendipity was the rule. In those days, after an hour of browsing, a person might leave the shop clutching a treasure unearthed in his random perusal, a tome never before seen perhaps. Maybe a book he always wanted to read, but had forgotten about, jumped off the shelf and shouted, "Read me!" The book he had come to the shop to find in the first place was erased from consciousness by the fun of the hunt.

In those days when life was simple, people didn't expect a used book to materialize at the press of a button. The enthusiast went to the most likely section in his favorite book store and looked for the needed volume, hoping also to find something of equal interest in the process - true serendipity. Sure, our society must be efficient, but is there anything wrong with retaining , where possible, a few of the pleasant old ways of doing things? Quiet backwaters can be pleasant places away from the rush and turbulence of the mainstream.

But I've gotten off the track. I started writing this piece about interesting people who come to the book shop. In the past twenty-five years we've had them all, from beggars to millionaires, from illiterates to Ph.D's.

I don't see the fellow I'll call Fred anymore since Michigan reduced some welfare programs; Fred was on welfare. At first he came to the shop on a bicycle, a twenty-five mile trip from his home in Benton Harbor, Michigan. When the bicycle broke he graduated to a large bicycle-size tricycle. When that died, his locomotion was reduced to walking, pushing a grocery cart. The grocery cart accommodated his personal belongings and the books he bought.

---Arriving by mid-morning, Fred spent the day in the shop. A good part of many welfare checks paid for his purchases; Fred liked books on far-out philosophy and Eastern religion. Once when closing the shop at seven o'clock, I asked my unkempt friend what he did about sleeping. He said he either found a protective doorway at a school where he was somewhat sheltered or, lacking that, he said the police would pick him up and lodge him in the local jail. Fred told me that sometimes a charitable institution wrote a check to a cheap hotel for his room rent. He never seemed to worry. Fred lived off the land.

If Fred never comes back it will be okay. His shaggy, unkempt beard, cloudy glasses and general disheveled appearance would turn anyone off. I'm sure he didn't improve our business. My major objection to him was not his fearful appearance but his frightful odor; he smelled bad!

Ronald Hull, a millionaire, was the opposite of Fred. Ron collected books about books. Lots of his money came to rest in my cash drawer, while many of my books were added to his enviable collection. We also talked for hours on end; he had led an exciting life. At his invitation, Doris and I went to visit him at his mansion near Niles. One of his antique cars was on display in the huge master bedroom. He could have added a couple more and still had plenty of rattle-around room. Ron's house, really an estate, is the kind of place where heads of state are entertained. The living room boasted six conversation areas, six davenports with matching chairs and end tables. Surrounding a show-place like this with many acres of land would have been quite appropriate. His wasn't. Neighboring houses were so close he could have spit on them with ease. Good judgment is not always packaged with great wealth.

The Englishman, Richard Booth, heir to the Booth Gin fortune, is a regular bookshop visitor. He sometimes stays for dinner. Several buildings in Richard's hometown in Wales, including a castle, house his huge book inventory. Not unlike many book people, Richard is eccentric. He told me he once proclaimed himself king of his hometown. This caper didn't work out too well though. When the British Royal Family objected vehemently, he had to remove his crown.

Philosophers by the gross descend on our place. One of them, impersonating Colonel Mosby, wears a Confederate dress uniform. I think he looks like Stonewall Jackson, not Col. Mosby. Whoever he resembles, he cuts quite a figure in his light bluish-grey coat with gold buttons and stars.

Another collector with big bucks to spend set himself the impossible task of tracking down the autographs of all Union Generals in the American Civil War. Invited to his house for dinner one night, we got to see his superb Civil War collection. This was fortunate, because his hoard was dispersed to the four winds when the man died.

Years ago Robert French of Buchanan gave me an interesting commission. "Put together," he said, "a collection of books that might have been found in the library of a cultured farmer living in Berrien County, Michigan in the mid-1800's." This proved to be a tough assignment; I spent one whole winter hunting up the books and building the collection. All of the books had to be dated during or before the time our imaginary farmer lived. In the spring I presented the finished library to Bob. It contained everything our farmer, living in this remote area, would have needed: Bibles, dictionaries, books on animal husbandry, agriculture, gardening, horticulture, and medicine (home cures mostly). Our farmer was a cultured person so books of literature, art, and music were there too; many other titles completed the library.

Our friend Bob French, an author in his own right and an interesting guy, bought the collection and gave it a home in his historic house by the St. Joseph River on River Road north of Buchanan, Michigan.

Many more people could be chronicled here but space limits me. My point is that if I ran my shop like a Kroger Store, there would be few memories and no stories to tell.

LARRY B. MASSIE, MICHIGAN AUTHOR

We are on our way to the Allegan Forest to visit Larry and Priscilla Massie, authors and publishers. Larry became my friend in 1975 when he and Vaughn Baber started the Bicentennial Book Shop in Kalamazoo. Our common ground caused Massie and me to become brothers from the first day. After patronizing their newly opened shop, Larry spent some time with Doris and me in a nearby restaurant. We began to get acquainted.

While breaking bread together, we learned about each other. Our common ground began to form a foundation for an enduring friendship. A combat infantryman in World War II and a paratrooper in Vietnam talk the same language. Nothing cements a friendship faster than shared military experiences. Though I served in an earlier war, we both had met the dragon.

My new friend was assistant archivist at Western Michigan University. My love for history is a part of me nurtured by a lifetime of reading. A degree in history from Western Michigan University gave Larry a more formal, firmer underpinning in the discipline. Differences in how we acquired knowledge are immaterial in the building of our relationship. We were both antiquarians.

The hour grows late at that restaurant table. As the minutes speed by, I find that my new acquaintance collects books, a sin that goes back, like mine, to his juvenile days.

Our values were similar too because we were brought up the same way. Larry was never handed anything on a silver platter. He was lucky to get his on a crude clay plate, and that only after he had put in the requisite labor. Neither he nor I ever received an allowance; we both did odd jobs and peddled papers. He acquired his formal college experience, which I lack, by taking advantage of the G I Bill. Lord knows, he earned this and then some. He brought back a lifelong disability from Vietnam.

Shared values and a coinciding of interests beget a caring for each other. A friendship blossomed that has endured for over twenty years. Other areas where our interests coincide surface as time passes, providing a pleasant cement for the major bricks in our house of commonality.

It was predictable that Larry would terminate his employment at the university archives. He is not an eight to five guy. His full potential would be forever submerged with someone else paddling his canoe; here again is a parallel in our lives. I, too, gave up formal employment to do my own thing.

A number of years ago Larry became a freelance writer and lecturer. He wrote the captions for the stations of the historic walk at Sault Ste. Marie, Michigan. His portrayal of a French voyager in the Chautauqua plays takes his audience back to the 1600's. Some who took his course in book collecting are antiquarian book dealers today. Articles from his pen on Michigan history have appeared in many magazines and newspapers around the state. He has written over fourteen books. Not only does he write the books, but he and his wife publish them through their own publishing house, "The Priscilla Press." He also sells and distributes his own books. He says he is running a trap line when he travels around the state calling on his retail book outlets. Other authors owe him a vote of thanks for publishing their books too.

The Massies and Caspersons have camped together in Michigan's upper peninsula. These trips have turned into writing and editing sessions for Larry's books. What could be more uplifting than working on a Michigan history essay, around a fireplace in a cozy cabin, in the wilds of Northern Michigan? This we have done together. We also enjoy each other's humor. Good-natured jibes at each other are ongoing, blended together with never-ending fantasies that only Larry and I can appreciate.

Back to our trip to the Massie home in the Allegan Forest. Pleasant anticipation mounts as we drive through the town of Allegan and turn off the highway onto the county road leading into the forest. After a few short miles the blacktop ends about two miles from our destination. This is appropriate, because Larry is an off-the-pavement type of person An old white, one-room schoolhouse is his abode. Here with Priscilla, a cat, one or two dogs, and a library of over 35,000 books, he lives and writes about the past. Lately baby Maureen has been added.

Anyone who collects books knows that the space available is soon filled with bibliographic treasures. So it is with Larry. His schoolhouse, now completely full, has been expanded three times. Like the pioneers, Larry did most of this work with his own hands. Larry's marriage to Priscilla necessitated running water and inside plumbing; he lived there for over twenty years with neither. The latest addition provides a kitchen, bathroom, and an office for Priscilla and her computer. They also built a huge space for storing the inventory of the books be has authored. Lastly, but probably first in Larry's mind, is space for his bound volumes of periodicals.

Most of the furniture and fixtures in the Massie home are antique; this includes things in the kitchen and bathroom. A cabinet made by the old Kompass and Stowe Cabinet Factory in Niles is still in use in the Massie kitchen. Tacked to the antique is a pamphlet dated 1910 advertising this cabinet. The bathtub is porcelain covered cast iron, popular during the boom days prior to the stock market crash in 1929; I could go on and on. A show place in its antiquity, the Massie household could be put together by no one else. It's inhabitants, Larry and Priscilla, invented it. The whole place is an uncontrived antique, but it is very comfortable, livable, and it is home.

Of Scottish descent, Larry does well living up to the reputation for which his ancestors are famous. He doesn't appear to be parsimonious either. On one of our trips to the Upper Peninsula of Michigan, our car developed a soft tire. The sign at a nearby service station said, "AIR 25cents". Larry would have none of it; he refused to pay for "free air." As he drove on, I said, "They aren't charging for air, but for the machinery needed to compress the air and for the hose needed to deliver it in usable form." I could only hope that in some way his Scotch stubbornness would somehow keep our tire from going completely flat. My friend persevered and finally prevailed when he found a station with "free air." This is the same guy who only reluctantly buys frozen water.

It will be a sad day for our Larry, with his Scottish traits, when he realizes that his antique refrigerator is using more "juice" than a modern one. I hope I'm not at his house when this intelligence is revealed. I would hate to see a strong man destroyed. Priscilla loves antiques too, but please, Lord, let me see her slightly-concealed pleasure when the old refrigerator dies.

By living up to his Scottish heritage Larry Massie has never had a mortgage or a car payment. A bank has yet to get its first penny of interest from him. In spite of this, or maybe because of his careful ways, his accumulation of worldly goods will far surpass those of most of his contemporaries. Also, when his siblings need financial aid, Larry is there.

The library that surrounds us at Massie's place runs heavily to Michigan and U.S. history. Books now completely fill the old schoolhouse and the library overflows into the new additions. Also included in this hoard are tomes on other subjects and many bibliographical and reference works.

The collection of books, periodicals, pamphlets, and paper ephemera collected over his lifetime now are the tools Larry uses in making his living. Put another way, we could say he mines his endless shelves searching for the golden nuggets of Michigan lore that appear in his books. Writing with a pencil, as I do, he feels (and I agree) that something is lost when a machine comes between the penman and his paper. The women in our lives use the machine to make our scribbling legible to our reading public.

Larry's periodical collection defies description. Row on row and shelf after shelf are loaded with old bound volumes of magazines popular one hundred and more years ago. Fashion questions back in 1865? His *Peterson's Magazine* and *Godey's Ladies' Books* provide the answers. What were people wearing in the eighteenth and nineteenth centuries? Bound volumes of *Harper's* and other literary magazines are at his fingertips. Do you want to look at Norman Rockwell's early illustrations? Larry has the old *Saturday Evening Posts*.

He has co-authored a cookbook with his wife, Priscilla. The recipes are those used by our forefathers and he continues to cook up at least one new book every year of his life.

My friend Wilber Jones, by far the unhappiest man I have ever met, disliked almost everyone. A listing of the people on his "I hate you" list might fill a book the size of a small dictionary. His emaciated body was tormented by an eczema-like rash that peeled like a dry onion when he scratched it. The itch, like a penance for past sins, drove him to distraction when he wasn't busy digging at it with the sharp fingernails on the end of his thin bony fingers. Cold nocturnal baths, he said, gave him some relief. The pure white ointment he used on his bare arms and face only served to make him look more skeletal. The way he looked, scaring children would have been a perfect occupation; he hated children.

Wilber carried a bunch of German shrapnel in his right leg. This gave him fits during damp weather. In 1944 the Army medics wanted to saw his leg off, but Wilber vetoed their plan. The part they wanted to remove from the rest of his body was the part that drove him to distraction now. Wilber's aversion to the Veteran's Administration, pharmacies, hospitals, and churches was almost palpable. He nursed an active dislike for lots of things including the Army, VFW, DAV, and the American Legion.

Like all of his relatives, Wilber's paternal grandmother had money to burn. She didn't use it to feed the fire or to fund bad habits. It reposed in the bank and was invested in real estate. Her investments included a rental farm in Berrien County. Meeting an untimely end in an auto accident, her robust estate went to Wilber. He didn't like the farmer folk who rented the farm. I sometimes felt he held them responsible for his grandmother's demise just because they occupied her old dwelling place.

Wilber showed up at the book shop in the mid 1980's. Plumbing the depths of their military careers is the first order of business for two liberators who fought in World War II. We were brothers-in-arms, having both received battlefield commissions. As Wilber fidgeted in my office, scratching his tormented body, he seemed to enjoy unburdening his heavy heart to me, and he lambasted his many hates.

A reluctant Wilber accepted his lieutenancy because he was

given no choice in the matter, leading his platoon until, collecting an assortment of shrapnel in his leg, he was evacuated to the states.

After the war my friend attended law school at the University of Michigan, graduated, and passed his Michigan Bar examinations. He spent not one day practicing law. He quite willingly rushed to Grand Rapids to help his parents operate their lucrative motel business.

Wilber reached the age when most men marry. Unhappily, he got spliced to a girl his parents didn't like, no surprise. The couple bought a house, set up housekeeping, and got a divorce. Wilber gave the unfortunate (or fortunate) girl the house and $20,000. He went back to his lonesome parents.

Time passed. Wilber's father died. The motel was sold. He had just buried his mother and inherited her small fortune when we made his acquaintance. His mourning for his mother and father, the only two people in the world he cared for, was a pitiful thing to observe; Wilber was a lost soul.

A highly-indulged only son, Wilber now lavished the only love he had ever had on the memory of his departed parents; his mourning was endless. Some days his mother and father were his only topic of conversation. Pathetic.

Many pre-teens could easily top Wilber's knowledge and understanding of the world. His know-how hovered near zero; his practicality tank was empty. Not dumb, he had a good intellect and was eminently qualified to learn, but his mind, from lack of use, was closed, rusty, completely shut up.

We grow and mature as we experience life, face and solve problems, forge relationships, provide for our livelihoods, build credos to live by, and develop our spirituality. Mothered in the home nest for so long now, past sixty and on his own, Wilber Jones was unable to fly. With next to nothing to live for, here was a man with over a million dollars, no ambition, no ideas, and no aspirations. He was completely devoid of imagination. Stuck with a wretched outlook on life and a disposition that would make a lemon seem sweet, my friend was one miserable guy.

Wilber harbored a malevolence as strong as his love for his parents, toward his mother's sister, his only living relative. He told me she was opinionated, mean, stingy, impossible to live with, and filthy rich. The cross that Wilber bore, ungraciously, was his promise to his mother on her deathbed that he would take care of her sister. He moved in with this aged aunt.

Continuing to suffer his aunt's unjust demands, overbearing conduct, and harassment, Wilber hung on. By now he had more money than he would ever need. Did "taking care" of her dictate living in the same house? His staying with the wretched woman who could well afford to hire someone to be with her made less than a little sense. Where money is concerned, it is difficult for some to learn when enough is enough; Wilber had that trouble. But then, of course, there was that deathbed promise. In one who had developed little character in other areas, his tenacity in keeping his deathbed promise is hard to fathom.

Wilber's aunt loved Florida in the wintertime. He hated the place all of the time. Adding to his misery, he drove her there anytime she wanted to go; beware of deathbed promises.

Wilber was obsessed with blizzards. He often drove aimlessly through the blowing and drifting snow for several hundred miles, staying in a motel overnight, coming home the next day. He came to the book shop in good weather and bad, but he always showed up when a winter storm raged.

Wilber never had anything to crow about because he never did anything. His achievement needle pointed to a permanent "O". One day, proud to bursting, he told me how he had set his aunt straight. He discovered two large pails full of pocket change in his aunt's bedroom closet. Before her retirement in 1960 she managed her husband's store in South Bend. Every weekend she unloaded her loose change from her purse into the pails.

"By God," Wilber boasted, "I turned the money in to the bank. Now it's where it will be drawing interest.

I said to Wilber, "Did you get face value for the coins?"

"Damned right I did," he said and seemed to strut a little, "no more, no less."

I couldn't say anything because it would have been cruel to bust his bubble, but I thought, "Yes, Wilber, you are a wise manager." The dimes, quarters, and half-dollar pieces in those pails were silver coins dated before 1965 and worth eight times face value at the time you turned them in to the lucky cashier. (After 1965 newly minted coins had no silver content. Before that date dimes, quarters, and fifty-cent pieces were partly silver).

Wilber approached a sustained state of happiness during the several summers he worked at the cemetery where his folks are buried. He lavished his energy almost full-time on his family plot, and when he had that shipshape, he directed his efforts to general cemetery improvement.

Enjoying a family reunion everyday by being close to his parents' graves seemed to rejuvenate him. The aunt he had promised to protect also rested in this cemetery by this time too. When the undertakers carted her to her final resting place, Wilber took her estate to the bank.

Curious, after listening to Wilber go on about the cemetery, Doris and I paid the place a visit. We found three headstones in the highly manicured "Jones" plot. Beside his parents' stones Wilber had his own, showing his full name and birth date. "Wilber Patton Jones. 1922." The last date was blank. The smooth, shiny, brown marble awaited the stone mason's final inscription.

Wilber, by then a walking skeleton, came to the book shop for the last time in July 1991. He didn't show up again, and when the weeks became months, we became concerned. I especially missed him during periods of blowing snow. Turning the calendar to 1992, I said to Doris, "I wonder what happened to Wilber Jones?" Doris tried to find out. His telephone was unlisted. Not knowing the exact location of his house, we couldn't inquire there. Doris's search availed us nothing.

1993 came but Wilber didn't. The man with the oversized bank account, uncounted stocks and bonds, pet peeves, and deep-seated hates had disappeared.

On a beautiful fall day in 1993, Doris and I were driving near Wilber's cemetery. I said to Doris, "This is the kind of day he would be puttering around his cemetery. Let's go there; maybe we'll find him."

We drove to the Jones's family plot. Our search was not in vain
Wilber was there! The final date had been chiseled into the smooth
shiny marble of his headstone "1992."

IVOR THE BRIDGE TROLL

Trolls, uncharming little people who live in caves and under
bridges in Norway, have, until recently avoided the United States.
These small ugly human like creatures lived among my Norwegian
ancestors for centuries. The leading characters in old Norse stories,
trolls add spice and warmth to tales from a land that is oftentimes
dark and cold.

In olden times bridge trolls lived under bridges collecting small
payments from people using the bridge. The local gentry, fearing
retribution, didn't deny bridge trolls this tribute. Norwegian people
know that trolls, when irritated, can do very disagreeable things; it
was all very simple, pay the troll toll or suffer the consequences.

Times have changed in northern Norway, thus changing the lifestyle of the troll. How do these little people collect their stipend from
the big people whizzing over their bridge in a speeding automobile?
Existence for the trolls was better when life was simple, when
people walked and crossed the bridges with reindeer pulling their
sleighs and carts. Trolls are largely ignored today. Some folks in
Norway go so far as to say that trolls don't even exist.

Most people put up with subtle change uttering only low-key
verbal protests. Then there are the activists. Ivor the bridge troll is
an activist, living like his parents before him, under a bridge in the
town of Polmark in northern Norway where my maternal
grandfather, John Garmen Schanche, was born.

In recent years, with his bridge toll income wiped out, only petty
theft afforded Ivor a sometimes exciting but otherwise bleak
existence. Ivor sought a better way; he left Polmark. Heading south
with his sister Olga and cousin Sven, before long the trio arrived at
the port city of Bergen. The three Liliputian people had little
difficulty stowing away in an empty pickled herring barrel aboard
the ship Roland Amundsen II. The original Roland Amundsen was
torpedoed by the Germans off the coast of Iceland in 1942.

Trolls preferred food is herring in any form - raw, fried, broiled, boiled, dried, pickled, and for dessert, creamed. But any life-sustaining food will satisfy trolls. Their diminutive bodies don't require many calories. Sustenance is no great problem with trolls, but they tend to became ornery when deprived of their herring for an extended time.

A one-hundred-fifty year old male troll like Ivor or Sven is about ten inches tall. It is said that trolls live to be five hundred years old; Olga is a bit shorter than her brother and cousin and about ten years their junior. Ivor's complexion resembles dark brown saddle leather. A sparse black beard sticks out like a long bristled brush from his pointed chin. His prominent ears, the color of Egyptian dates, look like old tree bark. Big powerful dark brown eyes stick out bug-like from his pinched face. An extra-long Pinocchio-type nose is his most prominent facial feature. Ivor, as a badge of his leadership, carries a stout staff clutched by the thin, bony, claw-like fingers of his right hand.

Comfortably stowed away in their smelly old herring barrel, the three cousins had an uneventful crossing of the North Atlantic. Meals squared with mealtimes on the fifteen day trip. Trolls are born thieves, so stealing enough herring to satisfy their small needs on a ship flying the flag of Norway didn't even begin to tax their capabilities.

Landfall was made at Montreal, Canada. The hardy vagabonds proceeded west to Sault Ste. Marie. Favorable reports prompted them to cross the border into Michigan.

In the confusion at the border, Ivor was separated from Olga and Sven. Something in Ivor made him head south out of Sault Ste. Marie, Michigan. The biggest thrill of his life awaited him ahead. The huge Mackinaw suspension bridge loomed out of the light fog. "Wow," he thought. "This one would house all of the bridge trolls in Norway!" After seeing government men collecting tolls at Big Mac, Ivor decided to give up bridges as his place of habitation.

How Ivor managed to home in on our book shop will remain a mystery to me forever. Even Ivor himself finds it impossible to explain. This strange happening and some subsequent events indicate that trolls have extrasensory powers. Many mysteries are hidden in their shrunken heads. One Wednesday morning in March of 1993 when I went to open the book shop, little Ivor stood waiting at the door.

Hearing his story prompted me to tell him that my ancestors hailed from his hometown in northern Norway. I tried the name Schanche out on him. Ivor said he remembered when he was a boy there was a businessman in Polmark named Karl John Schanche. Karl's little son, John Garmen, Ivor recalled, played around the bridge where Ivor's family lived. When John grew up he wasn't there anymore, but Ivor didn't know where he had gone. Heavens above! Karl and John are my great-grandfather and grandfather. John Schanche left the neighborhood all right. He emigrated to Minnesota.

I enthusiastically assented to Ivor's request that he be allowed to live in the book shop. Ivor wanted to live on top of the bookcase next to my desk, which he did.

Bridge trolls communicate with grunts, high-pitched squeaks, and weird facial expressions. For a thousand years and more, my ancestors lived near trolls. Our ability to understand one another must be in the genes. Talking with Ivor, right from the beginning, was for me easy and as natural as eating creamed herring.

After a week it became apparent that Ivor was not happy living on the bare top of the bookcase. His discomfort stemmed from the openness of his perch. He reminded me he was used to being surrounded by bridge abutments. Piling books around him made Ivor happy again.

Ivor became unhappy again in about a week because he said he had nothing to do. In Norway he kept busy stealing, collecting tolls, and fabricating gold jewelry. No one who knows trolls wants a disgruntled troll around; what could I do?

Some years ago Floriana Trigona, a citizen of Italy, gave me a Norwegian flag. Floriana's husband, Baron Francesco Trigona, Italy's Ambassador to Norway, received the flag from the royal hand of Norway's King. This flag, no ordinary relic, should be on display, but not without proper security.

Ivor has the job of guarding his nation's emblem; what could be more appropriate? Stout staff in hand, Ivor stands proudly atop the bookcase with the red, white, and blue banner of his native-land on its slender pole to his left. He is ready to do battle like a Viking of old with anyone who even contemplates harm to his priceless charge.

More than content now with his own situation Ivor, has been concerned about Sven and Olga. He tells me that his cousins have a "thing" for each other. Trolls are quite infertile. To avoid becoming extinct, the need to reproduce their own kind is great. Artificial social roadblocks are not erected to prevent sexual coupling between cousins. Premarital sexual congress is never practiced either; it is unheard of. Trolls either marry or nothing.

Another social custom dictates that a trollese couple cannot marry without the permission of the prospective bride's closest blood relative. That Olga and Sven can never marry unless they find him has worried Ivor considerably.

Ivor, though bothered, tells me repeatedly that his faith in Olga's and Sven's ability to find him is great. Troll's built-in instinct to home in on their own is strong.

During the last few days Ivor looks as though he has swallowed a bag of feathers; he is tickled to bursting. I have never seen him so happy, but he's playing it close to his ample middle and won't share with me the reason for his glee.

From time to time lately I hear strange unnatural thumps in various parts of the book shop. Until I started to wear my winter boots, I felt something under my desk tickling my ankles. When I looked under the desk I saw a fleeting shadow, nothing more; trolls move almost as fast as a beam of light.

The other day while in the office talking to me, Doris heard a sharp "thump" in the work area. Startled, she said, "What is that?"

My reply, "I don't know for sure, but I think it's Sven," puzzled her. Then I said, "I also believe Olga is living under my desk." After taking in this latter remark followed by my previous incomprehensible rejoinder, Doris put on her incredulous look and began walking briskly toward the door. To forestall her calling the loony squad, I hollered after her, "All right, if you don't believe me, ask Ivor."

Membership in the **Rotary** Club was mandatory for the manager of the gas utility. At a meeting in the mid 1960's, the noon program was a review of the book *Ring Lardner* by Don Elder. Elder's brother, Richard, was a prominent citizen in Niles at the time. Ring Lardner gained fame as a sports writer in Chicago, and his humorous books were best sellers. He had left the town, but Niles claimed him as its own. He was born here, graduating from Niles High School in 1901.

Some youngsters today are not acquainted with Lardner's writing. Older people still enjoy his humorous books and stories. Since my story took place, a school in Niles has been named for Ring Lardner. The house where he lived is an historic landmark and is recognized as such with a Michigan Historical Society marker

The book reviewer at the Rotary meeting said that in 1904 Ring went to work for the gas company. Having gained this intelligence, I felt good about presiding over some of the same facilities that were in existence when our local hero worked for the same company

The book reviewer read two passages from Elder's book. First, the author quotes Lardner's own words as follows: *"During the late autumn in 1905, the Niles, Michigan Gas Company was paying me eight dollars a week to read meters, make out bills, keep books, try to collect bad debts - and I never heard of a good one - handle all moneys, get new customers, and mop the office floor at least once daily."*

"The making out of bills and the keeping of books came under the heading of hard labor. The moping was kind of a game; I used to see whether I could do it today faster than I had done it yesterday. Trying to collect bad debts and get new customers was a set-up; I have always been a person who could take no for an answer. Reading meters was the rub, because meters are usually in dark cellars where my favorite animal, the rat, is wont to dwell. When I entered a cellar and saw a rat reading the meter ahead of me, I accepted his reading and went on to the next house."

Ring Lardner, being a member of the Episcopal Church, had ready access to that building. Elder goes on with the story: *"At the*

It is a well known fact among gas utility employees that each house, church, store, or other building is served by its own independent gas line from the main in the street. Gas line connections between two adjacent buildings do not exist, ever, never, never! The mischievous Lardner could not turn off the gas lights in the Presbyterian church from his vantage point in the Episcopal Church next door.

Doubting the book reviewer's word, I had to see the passages that carried this falsehood with my own eyes. Sure enough, pages 29 and 30 carried the offending paragraphs. The false information was there for all to behold.

I showed the book to my general foreman. He laughed to think that anyone would print such junk. He was adamant. He exclaimed, "No way, Boss." He made it plain that he knew about gas lines and such a prank could not be pulled on anyone, including Niles' favorite son. There is much Lardner lore. Many tales abound about Ringgold Lardner. Some are myths and some are verified. I classified the gas light caper as pure mythology.

Time passed. One quiet summer afternoon I was sitting in my office at the gas company, trying to stay awake, when a cyclone burst through the front door yelling, "Boss, Boss, Ring could have done it!" My general foreman was as excited as a kid at the circus. He told me that his crew had exposed various gas lines while excavating to repair a gas leak at the Episcopal Church. Remembering Lardner's alleged prank, my foreman investigated. He found an old line between the Episcopal Church and the Presbyterian Church next door.

The ruffled foreman took me to the scene. I looked it all over, too. The ancient lines were situated so that Ring could have done, in 1905, what his biographer said he had done.

In 1989 Ring's son, Ring Lardner, Jr., was in Michigan celebrating the 100th anniversary of his father's birth. A stop was made at our book shop. Ring's son was delighted to hear the story about his father and the gas lines. I'm glad I could make a small contribution to Lardner lore.

DISRAELI

A London book dealer sat in his shop one day conversing with a friend. Surrounded by thousands of used, out of print, and uncommon books, the bookman remarked that business left something to be desired of late. That subject wasn't belabored long when the conversation turned to other things.

The day began to look better to the proprietor when Benjamin Disraeli, the Prime Minister, a good customer, came through the front door. Disraeli browsed the shop for an hour or so while the two friends drank their tea and continued to visit. Seemingly satisfied after awhile the P.M. walked up to the owner of the book shop and said, "I'll take it. Same terms as last time I presume?"

The bookseller replied, "Yes indeed, Mr. Prime Minister." After this rejoinder the government man left the shop.

The shopkeeper's friend didn't know what to make of this strange conversation Disraeli had selected nothing from the shelves. He didn't lay any merchandise on the counter to be wrapped. What did the strange words mean?

The shopkeeper enlightened his friend as follows: "Mr Disraeli just bought the whole shop. He wants it delivered to his premises and will tender a cheque when the last book rests on his library shelves."

The bookman told his friend that this performance happened on two occasions in the past.

The above, not a fictitious tale, actually happened.

Recently the Japanese bought a book store in the middle-west in much the same fashion - lock, stock, and barrel.

Richard Booth, of the Booth Gin family, has a sizable used-book operation at Hay-on-Way in Wales. He buys used books in this country and sends whole ship loads of them back to England. He recently told me that the American mid-west is the last best used-book storehouse in the world. He should know - the world is his warehouse.

In our book shop we are trying to do our bit to inculcate the younger generation with the love of books and reading. A friend of mine, an American literature teacher at an area high school, requires that his students visit our shop and the Erasmus Book Shop in South Bend, Indiana during the school year. The students are given cards that entitle them to a 10% discount on any book they buy. Classroom credit accrues to them for making the visit. The response is something less than terrific, but some of the brighter ones make the effort.

This is not a merchandising ploy. My teacher friend and I believe that these kids should be cognizant of the fact that these storehouses of knowledge exist - off campus. We initiated and continue the practice in the hope that at least a few youngsters will learn about the gems that can be found in no other place but a used-book shop. Perhaps, we trust, some will remember the experience and will, in later life, frequent these cultural islands on a regular basis. Those who do will have a richer more satisfying life.

A few of my precious customers are making a non-contribution to their children's English training. Can you believe that these parents deny their kids the books the kids select off the shelves in the children's section? The offending parents refuse to pay the dollar or two which would put the treasures the little ones have found into their little hands for keeps.

While their parents are building healthy stacks of books for themselves, the children are also browsing. When the time comes to check out, the children excitedly show their mothers or fathers what they have found. They hold only one or two children's books. It is obvious that they want them desperately. The parents then lay out the fifty dollars for their stack of books and, in no uncertain terms, they command the child to return his meager choice to the shelves. The child is devastated. I cringe I am embarrassed for the stupid parent. It is difficult for me to suppress a tear for the rebuffed juvenile.

I'd like to shake the parent and shout, "Have you abdicated your mind? For goodness sakes, the kid has the desire to read and learn. Encourage him. Show some interest in his cultural development." Secondly, I want to give the books to the child and I often do this, thereby risking the wrath of the parent. The above scenario doesn't happen often, but once would be an excess.

I respect the necessity of a parent inspecting the books that a juvenile selects. They must ascertain that the books are not offensive. Many parents do this, but they allow the child to form the wholesome habit of searching for, and discovering, his own exciting gems.

It is important to bring up children in a home filled with books. Books of interest to the youngsters should be available in the home. Children should be read to before they know how to read by themselves. Many of my customers buy books for their children when they are mere babes. Some begin a children's home library prior to the "blessed event." later, after the kids have learned to read, the parents encourage them to spy out their own treasures in the children's section.

I never begrudge the time I spend straightening out the shelves in the children's bay. I know that the chaos I am repairing has been created by curious little hands grasping for knowledge and excitement.

A parent whose children are voracious readers will not have to worry about them being unable to express themselves correctly in later life. We should worry about the kids who have watched the "boob tube" for endless hours. They have developed square eyes and empty heads devoid of imagination. These are the ones who will make incomprehensible noises and grunts which pass for speech in some circles today. They won't be able to write the King's English either.

One of the more enjoyable functions in a bookseller's life is the trips he takes to buy books. My wife, Doris, always accompanies me on these happy sojourns. Quite frequently it is necessary to be away from home for an extended period and staying in motels is a prerequisite on these jaunts. It is high time that someone chronicle the motel experience. I have assigned myself this task, and address it forthwith.

"What do you know about checking into a motel? You never sign the card, nor do you tell the clerk what we want." That's the chatter I got from Doris when I told her I was going to write an essay about checking into and staying in a motel. A married man can't retain his self-respect if he leaves such wifely remarks unchallenged.

"I can write about checking into a motel," I say, "because while you are inquiring about the availability of a ground floor room with two beds I am listening and observing. You, my dear, are occupied trying to find your credit cards, running back to the car to get the license number, and making other demands of the clerk while I am quietly taking it all in. You, Doris, will never be able to write such a story because you are always too busy doing it all."

"I haven't mentioned," I continue, "Your asking about the old age discount, directions to the room, and the best restaurant and how to get out of this backwater and back onto the freeway if we are fortunate enough to survive the night. While you, dear one, are concerning yourself with these mundane details of life, I am pondering about how all of this will look on a typed sheet of paper. We don't live by bread alone you know." Now that I have Doris properly focused . . . .

Just about the time I become accustomed to a change in the rapidly shifting social scene, either society or government plasters me with another. The relatively new "no smoking" areas in restaurants have been around long enough so I reluctantly accept them as a norm. Now there is another one to challenge my capability. I wouldn't mind these new things, but they mostly require me to make major decisions, thus diverting mental energy from more rare creative endeavors .

My mind's eye envisions a volcano in eruption when I hear this query, "Do you want a smoking or non-smoking room?" Doris was having no trouble with this question. Such a strange interrogation stimulates me enough to break my reverie. I interject myself into the transaction. "I have never seen a smoking room," I say, "Why, do you have them? Is there a new kind of therapy afoot? Do you have clients who want to sleep in a smoke-filled room? Or are they only for the use of politicians? Do they ever stop smoking, or do they keep at it all night long?"

Finally, after it is all explained, I understand. I get the distinct feeling that Doris and the clerk are relieved when I assume my observer status. Non-smoking rooms are virginal as far as tobacco smoke is concerned. The girl behind the counter says, "The smoking rooms still carry the stale smell of smoked tobacco." I tell Doris to make the choice because I am prejudiced. The odor of smoked tobacco is a part of my heritage. This smell takes me back to the days of my youth when I peddled newspapers in railroad stations and pool halls. The air in those places was heavy with this pungent aroma. As a kid, this smell gave me a sense of maturity, almost as good as the smell of a recently discarded cigarette package we kids retrieved from the gutter. Doris always chooses the non-smoking room. So much for her sense of history.

I am not overly concerned with the past history or the personal habits of the room I am about to inhabit; it can smoke or not, I don't much care. I have other concerns. Motel rooms are sterile: no books or bookcases, no family pictures, and no newspapers or magazines scattered about. My jars of salted peanuts and M & Ms are also missing. I can overlook these touches of home. though, if there is a hook on the back of the bathroom door. I would be happy to stay in an unheated hovel if the bathroom door is equipped with a handy something on which to hang my night wear; heck, a rusty nail would do.

Did you ever stay in a room with no hook on the bathroom door AND no water tank back of the stool? What do you do when you stand half undressed in the middle of such a place with your hands full of stuff?

Engineers who design shower heads will be running lemonade

stands on busy freeways when I become king. The shower head on the end of a flex hose is the ultimate of misapplied talent. How do you apply the soap to the whole body while holding the bar in one hand and the hose in the other? Try to reach your right armpit with the bar of soap in your right hand. Visualize your problem when soap gets in your eyes. All motels should go back to the shower head that directs its product at a bare body without the assistance of the showeree.

I am a water faucet illiterate too. The damned things inhibit me. Why does a device that simply starts and stops the flow of water have to be so complicated. It was not always thus. And why is it that we are capable of standardizing the time of day and the measurement of gasoline, but water faucets in tonight's motel differ from the one we checked out of this morning? Is standardization dead?

Oh well, Doris says it's time to go home anyway. She keeps an eye on the van's tailpipe. When it begins to blow bubbles as we pass through puddles, she knows we have bought enough books and have a load.

A BUYING TRIP

Our book shop customers constantly ask us where we get our books. When I tell them that on occasion we go on buying trips to other parts of the United States, they indicate that they feel this is a glamorous endeavor.

I will not say that traveling to buy books is drudgery. It is, however, fraught with the same joys and mishaps experienced by travelers everywhere. Booksellers are not exempt from travail. A fellow bookman was wiped out in Toledo recently when thieves broke into his car and took everything .

We recently made a combination business and pleasure trip to northern areas of Wisconsin and Michigan. The pleasure part was successful, but we found out that high population centers generate more used books than beautiful lakes and pine forests., The wide open empty spaces are beautiful but they are also largely book-less. People are needed to accumulate our stock-in-trade. The book part of our trip was rather sterile.

Largely self-explanatory is a letter we wrote to the Chrysler Corporation after we returned from that dry trip too the North Country

One of my mother's favorite sayings was, "Put the flowers on the piano--don't wait and waste them on the casket." She meant that credit should be given when credit is due. I have tried to follow this sage advice--thus, the letter.

Customer Relations Manager
PO Box 1718
Detroit MI 48288-1718

Dear Sir,

We live in Niles, Michigan. In May 1988 we bought our Dodge Caravan mini van from Pat Abiney C/P/D 66036, in Dowagiac, Michigan.

In August on a trip through northern Wisconsin and Michigan's Upper Peninsula it was ascertained, after we experienced noise in the left front wheel, that we needed a "brake job." It was not convenient and the irritation was not severe enough to warrant a three day wait to get the job done In Ashland, Wisconsin. This is what we were told we would have to do. The job itself would not take three days, but it would be that long before the mechanic (not a Chrysler garage) could get to it.

By the time we got to Iron Mountain, Michigan at five o'clock a couple of days later, the problem had made itself manifest to the extent that we were afraid to travel farther. We were passing the Riverside Auto Sales of Iron Mountain, Inc. and saw their Chrysler logo. We drove in. The service department was closed but a salesman, after hearing our tale of woe, told us to come back at eight o'clock in the morning. "We have compassionate people here who, I am sure, can work you in," he said.

We were at the garage at seven forty-five when Greg, the service manager, took us in tow. The offending wheel was removed and we were shown where the trouble was located. In spite of a full schedule, Greg had the difficulty resolved and we were on our way by eleven-thirty that same morning. Greg served us coffee and provided a ride back to our motel where we waited in comfort. When the work was completed he had our vehicle delivered to the motel. All of this was accomplished at a cost that we thought was most reasonable.

We are senior citizen writers and book shop owners who don't know a brake job from a canoe paddle. We expected to be intolerably delayed, badly treated, and financially gouged. Instead, we were not delayed at all (used the time to catch up on diary entries and do our laundry). We were treated like royalty. Our bill was no larger than it would have been if we had been at home under normal conditions.

We thought you would like to know.

Very truly yours,

(Signed) Ralph and Doris Casperson

I hope we won't have to write another nice letter to anyone after we return from our buying trip to the Boston area. This time we are going where the people are. Car trouble may lurk there too, but I hope we also find some good books.

A BUYING TRIP EAST

In September 1992 Doris and I attended a military convention in Boston. I belong to the National Order of Battlefield Commissions-NOBC. The NOBC is made up of men who were commissioned as officers on the field of battle during WW I, WW II, Korea, and Vietnam. NOBC is a very small organization of unusual men. I count myself fortunate to qualify as a member of this fraternity.

After the convention was over, ar d because Doris and I found ourselves in New England, we went on a book-buying trip. I have written about a similar trip last August in northern Wisconsin and Michigan. In that report I exclaimed about the beautiful scenery and complained a little about the dearth of books. I came to the conclusion then that in order to find books one must go where there are large numbers of people. That is why New England beckoned. More people would mean more books.

Some years ago on a trip to Boston, I visited the gift shop at the Old North Church. A small card affixed to the wall next to an old musket there stated that the musket had been used at the Battle of Lexington on April 18, 1775. Engaging the attendant in conversation, I pointed out that this battle was fought on April 19. She told me, rather heatedly, that even today during the re-enactment of those sterling days, on April 18th, two lanterns are hung in the steeple of the Old North Church. They signify, as of old, that the British army had left Boston by sea and were headed toward Lexington. The British, I said, did indeed leave Boston on April 18, but they didn't get to Lexington to fight the battle until the next day. Reluctantly, the woman in charge of the shop agreed that this was true. She assured me that the card would be changed.

A year later, I again visited the gift shop at the Old North Church. The little card was unchanged. It still carried the date, offensive to me, of April 18th. I complained to a male attendant this time. He, too, resisted me. When my point was proved, however, he agreed to have the date on the card changed. I gave him my business card and a dollar, and asked that he let me know when the change had been effected. I told him that because I was a history buff, such errors adversely affected my sleep. My new-found friend kept my business card, gave the dollar back, and assured me that he would not be the cause of further insomnia. He would let me know when the date on the card had been changed. Time passed. I heard nothing. I slept badly.

Subsequently, on two occasions, I had people from the Boston area in our book shop. They too, being interested in history, agreed

that something should be done. They would not only see about it,
they would certainly let me know after the card had been corrected.
I waited. I heard nothing from Boston to cure my fitful sleep,
nothing but silence.

You can believe that I was anxious to get to the gift shop at the
Old North Church when we were at the NOBC convention. When
we had our first free time, Doris and I flagged down the jitney bus
which took us to the Church. Upon entering the shop, we
approached the musket with baited breath. It hung on the same wall.
A new, larger, card with big black letters fairly shouted at me. "This
musket was used in the Battle of Lexington on April 19, 1775."
Upon our return to the convention hotel, our buddies wanted to
know where we had been. When I told them the Old North Church,
they wanted to know how we liked it. They looked at us in disbelief
when I said, "We didn't go inside."

We found that people in New England talk differently than we
do. In Plymouth I asked some elderly ladies, who obviously lived in
the historic town, if there were any descendants of the Mayflower
passengers still living in their town. They were surprised to hear the
question, thought it was a good one, but didn't know the answer.
When our chat was finished, one of them said, "Have a good tuah."
(tour)

My favorite epitaph is carved on a rugged gravestone in the
Plymouth cemetery. This ancient stone carries the following
inscription, *"Remember me as you pass by. As you are now so once
was I. As I am now soon you will be. Prepare yourself and follow
me."* Neat?

Of course in Plymouth we found Plymouth Rock and marveled
at the old white houses. It was Sunday, but we found a small, but
good, book shop open where we bought two boxes of books.

I knew about Titcomb's Book Shop in East Sandwich on Cape
Cod. Their daughter had visited our shop a year ago. We bought lots
of things there. Stopping again the next day on our return from
Provincetown, we bought more minor treasures.

We wended our way on to Concord, Massachusetts, The Old
North Bridge, Walden Pond, Sleepy Hollow Cemetery, and some of
the houses of Concord's famous authors. We bought more books at

"Books With A Past" and a couple of other shops.

Continuing north to Portland, the picturesque village of Camden, Maine became our final destination. Stops were made on the way when we saw places that looked promising, or when we got hungry for another muffin. Finally, the mini-van was as full of books as we dared load it. And we were full of muffins. If you like muffins, New England is the place to go. Every eating place has them. Big ones, too!

Our thoughts about books and population were confirmed. New England _with_ its many people generates lots of books. We want to go back soon.

TROUBLED BOOK BUYS

During the last four months of a recent year I feared my magic touch had vanished. Buying household accumulations and private libraries, usually easy for me, suddenly turned troublesome. Five deals in a row, one after another contained flaws. Three of the five were good buys and provided good additions to our stock, but two turned out to be totally unproductive; complete zero, they produced nothing but a bad taste in my mouth. One of these two had the redeeming factor of being somewhat humorous. For me to walk away from a book buy empty handed, or with loose ends dangling, is most unusual. My deals are always clean cut. We always pay cash on the spot and after the last book has been loaded in our van, we say good-bye to the happy seller.

It is most unusual for us to have the slightest trouble with a book buy. Walking away from a deal rather than have the slightest trouble is something that I have done on infrequent occasions. Five flawed deals in a row got me to thinking I should refrain from jumping out of bed in the morning.

The first of the five deals I will chronicle here, though a bit funny, turned out to be a clear strike-out. We left the premises empty handed, but we didn't feel bad and had no ill feelings against the person we were unable to deal with.

An elderly woman we have known for years called and said their children were pressing her to start disposing of some of the household effects she and her husband had accumulated over the years. This included a lifelong accumulation of books. Obviously I can't use these folks' real name We'll call them John and Wilma Jones.

Our appointment was for mid-afternoon. After passing the time of day and agreeing that modern society and its attendant political system is going to hell by fast express, we got down to the business of book buying.

After glancing at the books on shelves in a small room upstairs, as we always do, we set forth our modus operandi. We would select the books we wanted, remove them one by one from the shelves and stack them on the floor. Mrs. Jones said there were some books she may want to keep. This is standard procedure. We told her to remove these titles from the stack we were building and set them to one side. After all of the shelves had been worked, we would know that the books in our stack on the floor were to go and we then would make our offer accordingly. If she then accepts the offer, we told her, Doris would write a check and we would remove the books.. This is the procedure we have been using for years.

Mrs. Jones agreed with this plan and I began to pull books from the shelves. About every fourth book provoked a tale of woo. Instead of quietly removing the book "from my stack", Mrs. Jones grabbed the book, hugged it to her breast, and cried, "Oh, no, not that one." I began to feel like a slave auctioneer might have felt when separating little slave children from their mothers.

Mrs. Jones's lament continued, not just pulling the book from the stack, but reciting the book's provenance as well. "No, no, not that. John got that for me the day I told him I was pregnant with Nan."

"Mr. Casperson, not that one! We bought it in Petoskey on that Saturday during the war when it rained so hard. Don't you remember we took shelter in the book-shop."

I kept my council and said nothing but I thought, "Of course, I remember it well. It was in 1944 and I was nursing a machine gun on the Italian front, but , yes, I remember it well."

Trying to pull more books from the shelves was fast becoming a nightmare. There were tears in her eyes when she grasped and tore a battered, leather-bound, poetry book from my hands I didn't want the book 'cause it looked like it had been beaten with a rusty chain. "That one," she blubbered, "oh, don't tell John - not that one. My true love brought it to me the night we - oh, no, not that one -." Clutching the poor fragment to her ancient bosom, she pretty much broke down and sobbed, "John doesn't know - don't tell him - oh, no."

At this point I stopped. After a fashion Mrs. Jones regained her composure. Not wishing to hear anymore confessions or anymore of Mrs. Jones's autobiographical tales and not caring to put her through any further anguish, I stopped. I told her I would put all of the books back on the shelves, being careful, I said, to hide the battered poetry book.

"Mrs. Jones," I said, "you can look your library over at your leisure. When you come to an irrevocable decision concerning what you want to dispose of, please call us and we'll comeback." I put all the books back on the shelves.

Mrs. Jones's kids should never have put their mother in this terrible position. Let the old folks live undisturbed with their memories. We went downstairs where Mr Jones sat. He is largely incapacitated. When we said good-bye to him I felt guilty, the keeper of a terrible secret.

We will never hear from Mr and Mrs. Jones. After these old folks pass from the scene we will probably get a call from their kids. It will sound something like this, "We told Ma to get rid of the damn books and she didn't do it. Please come and get them out of here. The house is sold and we have to turn over the keys next Tuesday."

The second cloudy deal was with an aging friend. Having dealt with him before, we were looking forward to a pleasant interlude. Before he became partially disabled he was a regular in our bookshop and we had been entertained in their home. He, on a couple of occasions, had recommended us to others who had books to sell.

Arriving at our friend's house, we reviewed our conditions of the sale which were actually well known to him because we had done business together before. As he had on past occasions, my friend told me there were books he wasn't ready to part with. Again I reminded him to set these books aside as I pulled them from the shelves. Standard procedure.

Mr. Schmidt (not his real name) sat and watched as I pulled books from his shelves, surprised it seemed, that I was taking so many. This should have come as no surprise. I was there to help solve a problem, which was to move as many books as possible out of his house so the place could be put up for sale. I was doing what he called me there to do. This should have surprised no one. Mr. Schmidt made no move to pull our any books to keep. We did talk about one *Limited Edition Club* set. He told me not to take it as he wasn't ready just yet to part with it, so I left it on the shelf. That set was the only books he evidenced any desire to keep for himself.

Finally I was finished. All of the books I wanted were stacked on a tea table and on the floor around the rocking chair where Mr. Schmidt was seated. Most of the stuff was within easy reach of where he was perched. We agreed on a price and Doris wrote him a handsome check in four figures. The deal was made, consummated, finished. The books were mine. Mrs. Schmidt, at this juncture, brought in refreshments.

As we visited and passed the time agreeing that the world was in a tailspin to ruin I noticed Mr. Schmidt plucking books from the stack I had created. As he did this he kept telling me about each book saying he just couldn't part with this one and that one. The fact is, he already had.

At other times when the sellers realize they can't live a happy life without a volume or two, they offer to buy them back. In these past cases I have always just given the volumes to them and promptly forgotten about it.

Mr. Schmidt didn't take one or two non-descript volumes but a dozen or more of very good fast-selling items. He also didn't offer to buy them back. Had he not been a friend, I would have asked for my check back or would have walked out of his house and stopped payment on the check. We did neither.

Hurriedly draining my teacup, I signaled Doris and we hurriedly loaded the books and promptly escaped. Mr. Schmidt has lots of books in another house and when the time comes, I hope he offers them to some other dealer.

Our buying a fairly large library of Americana was the next one to be tainted by a flaw at the very end. Both Bill and Mary Wilson were book collectors of long standing; Mary was a more sophisticated accumulator than her husband. Through the years, many of their books had come from our shop. Mary Wilson, after a long fight, finally lost her battle with cancer thus leaving her husband with a two-pronged problem. He decided to leave the area and had to dispose of a happy lifetime accumulation of possessions; the bulkiest was his huge accumulation of books. The second task was to erase the memories the books resurrected of Mary. He recalled the time and place where most of the books had been acquired. Each volume, he said, triggered a once fond memory that now pained him. The first step in his effort to solve his dual problem was taken when he called us. Remove the books and his pain would become more tolerable and he could move on and start his life over with a clean slate.

Bill and I had a little trouble arriving at a mutually satisfactory deal. But then the books were paid for, loaded into the van, and we were on our way. This load took up all the space in one of the aisles of our warehouse.

One of Bill Wilson's daughters called me the next day. Her accusing voice coming over the telephone wire made me feel like some sort of criminal because I had taken her mother's books away. "I want some of those books," she cried. "After all they were my mother's books." This irate daughter lived not over a dozen miles from her parents" house. I can only assume that she knew her dad was moving and had to get rid of everything. Or don't people talk together any more? I also guessed that this creature had been around the house before, during, and after the funeral. She had ample opportunity to remove the books she wanted from the premises before I was called in. As is often the case, the desire for the deceased person's property seldom seems to seriously manifest itself until some outsider shows an interest.

I asked this irate person to give me the names of the books she wanted. She responded with six titles. Calling her back, I reported I had the books she wanted. Rather than have her come to the shop to pick them up, which is what she wanted to do, I offered to ship them to her, which we did. As little as possible to do with this person fitted my agenda perfectly. No charge was made for the books.

Two sisters were handling their mother's estate. When we responded to their call to look at the books, one of these worthies was busily engaged pricing junk for an estate sale. We arrived at the scene highly recommended by a third person as a firm that would treat them fairly. The books in this estate weren't numerous or valuable.

The sister on board at the time assured Doris and me that she was authorized to deal with us, an ascertation that must be made in cases of this nature. Our offer for the items we could use was accepted and I began to load the books into the van. After I had carried several armloads to the car, the other sister blew in like a mid-summer cyclone. "These books," she yelled, "are valuable. They're worth more than that." Continuing on in an abusive voice that would cause a lion to tremble she screamed, "You intend to sell Mother's books and make a bundle "

At this point, as I headed for the car, I whispered to Doris, "Don't write the check." Two round trips to and from the car and the books were back in the house. The daughter with "the voice" became falsely pleasant when I told her she needed the books more than I did. "Oh, no, I didn't mean to offend you. Don't get mad. I'm sure we can arrive at a fair price," she purred.

I assured her that we had already arrived at a fair price. "That's not the issue now," I said. "The point is that we don't care to do business with you." Whereupon we exited the troubled premises.

Before this spate of troubled buys passed I had yet another experience that turned out bad because of the deceased's grand-kids. This one was a little hard to do anyway because of our friendship with the lady who had accumulated the books. It's always a sad experience to go through the library of a friend who has passed on. We were dealing with a daughter, who, though we didn't know her, was a delight.

The daughter, Ann Ganning, was here from the eastern seaboard to settle her mother's affairs. Her main burden consisted of emptying out her mother's apartment, which housed several hundred books.

Mrs Ganning's children had come to Niles to attend the funeral. In looking the library over before returning east, they had pulled out six or eight books that they wanted for themselves. Ann assured us that the remaining books were for sale.

When things go awry on a book purchase, I don't waste time or emotions feeling sorry for the person selling the books. In this final episode of troubled buys, I did feel sorry for Mrs.Ganning. Her kids put her into a most embarrassing position.

We unloaded Mrs. Ganning's mother's books into the work area of the shop. Being late in the day nothing more was done with them. A troubled and embarrassed Mrs. Ganning was on the telephone bright and early the next morning. In talking with her children the pervious night, she caught Hail Columbia for selling Grandma's books. She wanted to come to the shop to retrieve some of the volumes in an effort to pacify her offspring.

Asking a few questions when Ann got to the shop revealed that her children wanted all of the history books. Showing her where the books were stacked, I told her to help herself. Visibly upset, the good lady picked out a dozen books thinking that she had skimmed all of the history out of the lot. I knew differently and told her so. I then virtually destroyed the lot by removing all of the history books. Of the original lot there were only about fifty books left. I helped Mrs.G. load the history books into her car.

I wondered how we would resolve the financial end of this debacle. Ann walked back to the shop with me, whipped out her check book and wrote a check in the exact amount I had paid her the day before. She was also full of apologies.

Here we have one more case of folks having no interest in a property until someone, usually an expert in the field, shows interest. Mrs. Ganning's kids acted inappropriately, but not unlike many others given the same circumstances.

After these five buys I was convinced I should quit answering the telephone. Two weeks after the Ganning debacle I was called in to look at a large Civil War and military lot. Almost reluctant to make the appointment, we did go. We bought the lot, a nice one, with no trouble at all. The spell was broken.

An outstanding private library came up for sale when we were vacationing in northern Wisconsin. The man who owned and had put this accumulation together was a well-known local historian. His library reflected a lifetime spent in reading not only history, but a wide range of other subjects as well. His hoard of fine books was heavily tilted toward history, his first love.

The fellow had gone to his reward and hopefully was spending full time indulging his historical interest in the library of the celestial city. A committee of elderly women had either taken it upon themselves, or had been appointed by someone to oversee the disposition of the local historian's treasures. These worthies had little or no knowledge about the printed word between hard covers. Maybe some of them, if pressed, could name four or five titles they'd read since leaving the local high school fifty years since.

One of the group, a member of the local historical society was more or less in charge, though timidly. This historical society, in spite of the fact that the area had a rich history, was only that - a society, a small group of citizens held together by their interest in things historical. They met irregularly, at the behest of the chairperson, at the houses of the members. There were no headquarters, no premises in which to store anything, and no archives.

The library I was looking at contained a mere handful books about the area. Local history. The women had segregated these few books, stocking a good sized bookcase with them along with a large number of other works of a general historical nature. Naturally the books in this bookcase were the ones I wanted. However, I was told that these books were not for sale. Because they were of local interest, the women said they were going to be given as a gift to the Historical Society. I agreed that books about the local area should be retained in the community. Not having a place to house anything posed a problem but the material should be kept someplace so the locals would have access to them; no argument from me on that score.

A quick glance at the bookshelves housing the segregated

volumes told me that most of these books were not about local history at all. The books dealt with history in general. In addition to the other things the Society didn't have were funds. The society had no treasury. Because of this rather important lack the women handling the estate, in their wisdom, decided that the local history books should be given to the society as a gift. One of the ladies' problems was that they could not distinguish between history in general and local history.

My nephew John, who is somewhat knowledgeable about books, was with me on this occasion and his help in sorting and carrying was of great value to me. Books that held no interest were carried to an empty part of the room in which we were working and were stacked out of the way. Along with me, John stole a glance from time to time at the books in the "off limits" bookcase. Realizing the value of these, as I did, he whispered, "You've got to get those, but how?"

My whispered reply, "Yeah, I have to have most of them, but the local history should be left in town." Continuing our quiet conversation, I said, "Wait and see, John. I have a plan. I'll use human nature against these good ladies. I'll bet you'll be loading most of those books into the van before we leave."

John's reply to this was an incredulous look. Nothing more. Likewise I kept my own counsel and we continued to work our way through the library. John looked puzzled as we continued to sort through the stacks, boxes, and shelves.

In order to work my plan, I had to figure out who headed up the ladies' group. close observation of a group at work will, in time, reveal the group's leader.

After awhile the head hancho of the group became manifest. Going over to the bookcase where the "not for sale" books were shelved, I asked Mrs. Leader if she would allow me to do some snooping in the bookcase. I assured her that I was well aware of the intention to give these books to the Historical Society. I am also telling her that because of my interest in history books I wanted to give their gift a closer look. My request was readily assented to and, feeling John's eyes boring holes in the back of my head, I set to work.

John saw me inspecting each book. Mentally he asked a million questions as he saw me pile the local history books on the floor, leaving the others that had nothing to do with the locale, on the shelves in the bookcase. John could readily see that pile of books on local history made a very small stack.

After engaging the matriarch in conversation, I pointed out that having looked the books over carefully, I deduced that the small stack on the floor was strictly local history and should by all means be kept in the community. I would like to have them, I told her, but they should rightly be given to the Historical Society. Out of the corner of my eye I could see John drifting closer to us trying to listen in on the conversation.

Trying to put John out of my mind, I continued my conversation with the lady. "Furthermore," I added, "the books in the bookcase, though desirable, are not local history books at all and should not be given away."

At this point, when I felt John was close enough to hear me, I dropped the bomb, or maybe more appropriately, I played my ace by saying, "I will pay you $500 for the books that are left in the bookcase."

Without hesitation I heard the woman say, "Sold", as I searched my various pockets for the checkbook.

After agreeing to sell those books, the woman seemed relieved. An important decision had been made for her by a third party. I really believe that the women were in deep water, not completely happy about giving these books away, but they didn't really know what should be put in the hands of the Society and what should be sold. My action delivered them to dry ground; their dilemma was behind them.

The other moral to this story is the part that I tried to rely on to turn the trick in my favor. This is the human nature trait I told John I would use to get these books. I have used it before in various guises in buying stamps and books. Experience tells.

Acting the role of the philanthropist is easy when the actor is unaware of the value of the gift. Translating the ladies' largess into language they readily understood was necessary. It was incumbent on me to do this to achieve my goal. When it became apparent they were giving away $500, the attitude of the Historical Society's benefactors changed. Giving away several shelves of books they knew next to nothing about was one thing. Giving away $500 was something else, something they were unwilling to do.

I can still see John shaking his head as we loaded the books into the van. To this day I'm not sure he realizes what happened.

READIN' WRITIN' AND SPEAKIN'

An excerpt from a commencement address by James Lehrer to a graduating class at Southern Methodist University at Dallas, Texas:

"I urge you to please keep in mind what the diploma you are about to receive does not mean you are educated. Quite the contrary. It means, I hope, that you have been opened up to a perpetual state of ignorance...and thus a lifelong hunger for more - more ideas, more information, more good thoughts, more challenges, more of everything.

I must tell you that some of the dumbest people I know went to great, prestigious colleges and universities like SMU...They walked across a stage as you are going to do, with diplomas in their hot little hands, pronounced themselves well-educated...and proceed to never read another book, entertain another fresh idea or tax their minds in any way beyond what was minimally required to make a living or make it socially, or both."

Some years ago a friend came to me complaining that in spite of repeated trials she couldn't get her high school aged son to read. The idiot box, she was telling me, consumes him, claiming his total time and attention. Even comic books, the lowest denominator on the reading scale, hold no interest for him. His square bug-eyes are true testimony of his emptiness. He speaks in disconnected grunts when he communicates at all. This offspring's odd habits are especially sad for his parents, voracious readers, who devour a book and more a week.

On a return visit sometime later, this distraught mother, visibly disturbed, was figuratively tearing her grey hair out. Her high-pitched plaintive voice dramatized her frustrations when she exclaimed, "Ralph, I wouldn't care what he reads even if it is pornographic, if he would just read something!"

Some weeks passed and the disturbed woman visited me again. She was holding an 8-1/2" x 11", sheet of paper in her hand. Exasperated, she handed it to me and said, "Read this, but first note the teacher's mark in red ink at the top." A bright "A-plus" on the head of the sheet stood out in glaring contrast to the grey words scrawled in pencil on the white neatly-lined paper.

The composition, containing no complete sentences and no paragraphs puzzled me; it was a spelling teacher's nightmare too. Worse than that, it was meaningless; it contained no message. Scratching my head and pulling my white beard, I handed the thing back saying, "What is it?"

My angry friend replied disgustedly, "It is nothing, really, but I am told it is a book report, and the kid thinks he is doing A-plus work."

"What are you going to do?" I asked.

Throwing her arms in the air in the gesture symbolizing surrender, she resignedly replied, "Private school." This episode dramatizes the linkage between reading, writing, and speech, the subject of this chapter.

Continuous observation in the book shop convinces me that reading good literature begets better speech. I have found from personal experience that such reading causes writing to improve too. The self-expression of those who are well-read is in marked contrast with the non-readers I meet in other environments. It is a pleasure for me to have oral communication with the highly literate. Trying to talk to those who aren't is a chore.

Some of the babies whose diapers were changed on the davenport in the book shop office are college students today. Watching their communication skills develop over these twenty-five years has been a rewarding experience. These young people, children no longer, brought up reading *Robinson Crusoe, Treasure Island, The Bobbsey Twins, Heidi*, the *Nancy Drew* stories, etc. are eons ahead of the comic book crowd in their ability to communicate with others. Also left in the murky dust of ignorance are those poor kids denied the children's classics because of their parents' corresponding stupidity.

One of the saddest things I have experienced in over twenty years in the bookshop is parental denial of good books to their children. While the child is hunting in the child's section, the parent is building his own stack of volumes. In contrast to Daddy's fifty dollars worth of books, the child's dollar paperback of *Black Beauty* is pretty insignificant. But sadly, the excited kid is crushed by the parent who says, "Ya don't need that. Put it back."

Instead of counting their blessings when their junior shows an interest in reading, the budding curiosity is killed. Seeing the expression on the child's face change from smiling exuberance and wonder to blank disappointment and defeat wrenches my heart. Feeling the hurt of the devastated child myself, I feel like shaking the offending parent. If it can be accomplished without offending my customer, I slip the rejected treasure into the child's hands, reinstating the smile so recently extinguished.

Over time good reading is internalized. Complete sentences are the norm and we see how the author marshals his thoughts by using paragraphs. Correct sentence structure and proper word usage becomes obvious. The reader carries this syntax over into his own writing and oral communication. Our writing and talking, in time, reflect the good books that have become a part of us and we profit from such reading.

The reading of good books contributes to the art of intelligent conversation in another way as well. Reading widens our fund of interesting knowledge which we share with our conversational partners; a well-read person never lacks for things to converse about.

It is difficult for me to carry on a meaningful far-ranging conversation with some who have formal academic training. If their academic and professional specialty is necessarily narrow, and if they have abandoned the pursuit of the printed word outside of their specialty, they have nothing much to contribute to general conversation. Such folks do well conversing with their peers in the same specialty. They will again become interesting general conversationalists when they expand their horizons of knowledge and experience.

The book shop spawns superb and humorous conversational partners. Such is not the case when I find myself in other environments. 'Phone conversations with people who want to sell books they found in a house they are wrecking can be particularly exasperating and ear shattering to one who appreciates good English properly used.

Letter writing, now becoming a lost art, is an excellent tool for the writer. Writing itself goes a long way toward improving writing. You want to become a good writer? Then write! And then write some more. Write something everyday. Write letters to friends. Write to a relative: Aunt Elaine, Grandma, Grandpa, or surprise your cousin with a four page essay on the affairs of the world. Write to the Voice of the People in your local paper. Write a piece and file it. Write another and burn it. Write, and write some more.

Much of the writing in modern novels is writing at its worst. Writing in periodicals is at least grammatically correct most of the time; it is utilitarian only. It's quite adequate for its purpose and you must read it, but it won't make you a better writer. It is a joy to read something I don't have to correct (edit) as I go. Steinbeck, Hemingway, Faulkner, Hawthorne, Thoreau, Twain, Ferber, Cather, and E.B. White, to name only a few American authors, can be read without mental editing. This type of writing is the kind that soaks into your skill bank and will eventually flavor the words that emanate from the end of your pencil.

So if you would a writer be .... hang up the 'phone, shut off the tube, silence the radio, and stick your head in a book, or write a letter. Hunt up a partner or two and talk about something substantial, unlike your latest golf score, the features on the latest automobile or the high cost of groceries. Participate in a conversation where you must parry your partner's thrusts, where you must think before putting your tongue in gear.

Author in the book shop Nov. 1977. Before the beard.

A browser's heaven

Book dealer Ralph Casperson and his wife, Doris, together have run their book shop for the past 10 years behind their home at 1303 Niles-Buchanan Road. They sell used books, first editions, paperbacks, prints, maps and anything "made out of paper" in their shop on Wednesday, Saturday and Sunday from 9 a.m. to 7 p.m. Mrs. Casperson said there is over 2 miles of lumber that has been turned into book shelves and she has personally stained each and every one herself. Their shop offers 30,000 books to choose from and the book dealer told of one young man who came on a Tuesday at 4 p.m. and stayed until Thursday morning "just browsing." Shelf after shelf offers anything and everything the reader could possibly ask for and they are all categorized for easy locating. (Daily Star photo by Barb Hosterman)

"Niles Daily Star News Article July 1980"

ONIONS 1975

A 1970's picture of the shop and part of the garden.

About one-half of the warehouse shelving lumber

Doris staining the shelving for the warehouse

Biblio - the official greeter at the shop.

Doris and Ralph at the signing party for their first book, *A NORTHERN BOYHOOD* in the author's home town Ashland, Wisconsin Aug. 1993

The sign at the Niles, Michigan HOLIDAY INN where the first signing party for the author's first book was held March 1993

Author and display at the "coming out" party for *A NORTHERN BOYHOOD*
Niles, Michigan March 1993

Label on the package of books from the Kansas Historical Society. Note the date (May 10, 1973). Now, in 1997, the box is still intact.

This one will soon join its brothers in oblivion

The Modern Library Collection

A Bookman's dinner party at our home in March 1985.
Harriette Barnette at the far right. Lew Barnette is at the author's right.

Ivor the Bridge Troll guarding the flag of Norway. His sister Olga is content to occupy a lower position on his left.

Karl John Schanche, the author's great grandfather who Ivor the Bridge Troll remembered.

Wally Bernhardine Ullich Schanche, wife of Karl John. 1825-1845

John Garmen Schanche and Christine Olsson Schanche, the author's grandparents. Ivor the Bridge Troll knew John who as a boy played around the bridge where Ivor lived.

The Modern Motel

Example of what the bookseller sometimes gets in his mail

Don Allen at his desk

Don Allen's barn and garden

Don Allen with Rockwell Gardener, a well known book dealer from Connecticut. on his right at the Chicago Book Fair

The author in his book shop about 1974

In the shop before the author found out that a beard needs an occasional trim. 1980

The author in his shop in February 1990

The "Mug Shot" used on the author's newspaper columns

The by-line from the author's newspaper column

Ralph and Doris in their home library in 1977

Ralph and Doris in their home library in 1997

Doris - 15 gallons later - she painted all of the book buildings

OUR MOTHER TONGUE MURDERED

In this chapter I continue to bemoan the ongoing murder of our mother tongue. Properly utilized our native vernacular is a beautiful tool. We use it in making our living. Its proper use makes our lives richer and more meaningful. The written word is a vehicle for communicating, but its use goes far beyond that necessary chore. Charming word pictures can be painted in our language. It is, in the hands of the literary artist, the brush with which he creates works of art.

Our communicating skills improve commensurate with the quality of the stuff we read. If we want to speak and write well we must read good literature. Show me a person who speaks well and I will wager that he or she is well-read and can write well too. Conversely, folks who read little are unable to express themselves either vocally or in writing. So often what passes for conversation today is a series of mispronounced, unconnected words interspersed with ill-timed grunts and groans. Well-worn clichés of the moment such as, "you know" and "I mean" are the glue that makes it all fall apart. Because of the dearth of reading today, much that passes for writing screams for an editor's blue pencil. But then many contemporary editors don't recognize misused language either.

In some past essays I have given examples from personal experience of the bad English usage.

The following quotes are from some one else's experience.

THESE SENTENCES WERE TAKEN FROM ACTUAL LETTERS RECEIVED BY A WELFARE DEPARTMENT IN APPLICATION FOR SUPPORT:

I am forwarding my marriage certificate and six children. I have seven but one died which was baptized on half a sheet of paper.

I am writing to the Welfare Department to say that my baby was born two years old. When do I get my money?

Mrs. Jones has not had any clothes for 4 years and has been visited regularly by the clergy.

I cannot get sick pay I have six children. Can you tell me why?

I am glad to report that my husband that is missing is dead.

This is my eighth child. What are you going to do about it?

Please find for certain if my husband is dead. The man I am now living with can't eat or do anything until he knows.

I am forwarding my marriage certificate and my three children, one which is a mistake as you can see.

My husband got his project cut off three weeks ago and I haven't had any relief since.

Unless I get my husband's money pretty soon, I will be forced to live an immortal life.

You have changed my little boy to a girl. Will this make a difference?

In accordance with your instructions I have given birth to twins in the enclosed envelope.

I want my money as quick as I can get it. I have been in bed with the doctor for two weeks and he doesn't do me any good. If things don't improve, I will have to send for another doctor.

I am very much annoyed to find that you have branded my son as illiterate. This is a dirty lie as I married a week before he was born.

HERE ARE SOME SENTENCES THAT APPEARED IN CHURCH BULLETINS:

This afternoon there will be a meeting in the South and North ends of the church. Children will be baptized at both ends.

This being Easter Sunday, we will ask Mrs. Johnson to come forward and lay an egg on the altar.

The ladies of the church have cast off clothing of every kind and they may be seen in the church basement on Friday afternoon.

SIGNS OF THE TIMES

Once again I position my pencil above a blank sheet of paper and wonder if I should write yet another essay about the misuse of our beautiful language. Continue this criticism, this negativism, and my readers may abandon me. Negative or no, I have to press pencil to paper in this vein as long as our mother tongue suffers abuse. Like wielding a sword in her defense, my pencil will lash out in her behalf as long as this malediction continues.

When writers of the world get it right, when the glaring linguistic errors dry up, I will put my pencil back in its cup. I wouldn't write essays about the misuse of it if those who use our language did it correctly, thus making criticism unnecessary.

In my mind I edit everything I read, except fine literature. The daily papers, news magazines, and some books are all read with a critical eye. My sympathy goes out to the folks who put the daily paper together. They don't have much time to get it right and quite often they don't, but I make allowances for them. The deadline they face each day would terrify me.

My sympathy doesn't extend to those writers who have time to do it right, but don't. Those who write signs are included in that group and they are the subject of this essay. When a branch of government has trouble correctly putting one word after another, I get almost violent. This is especially true after the shoddy work has been made permanent on a steel sign, highly unerasable. How many hands does the message on a road sign go through? Doesn't anyone have the gumption to say, "Hey, hold it, this doesn't make sense," or "My God, can't we say it better?"

I shudder every time I see this sign on U.S. 131 north of Cadillac, Michigan: "Do not pass when opposing traffic present." Did the state pick this as the winner in a contest of third graders? How about, "Do not pass against oncoming traffic"? This says it better with 37 characters and five spaces against 41 in the state's effort.

I am ashamed to admit to myself that I am a citizen of the "say yes to" state. What, I often ask myself, does "Say Yes to Michigan" really mean? Another absurdity at the entrance to our state is a steel sign that proclaims, "Michigan requires seat belt use." Some states with mandatory seat belt laws have very clever signs at their borders such as, "Buckle up, it's our law." What's wrong with "Fasten seat belts, it's the law." The latter message gets the point across without murdering the king's english and it contains fewer letters and spaces (29) against our present nightmare with 35.

There are many ways to say or write something. How dead and uninteresting our language would be if all writers had to use the same words to express similar ideas. I'm complaining about the misuse of words, bad composition, or the expression of the unintended.

Examples of words used to state the unintended can be found on road signs all over the state. You are in violation of the state's dictates if you don't stop your car and, "Watch for ice on bridge." Without stopping you can't very well do what this sign commands. Maybe the highway department really meant to say, "Bridge may be icy." (18 characters and spaces against 23) It is to the state's credit that the "watch" signs are being replaced.

Every time I see the sign near St. Ignace I am tempted to pull over and "Watch for falling rocks." If I did what their employer is telling me to do, the State Police would probably apprehend me for loitering. To forestall this, how about changing the sign to "Danger, falling rocks", or "Rocks on roadway", or just simply "Falling rocks"?

This spring big banners throughout one of the big mall stores proclaimed, "The Rights of Spring." I thought that they had spelled it wrong, meaning the "Rites of Spring." That would make a modicum of sense. Inquiring at the head office, I was told by a pretty, bright girl that "Rights" meant "Trend." I don't get it and neither does my well-used *American College Dictionary.*

Sometimes, if a single simple word is added, a sign will convey its meaning correctly. A two letter word added to a sign on a U-Haul truck would make it more effective and grammatically correct. The sign said, "Move yourself and save." We move ourselves very well without the aid of a big orange truck. How about adding a two letter word? There is plenty of room for it, "Move it yourself and save."

I saw another sign where the change of just one word gives a sharper clearer meaning. The sign stated, "On sale now, coupon books just $2.00." How about changing the "just" to "only"? It makes for a clearer smoother thrust.

Eliminating words sometimes strengthens the message too. A local restaurant wants us to "Try our daily specials." The "Try our" is superfluous. The message shortened to "Daily specials" says it all with more punch.

Here is another example where the elimination of one word sharpens the message and says what the entrepreneur really wants said. "See us for your life insurance." How about your kid's or your wife's life insurance? Maybe your wife wants to insure her aging and infirm uncle. Come on - drop the "your." "See us for life insurance."

Rearranging words sometimes gives a correct sharper message. "Try a hot bowl of soup" becomes "Try a bowl of hot soup." I'm sure the restaurant is trying to sell hot soup, not hot bowls.

Some signs should be redone completely. "Great Prime Rib at great prices." Our language provides us with many words to work with. Why in such a short message is one of them used twice? Let's get rid on one "great" in this sign. Maybe both of them should go. The second "great" might be misconstrued to mean big or large. Are the "prices" big or large? Is this what the restaurant wants to say? How about "Great Prime Rib at a moderate price" or "Super Prime Rib at low, low prices"?

Everyone has seen this one. It was on huge billboards and even on TV. The fact that it was sponsored by some outfit promoting education makes it especially shocking. "A mind is a terrible thing to waste." Remember seeing it? A mind is not a terrible thing. Certainly the people who wrote this thing had access to someone who knows a little about the English language. There are a couple of ways to say it without even working up a good mental sweat. "To waste a mind is a terrible thing", or, "It is terrible to waste a mind."

A big boo-boo showed up in downtown Niles, Michigan near the Main Street bridge. A large sign there stated, "Future site of Niles river-front amphitheater." The "Niles" is probably superfluous. Certainly the edifice won't be in any other city. But the major error on this sign is the "Future site." That location **is** the site, not the future site. How about, "Site of our future river front amphitheater"? The amphitheater is in the future, the site is now.

This critique includes only signs. The temptation is great to extend my remarks to periodicals, but I prefer a greater challenge. Columnist James L. Kilpatrick does a good job detailing some of the slips of the print media. I will not invade his province here.

Is the ill usage detailed above mere sloppiness, or is this more evidence that something is "on the blink" in our society? Is this the result of our failure to teach English properly in our schools? Do our signs now reflect this failure? We hear that Johnny can't read or write, even with a high school diploma in his hand. Is Johnny now writing signs in the real world?

NEW WORDS

The English language was not handed to Adam and Eve in the Garden of Eden. It wasn't created all at once at some time in the distant past like Henry assembled his Model-T Ford. Our language didn't come off an assembly line a finished entity. The body of words we use today has grown over eons of time. Like a live green plant, its roots grow deep in the old fertile soil of Greece and Rome. Other lingos nourish our plant as it grows into what it is today. Who is to say it is mature even yet?

Compare any late edition dictionary and you will find a number of new words that did not appear in the preceding edition. An exciting feature of our mother tongue is that it is not a fixed product. A vibrant tool or institution, if you will, our verbiage continues to grow and expand. While new words and expressions are being created, old ones, with increased usage, are coming into vogue.

Our English language is beautiful and lively. Like viewing the destruction of a classic painting, it hurts me to see our language abused. When not used correctly, it is indeed abused. It is beyond my understanding why folks today abdicate this useful tool and adopt a series of incomprehensible grunts, groans, and hisses as a means of communication. Or they put the words together so rapidly that they are delivered without enunciation. The result being a mouthful of noisy mush. Then we have the incomplete sentence freaks. A single word here and an unrelated word there without connecting consonants and vowels is really incomprehensible gibberish but it passes for communication; and our incomparable language is cast aside unused.

My space is limited, so I will not devote much space here to the rape of the <u>written word</u>. Here too the language is badly fractured. Among the young, letter writing is almost a lost art. Even our public prints, including books, abuse the glorious tool that is the English language.

But as usual I'm getting off the track. I started to write about those new words that constantly creep into and energize our language. A friend of mine, who has a way with words, has a virtual love affair with the English language. She wants more of it to love, so she tries to make it bigger by inventing new words. The other day she invented three. The first is "jibby jab." Agreeing that this is a summeyumptious expression, I asked her to define it. "Definition", she replied, "it has no fixed meaning. That's the joy of it", she bubbled. "It's a little like modern art. It means whatever you want it to mean."

So much for "jibby jab." On the heels of that one she came up with two more: "thing-a-ma-hochie" and "thing-a-ma-jig." These two have a familiar ring, particularly the second one, but her veracity has never been impeached, so who am I to question it? Again, when my scribbling grows stale, I like to have a little-used veribiage to spiggle it up a bit. I asked about the meaning of "thing-a-ma-hochie" and "thing-a-ma-jig." Darlene, my friend, would only tell me that the first word was female and the second was male. (Her dabbling in foreign languages gives her these notions.) As to the meaning, she said, "Ralph, just play with them a bit and the meaning may become obvious."

I'd do what she suggests too, but I must get these lines typed and Doris, though not a Puritan, is rather smeekey and she may rebel. Who 'da hell would do my typing then?

I have, by writing this piece, and using Darlene's new words in it, let myself in for another problem. She will get absolutely weemish when she sees her words in print. Her anguish will be a legardable thing to witness. She will know that in one-hundred years the Oxford English Dictionary will give me credit for using her inventions for the first time. "Piggledash, Darlene!" That's the way the rubber sphere rises rapidly into the air after coming forcefully into contact with the pavement. Or, to use a much too trite expression, "That's the way the cookie crumbles."

Men of old or of yesterday don't have a monopoly on the coinage of new words; neither does my friend Darlene.

SO WHAT'S NEW?

One June day in 1992 an elderly lady brought several Civil War books to the book shop. The books once belonged to her great-uncle who fought in the Union Army. She realized that books such as these should be passed on to younger family hands. But the soldier boy who had gone off to fight in the Army of the Potomac in 1861 had no more descendants. She was the last of the line. She told me this with a shade of sadness in her voice.

I bought the books. After the kindly old woman had left the shop, I sat with the books, slowly turning their pages, looking at the pictures and pondering. One of the books was a memorial to a Union general with an account of a reunion of his division at Gettysburg. After a while I began to have a feeling of deja vu.

One book dealt with the dedication of various monuments to military units that fought in the Civil War. I was looking at pictures of tablets and plaques, stones, and arches commemorating various fighting units of the Union Army at Andersonville, Antietam, Bull Run, Gettysburg, and Shiloh. There were pictures of aging veterans with white beards, too. These old men came from afar to a central meeting place to reminisce with the buddies of their youth, men grown old but sharing faded memories of experiences in a big war many years ago. They belonged to an exclusive fraternity open only to those who had met the dragon. Some wore medals on their black broadcloth suits. Many had broad-brimmed dark blue hats sitting squarely on their heads, the hat of the Grand Army of the Republic (GAR).

As I continued to turn the pages, it seemed that the old grey and black tomes were trying to tell me something. A strange feeling had overtaken me. What was it and what did it mean? I began to feel at one, a kinship, with the Civil War Veterans who looked at me from their places on the old pages.

I read some of the text in the old volumes too. A section of one book had copies of letters of congratulations from one veteran to another. The congratulated recipient had just had a book published about his Civil War exploits. When I read this letter I felt even closer to these old people. But why? I was looking at a book published in 1904 about a war that had ended over one-hundred years ago. Yet I had this feeling of fraternity. Where did it come from?

Slowly the dawn came. I was looking at pictures and reading about men who were reliving their war, the most exciting experience of their long lives. Like the fellows in the book, we veterans of World War II (my war) were doing the same thing. In April Doris and I had attended a monument dedication at Arlington, Virginia. This moving experience was still fresh in my memory.

On April 8, 1992 our group gathered at the Arlington National Cemetery where we dedicated a plaque to recipients of Battlefield

Commissions. My comrades in the National Order of Battlefield Commissions (NOBC) were doing the same thing in 1992 that the Civil War Veterans were doing in the late nineteenth century. The old soldiers of yore are gone now, as we soon will be, but our monuments will endure. The country is full of granite shafts and brass plates erected by the participants of our wars. When the elderly military men of old met together for their dedications, they reminisced, took pictures, and left a written record for us to read. We are doing exactly the same thing.

I had just read a book by an NOBC member about his combat in Korea. The ink was scarcely dry on my letter congratulating him on his literary effort.

Is it any wonder I felt close to the old men in the books? I read about their reunion in Gettysburg. In August and September I was scheduled to go to military reunions. These get-togethers will continue as long as today's old soldiers are mobile. We, too, will wear our medals and funny looking caps. We, too, will reminisce, take pictures, and dedicate monuments; we will continue to leave a written record also.

It has ever been thus. War veterans must get together to relive the most exciting part of their lives.

OLD LAWS OF MICHIGAN

The used-book business provides one benefit to the shop proprietor not enjoyed by the operators of other enterprises. This dividend goes a long way to balance the scale not overly weighted, at times, with monetary rewards. We in the Antiquarian or Used-book trade can utilize our merchandise for our own benefit and pleasure without diminishing its usefulness or lessening its value. After all, a used book is not virginal when we acquire it. As its name implies, it has been used. Further careful perusal does not make it less desirable in the eyes of our customers.

It is quite necessary in the pricing process to sometimes read parts of a book in order to ascertain its worth. But pricing aside, the great luxury of the bookman's occupation is his access to the endless stream of books passing through his hands that can be set aside for his future reading pleasure. Interesting and sometimes strange books constantly drift across my desk. I dip into these tomes in the process of getting them ready for the book-shop shelves. This ladling pours a great deal of knowledge into my sparsely-covered head. Almost all of this information is interesting - some is useful and some has no practical value whatsoever. You, gentle reader, are the judge of the material I will share with you in this essay. It is the result of my sneaking a peek between the covers of one volume in the river of publications passing across my desk.

In looking over a newly-acquired stack of books this morning, checking their condition, removing extraneous material from between their leaves (bobby pins, paper clips, tooth picks, and autumn leaves) and ultimately arriving at a price, I find myself looking with interest at a rather badly-beaten leather-covered volume dated 1846. I am leafing through *The Revised Statutes of the State of Michigan* approved by the Legislature on May 18, 1846. These law-giving people are a busy group. A record of their labors now lodged between these dusty covers fills 724 pages with small print. The state had only been in existence since 1837. All of this law-giving in only nine years. Whew!

I don't go out of my way to hunt up laws to obey, so it's quite uncharacteristic for me to peruse such a book. In this case my native curiosity overcame my lawless nature. I was compelled to ascertain what type of yoke their elected representatives in Congress had fashioned for the citizens of 1846. Some of my findings are recorded below.

An astounding departure from today's practice is provided for in chapter 37. The care and maintenance of an indigent parent, it says, is the responsibility of the parent's children. Such support can be ordered by the county. The court, after ascertaining that the offspring of the poor parent is able, will dictate the amount the son or daughter <u>must</u> pay toward their parent's support. If the offspring are unable to support the parent, <u>any</u> relative can be ordered to do so. It's no wonder that people had a lot of kids in those days. The incentive certainly existed, better than a bank account in a shaky rural bank.

Chapter 41 prohibits the sale of spirituous liquor to the Indians

(Native Americans). Also, anyone who imbibed at a tavern was not legally obligated to pay a bar bill in excess of seventy-five cents. Extending credit for spirituous liquor in excess of that amount was not illegal, but was done at the peril of the tavern keeper.

Chapter 42 provides that the father of a child conceived out of wedlock is responsible for the child's support. If the father's performance didn't suit the court, the fellow was locked up in the slammer until he mended his ways.

Quoted here without comment is Section 1 of chapter 43: *"No person shall keep open his shop, warehouse or workhouse or shall do any manner of labor, business or work, except only works of necessity or charity, or be present at any dancing or any public diversion, show or entertainment, or take part in any sport, game or play on the first day of the week; and every person so offending shall be punished by a fine not exceeding ten dollars for each offense."*

It was against Chapter 44, Section 5 for any driver of a horse-drawn vehicle used for hire to cause his horses to run, with or without passengers in the vehicle. Break this law and you were subject to a fine up to one-hundred dollars. No pennyante ten-dollar penalty here. This was serious business. If the driver happened to be short of greenbacks he would be obliged to sit in the local calaboose for up to thirty days.

Chapter 47 addresses lost articles and stray beasts. This chapter gets long and involved. Suffice it to say that it was against the law to keep money or any lost article without first reporting it to local government authority. If the proper owner didn't surface, the finder got to keep the goods after paying the government half of its value.

Chapter 48 deals with firemen. If a worthy citizen wanted to be exempt from jury or militia duty all he had to do was become a volunteer fireman. He could be called for militia duty only in the case of domestic insurrection or foreign invasion; was Canada a threat?

Chapter 51 provides, not simply, for the payment of bounty for killing wolves. Section I ends by stating. *"... and paid in the manner herein provided."* Following this is almost two pages of small print detailing the method of payment.

Chapter 83 is the marriage chapter. Section 3 spells out in no uncertain terms who a man or woman cannot marry. *"No man shall marry his mother, grandmother, daughter, granddaughter, stepmother, grandfather's wife, son's wife, grandson's wife, wife's mother, wife's grandmother, wife's daughter, wife's granddaughter, nor his sister, brother's daughter, sister's daughter, father's sister, or mother's sister."* Similar prohibitions are listed for women. It seems strange that cousins who are related by blood are not prohibited from occupying the marriage bed together, but several non-blood relatives are banned from joining in Holy Matrimony: stepmother, son's wife, grandson's wife, wife's mother, wife's grandmother. Why? This section forbids the marriage of black and white persons. The section also attempts to keep our gene pool pure by providing that *"no insane person or idiot shall be capable of contracting marriage."*

The marriage chapter provides for instant divorce when either party is sentenced to life in prison.

Moving on, Chapter 158 provides for a $500 fine or incarceration up to a year for *"every person who shall commit adultery."*

Section 13 deals with obscene material. Anyone, this section provides, that imports, prints, publishes or sells any book, pamphlet, ballad, etc. that contains obscene language or pictures *"manifestly tending to the corruption of the morals of youth..."* shall be jailed for up to a year or fined up to $1000. What would these solid legislators think if they turned on a TV today?

I could go on but I have come to the conclusion that it is the nature of man to meddle in his fellow's business. It's still going on.

My point in writing this piece is to illustrate that good used-book stores are filled with works of similar interest. Diligent browsing is its own reward.

THE OLD FRONT PORCH

My mind is tuning out the drone of a distant airplane and the abrasive sound of an occasional semi-truck on the concrete by-pass about two miles away. My being is dealing only with the rural silence as I am drawn to the wicker arm chair on the shaded front porch of the old farm house.

Old farm house, indeed, but modernized by its present owners with a large swimming pool in the back yard. So why am I here? The lovely teenage daughter of the present house holders, successors on this farmland to its original farm folk, is an exceptionally fine swimming instructor. I am here delivering my granddaughter for her swimming lesson. But after spying the old fashioned front porch with its comfortable looking wicker arm chair and swing, the pool and other modern fixings on the place cease to exist for me. The porch on the front of the white clapboard-sided house, with its decorative spindle railing and old-fashioned gingerbread decorative dowels, draw me like a magnet drawing iron filings. The sculptured glass in the front door seems to take on a human quality beckoning me to this quiet haven secluded from the busy, noisy harshness of the modern world, a calm backwater, a place out of the past.

The feeling that I have been here before possesses me as I sink tiredly into the deep cushion of the rustic chair. I have an hour to while away and with every passing minute the feeling of deja vu grows stronger.

The day is full of sun, a hot summer afternoon. The slight breeze coming to the deeply shaded porch cools a bit as it passes through the thick leaves of a gigantic maple tree. This pleasant breeze seems to come out of the past. It strengthens my nostalgic feeling. This massive natural air conditioning is carrying me back in time. Looking at the tall green corn in the field across the narrow country road further reinforces my feeling of times gone-by. The road I am facing, though blacktopped, seems to shed its surface. It becomes dry gravel. I can see brown horse droppings here and there on its light tan surface. I can hear the slight rustle of the shiny leaves on the tall corn stalks as the small breeze drifts through the field across the way.

The loud buzzing of a fly sends my already aroused memory reeling backwards in time. Prevented for many years by our noisy world from hearing this rasping sound, the sharp buzzing completes my memory trip and I am back on the front porch of the house where I first saw the light of day in Deer Park, Wisconsin. My seventy-five years have evaporated. I am a boy again, sitting on the front porch of that old white house in the farm village of the 1920's.

Reading a modern magazine during my first visit to the old front porch didn't seem to be in keeping with my journey into the past. On my second visit I brought along Hamlin Garland's, *A Son Of The Middle Border*. Garland's autobiographical work is much more in keeping with my dream trip to that old front porch of yore. Garland, too, stemmed from Wisconsin a few years prior to my toddling onto the stage of life in America's dairyland. The change in reading material stimulated my thoughts of the past.

Reading this antiquarian book helped me to focus on the front porches of yesterday that played important roles in our lives. But my reading ceased as I slowly closed the book. My eyelids drooped and, entering a state of semi-conscious reverie, I began to feel the presence of those who once whiled away a lazy hour on their front porch long ago. These people I was remembering are long gone to the verandah in the sky where they still rock and visit with their own kind and will do so for all eternity.

A host of scenes floods my memory screen. The front porches in my recall are places much used. Many of the happenings there seventy-five years ago don't take place anymore. Our modern houses are completely devoid of this charming, useful architectural appendage.

Nowadays front porches, if they exist at all, are not used. The advent of television, central air-conditioning, and the dearth of spare time to sit quietly reading, reflecting, and visiting have efficiently killed the old front porch.

Many are the books my parents read in the quiet time of early evening when that interlude wasn't filled with the screams of the daily newspaper. A weekly news sheet was sufficient to keep them abreast of the small happenings in their little town and the much larger world of their day. Books by Peter B. Kyne, Jean Stratton-Porter, Sigrid Unset, Mary J. Holmes, and Grace Livingston Hill held their interest while we kids devoured Tom Swift, The Bobbsey Twins, and books by Henty.

Like a huge family picture album or scribbled journal, those old front porches recorded the comings and goings of the family who lived and loved behind the massive front door with its bevel-edged glass panes.

Here is where the mother is hugging her son for the last time as he is leaving for the wars. I can imagine the happy reunion when he returns a hero with his uniform jacket ablaze with bright colored military awards. The hero is welcomed home again on the front porch.

Perhaps circumstances dictate that we focus on a different scene. The Western Union messenger in his high-topped boots and olive drab uniform, parking his bicycle and hurrying up the front steps to deliver the yellow telegram - "The War Department regrets to inform you - -."

Sometimes the newly painted grey porch boards were slippery with rice thrown at the bride and groom after the daughter of the house got married in the parlor. Or maybe it is a new house and the groom proudly carries his bride across the front porch.

Now I envision a summer evening in a more silent world and the soft drone of voices is heard in the neighborhood as folks sit on their front porches visiting, talking to each other and rocking, or slowly swinging and talking, rocking and swinging and talking. I also hear the squeal of children as they play their evening games with the front porch steps as the goal: hide and seek, pompom pull-away, poke in the ribs, tag, and other games. The children tire and grow quiet and it's time to listen to the night birds and the chirping of the crickets as the soft talk continues on the old front porch.

Maybe the night is warm. A slight breeze rustles the oak leaves from time to time. Quietly the lady of the house leaves her family group and disappears into the house reappearing with a tray laden with tall glasses of freshly made lemonade with pieces of bright yellow lemon floating among the slivers of ice.

On another humid evening the man of the house silently slips away. He returns in a half-hour with a quart of ice cream from the local confectionery store four blocks away.

At another time a home-grown watermelon that has spent the day on a block of ice is shared. Be it ice cream, lemonade, watermelon, homemade cookies, or just plain talk, they all go far in cementing the family together on the old front porch.

A wreath of flowers adorns the front door when a family

member passes from the scene, a sad warning to all not to intrude on the family during its bereavement. The same porch is also off-limits when a bright red quarantine sign is tacked to the side of the house, warning of a contagious disease within.

The timid teenage boy can be seen greeting his date on the front porch. Upon their return from the movies or the ice cream store, while swinging on the porch swing with the fireflies blinking around them, maybe she allows him to hold her hand. When all too soon the time comes to say good-night, nervous lips meet and touch timidly as the date ends on the old front porch.

It's called progress and maybe it is; but with all of our busyness, our electronic devices, decks, patios, and pools, something precious was lost when we abdicated the old front porch.

THE HERMIT COMPLEX

Is it not true that almost everyone harbors the latent desire to run away to some remote spot and, once there, to lead the uncomplicated life of a hermit? Such a fantasy has always lived in one of the back-rooms of my mind, to be called forth to fill those infrequent but endless hours when sleep eludes me. Long ago I gave up counting sheep - much too unproductive.

In my youth, playing with the Thoreauian Philosophy, I settled on the idea of erecting a tiny cabin in the woods, planting a bean patch, and there, solely with my thoughts for company, living a self-sustaining existence. As the years passed, further study of Thoreau's works convinced me that the close proximity to Emerson's house made Henry David's solitary existence more possible and pleasant. I'm sure that the mistress of the house where Emerson wrote his books and hung his hat saw to it that 'The Hermit' of Walden Pond got a square meal when he wandered through the kitchen door of the big white house in Concord. These suspicions aside I continued to harbor the desire to emulate Thoreau. At times the subject even dominated my discussions.

In one conversation my sister, Margaret, brought me back to stark reality with a few short sentences outlining my lifestyle and mode of living. She pointed out that it was easy to dream of a life of self-denial devoid of most material things and all modern-day comforts and friends. "This is easy," she said, "surrounded as you are by your private library and other creature comforts in your modern well-appointed dwelling." She continued with her wise counsel by telling me, "it's all right to dream, but it might be difficult while you are eating your boiled beans and fat pork for the seventh time that week, to forget all of the nice things you have given up."

She continued to badly fracture my bubble by saying, "try not to remember the supermarket as you wrest your vittles out of the ground and the dark forest." "Forget," she said, "your central air conditioning, automatic furnace and swimming pool as you swat the mosquitoes in the heat of the night in your un-screened cabin."

I pointed out to my sister that anything can be fantasized. "My fantasy," I told her, "doesn't include leaky roofs, obnoxious bugs and mud " So the fantasy, even after our conversation, though a bit tarnished, still exists. In the real world I know that the practical way to lead the life of a hermit is to be independently wealthy.

My Robinson Crusoe complex has lead me to an extensive interest in the islands of the South Seas too. *Robinson Crusoe* and *The Swiss Family Robinson* are books I read in my youth and they pointed me toward the dream islands of the South Pacific. My interest in these precious atolls has never flagged.

This fantasy about living the lone existence takes me on mental journeys to Northern Wisconsin and Michigan. The Pacific Islands may provide a more hospitable climate, but not until recently have I been able to relate to these remote places when I dream about escaping. I'm interested in these islands, yes, but I've been unable to visualize myself living in a grass shack. A tight log cabin in the north country has always been my dream; I repeat, until recently.

My reading takes me on repeated trips to the South Pacific. A foundation for this reading was built by reading substantial works about the area. From Beaglehole's *Life Of Captain James Cook* to Mitchener's works as the beginning building blocks, I have continued to read widely about this area.

The books of my Norwegian hero, Thor Heyerdahl, *Fatu-Hiva*, *Aku-Aku*, and *Kon-tiki*, are required course reading for South Sea Islands 101. These books serve to broaden my knowledge of this mysterious area and each one whets my appetite for more.

A debt is owed to Charles Nordhoff and James Norman Hall too for authoring *Mutiny on the Bounty, Men Against the Sea,* and *Pitcairn Island.* Also their picture of early Australia in *Botany Bay* is surpassed only by Robert Hughes's epic of Australia's founding in *The Fatal Shore.* Huge's accounts of conditions on the convict ships filled with England's worst, the first settlers of Australia, are barely believable. *My Island Home* by James Norman Hall takes me to Tapai and as close to an island existence there as I have ever experienced. These books are only a few of the ones that have nurtured my interest in these islands.

A few more I recommend to anyone curious about this interesting part of our planet are Ian Ball's *Pitcairn: Children of Mutiny* and *Two Thirds of a Coconut Tree,* by H. Allen Smith. Smith mixes his humor with delightful information about Tahiti. Peter Buck in his *Vikings of the Sunrise* attempts to solve the mystery of the original settlement of these islands. Lastly to cap off this very incomplete list is Bengt Danielson's work *Love in the South Seas.* I have enjoyed all of these books, but none have really ignited my desire to include the islands as a place of escape and settlement.

In past essays I have scribbled about the luxury enjoyed by used-book dealers in being able to read their stock-in-trade prior to offering it for sale. The good fortune of finding unusual books also accrues to people who browse in used-book shops. In both cases treasures unknown to us fall into our hands. I laid my always-curious hands on such a little volume this morning as I was pricing a box of books. Ross Norgrove, the author, calls his little paperback volume *Blueprint for Paradise.* This How-to-do-it book about how to live on a tropic island has changed my interest in these island gems to a desire to live on one of them. In the past, not being able to perceive the problems one would encounter in establishing an island haven I could not visualize an existence there. Therefore I had no fantasy as an islander.

Now this slim paperback will power my flight of fancy. To start, it tells me how to choose my island. The choices range from a place to practice a truly primitive existence to one where civilization rivals my present homestead with electricity and telephones. The book explains the problems encountered and gives solutions in each type of existence.

Norgrove's book really covers the waterfront: Can children be included in your plans? What is the language problem? How you deal with medical problems is addressed. The book tells about one fellow who had his non-troubling appendix removed before he set sail for the islands. Another had a badly broken little toe chopped off because it might cause trouble where medical facilities are limited.

The author reminds us that in spite of their romantic visage, thatched roofs provide a home for crawling bugs from scorpions to big healthy cockroaches. There are better ways, the author writes, to start a day than by having a spider descend with a splash into your morning cup of coffee.

This book gets into important details such as the disconnection of cistern down-spouts on the approach of a hurricane, because salt water carried by the intense wind will contaminate the water supply.

My departure for the South Seas is not imminent. It is not even a possibility. The new information will merely give my log cabin dream in the north woods a little competition.

Once again I have tried to show that diligent browsing in a good used-book shop will invariably turn up unknown treasures.

DONALD CHARLES ALLEN - MASTER BOOKMAN

Donald Charles Allen was a character and a nonconformist during a time when a homogenized society quit making such things. Smashing the mold after making him God could never duplicate Don Allen. It can be said without fear of contradiction that he was a unique person with a compulsion to do his own thing, in his own way, without interference and at his own convenience. Being different exacted a price but not one in excess of what he willingly continued to pay.

His scale of values, heavily influenced by deep general scholarship, his uncommon lifestyle, the book trade and large sweet cantaloupes totally rejected the turn-ons of conventional society. He wouldn't note the slight if the local banker snubbed him when they met on the street. The clergy meant nothing to him except as casual customers in his book shop. His circle of friends didn't include the so called "right people" in the community, all crashing bores and a waste of time, to hear him say it. A good father who loved his own kids, Don held no special feelings for anyone else's. He let others bother with Boy Scouts, Little League, and other highly structured juvenile time fillers. He and his wife, Edith, raised their six kids without the aide of TV. Oh, they had a set, but it wasn't the central stimulus in the children's lives. He actually took pride in not concerning himself with the PTA and other organized social entities. Don took care of his own, lived his life as he pleased, and expected others to do likewise. Don could be tenacious, but he didn't fight. In an adversarial confrontation, which he almost always successfully avoided, he became downright timid. At the Antiquarian Bookman's Association of America (ABAA) Chicago Book Fair it became necessary to ask an undesirable character to leave the premises. Having no stomach for this disagreeable task, Don shunted it off onto his wife Edith and me. As chairman of the affair, Don should have performed this dirty task, but typically he didn't do it. No one thought less of my friend for his lack in this area because he excelled in so many others.

The House of David sect in Benton Harbor, Michigan, held such an allure for Don that he began to resemble them in appearance. Like them, his beard was unkempt and he wore his long hair in a pony tail. I'm sure their metaphysical beliefs were not a part of his credo, but probably the attraction existed because the Israelites dared to be different; Don accepted that. Over the years he accumulated a vast hoard of paper material concerning the House of David, none of which he ever offered for sale. I never set eyes on a House of David piece in his shop except a little green pamphlet about vegetarianism readily available at the House of David compound. Don, in reality, rescued this vast accumulation from the slowly-dying group, donating a large amount to the Benton Harbor Library and selling the balance enblock to a university a few years before he died.

Don's entertaining Willie from the House of David every Thursday night became almost ritual. No other friends sat in on these sessions. Should I happen to be at Don's house on Thursday evening, the distinct feeling existed that even I, Don's star pupil and best friend, would not be welcome at his sessions with Willie. What transpired between these two week after week? No one knows. Though I know he frequented the place, Don never once took me with him to the House of David. Why? We went together every other place under the sun, but never to the House of David. My feeling at the time? Don't ask questions. I listened to my feelings, gleaning no answers.

He visited the House of David compound every Tuesday afternoon week in and week out until his illness prevented him from driving. Only then did he quit.

I was in my late forties when I met Don. He was ten years my junior. The distinguishing feature of Don's physique at the time of our meeting? Rotund. Not very tall, about 5'10 1/2". He tipped the scale at well over 200 pounds prior to his terminal illness that continued to waste him during the last years of his life.

As that inner animal in us all does to a greater or lesser extent, Don's ego needed feeding, but his didn't thrive on the nutrients commonly used to inflate most people's self-esteem. Don blossomed when his peers in the book world recognized his genius or when those in the world of letters, that he considered his superiors, noticed him in one way or another. A few of these lettered people summered on the Lake Michigan shore near Three Oaks. On occasion when he was invited to break bread with them, I found him strutting a little; not perceptively perhaps, but a lightness invaded his spirit at these times and it looked like he was carrying his head just a little bit higher. Following the invitation or recognition, his smile brightened, and became a little wider with just a small sneer as though he whispered just above a thought, "Look, even those conforming tides are reaching out for me."

The optimum of ego trips came to Don in three parts: his selection for membership in ABAA, his election as president of the Midwest Chapter of that group and the chairman of the ABAA Book Fair in the Prudential Building in Chicago, Illinois. The fair became the capstone of his career. Putting on this affair, no mean achievement, taxed his executive ability, but as it came to the fore, he very successfully directed the efforts of others in a truly pioneering effort. A trailblazer, he had no road map to follow in setting up the fair. Copied by others, his methods are now the blueprints used in conducting the fairs today.

Doris, Harriette Barnette (a book dealer from South Bend, Indiana), and I traveled to Chicago for one day at the fair, re-acquainting ourselves with exhibitors from the Midwest such as Van Allen Bradley, Don Vento, Ash Kennedy, Titles Incorporated, to name some. We also met others from all over the United States and abroad. I sprout goose bumps reliving the thrill of this experience and I'm sure it showed that I was mighty proud to count Don Allen, boss-man of this event, my very good friend.

So these things gave satisfaction to Don Allen, along with a good melon crop and a cob of corn drenched in salted butter and freshly harvested from the towering rows in his fertile garden located row on beautiful row in back of his old red book-filled barn.

Late model cars, a low golf score, large financial assets, and over-priced restaurants didn't tickle the inner Don Allen. He preferred truck stops. Anyone searching for him would not be apt to find him anyplace haunted by mass man.

Don Charles Allen shared the town of his birth with James Oliver Curwood, author of adventure stories for boys. A distant relative of Ethan Allen, Don Allen hailed from Owosso, Michigan. Along with his famous townsman, Curwood, Don became attracted to letters at an early age, reading the Encyclopedia Britannica from cover to cover; retaining it all, too, I'm sure. The type who may have been spoiled by higher education, Don never experienced much formal training past high school, but he never stopped reading and learning. Don's mind, if not photogenic, had sponge-like qualities soaking up information until he knew at least a little bit about everything and a great deal about some things.

To illustrate his mental prowess the following antidote is in order: In his youth Don wanted to be a watchmaker. He finished an eighteen month course in watchmaking in nine months. When he took the entrance examination for this course he had to write it five different times. Finally he exploded stating that if this is what he had to go through to be admitted he didn't want any part of their school.

The authorities were amazed because he had missed no questions on any of the exams They had continued to give him exams to see if he would miss a question. He hadn't.

The upshot of this successful testing was that he was offered scholarships to any university of his choice in the country. "No," he said, "I want to be a watchmaker."

I became the beneficiary of this learning. Plumbing his vast store of knowledge, he began to unload it on me. In the process of his endless discourse he aimed to teach me the rudiments of the used-book business. Most of what I know about the used book and antiquarian book trade I learned from this tough but effective professor of bookmanship. He retained me in Bookmanship 101 for a number of years because he continued to expand the prospectus; he never, to his dying day. let me graduate, teaching me to the end of his life Other teachers besides Don were contributing to my education, but he continued as my chief mentor. His task, because he worked in fertile ground, was easy. Fertilized with a lifetime of reading and nurtured by a long-standing enthusiastic desire to own a used-book shop, the seed he planted took immediate root and Don's efforts bore fruit for both of us in many ways.

My sister, Margaret, librarian at the Iron Mountain, Michigan High School Library, sent me a copy of one of Don's early book catalogues. Impressed, I went to see Don at his place in Three Oaks, Michigan; this was in the late 1960's.

As in most bookmen's dwellings, the major decoration in Don's house was books. Merely an extension of his book-shop, his house overflowed with books. If he took a fancy to you, or if he sensed that you were a serious book buyer, you graduated from his book barn and shed shop to the house where your browsing continued. Passing muster on my first trip, Don gave me free run of the place from the start.

Trying to get involved with the Allens socially though didn't come easily. Don told me in later years that he avoided my initial invitations to dinner at our house because he knew I was a utility company manager; thus turned off, he spurned my social advances. No time existed in his scheme of things to become involved socially with a middle-management bore. Only after he found out about my consuming passion for the book did our social life begin to grow. Friendship began to blossom when he discovered my unconventional side as well.

Again, from the start, I could be found browsing the shelves in the barn, the shop (once a milk house), and the house. More importantly, Don began to open his mind for my perusal. Figuratively sitting at his feet in his cluttered office, surrounded by shelves full of book treasures in fine bindings, I listened enthralled as Don, like a king on his throne behind his intricately carved wooden desk, his large graying head wreathed in blue cigarette smoke, expounded book-lore hour after endless hour to this willing novice. The attention of the new kid on the block never wavered.

While I was soaking up knowledge gleaned from the mind and delivered by the tongue of my mentor, Doris, not as fortunate, sat in Allen's overworked kitchen swapping recipes with Edith Allen while listening to her recitation of the travails of trying to raise six kids on the uneven income of a master book-seller. Not really bad, their income trail was plagued with hills and valleys, flooding when the big checks came in from universities and returning again to dry deserts between catalogues.

Listening to Don at first was like attending a lecture, but over time I combined his tutoring with other study and our sessions became conversations, the student learning enough as time passed to ask questions. Further on down the road to bookmanship, I began learning by doing, a favorite teaching method of my newly found teacher.

Don began to take me with him on buying trips. In time, whenever he went to buy books, I went along. Part of the reason for taking me along was friendship coupled with further instruction. The other part was more practical from Don's standpoint; I became his banker.

Don Allen harbored some strange notions about money, ideas held by him and very few others. Strange though it was, he made his credo work for him. He verbalized the foundation of his monetary notions quite often by saying, "When a book seller has money, he is not buying enough books." In our many conversations about money I tried, without success, to convince Don that there are many kinds of money: Walking around money or cash in the wallet, ready money in the business, business reserves, household money, surplus capital invested in liquid instruments - not books or other stock-in-trade and household reserves to name some. Disagreeing with me vehemently, Don said, "No, no, I either have money or I don't. 'Walking around money' is the only kind of money I have. When my pockets are empty, I'm broke." He often suffered the latter. He only opened a checking account near the end of his life. Then, while liquidating his inventory, he, for once, needed the banks help. His pockets were not roomy enough to hold all of his 'walking around money.'

I must repeat that Don's concept about money worked for him. His family was well taken care of and well fed. This I know from personal experience having put my feet under his and Edith's table on many occasions. One time even for Thanksgiving dinner. Don was not in need of a sterling credit rating 'cause such was not needed in the way he conducted his affairs. Should anyone have occasion to inquire though, they would have come up with a rating of triple A one. Don discharged his financial obligations in full, and on time.

Don's strange concept about money often left him bereft of this necessity and led us into a loose partnership. He furnished the know-how and I came up with the dough to finance our book purchases. When Don owed me dollars, the debt always got paid with books. I was acquiring a lot of good books. Boxes of those books began to accumulate in the Casperson household. This arrangement suited me fine. My lust for books was then, and still is, insatiable. The inventory accumulated though without any concrete idea about their ultimate disposition; I had only a hazy notion about going into the book business - someday.

Immediately after paying Don fifty dollars for forty pounds of government documents, I proclaimed to him that I had become, with that purchase, a dues-paying, card-carrying member of the book selling fraternity. This box full of government publications about railroads, canals, lighthouses, breakwaters, harbors, and other things that the government gets excited about held little interest for me. But my strong feeling that a market existed for this officious hoard prompted me to take it off Don's hands, and by so doing, I launched myself on a most pleasant commercial enterprise. For years thereafter anyone who came near me left with a handful of these precious things. The fifty dollar investment spawned many additional dollars to invest in books. Finally, after taking my original investment tenfold or more, I still had five pounds of paper pamphlets left. These were lotted off to a dealer for fifty dollars. After all, I had to get my original money back, didn't I?

Every summer Don and Edith Allen hosted a Bookman's picnic on their spacious grounds in Three Oaks, Michigan. Their six kids provided cheap labor for the toting and carting. Book dealers and book people flocked to this affair, the place to go to meet birds of a feather from the whole Mid-west. Dealers displaying their books on the tailgates of their station wagons munched juicy sausage sandwiches while hawking their wares. The most successful merchant at these affairs was the host; he could hardly miss with his entire stock on display to a captive audience who had to feel at least a little obligated to him. At one of these affairs, several bushel-baskets full of green and red Lakeside Classics and about five boxes crammed full of early Modern Library books passed from an Evanston, Illinois dealer's hands into mine. (This became the nucleus for my Modern Library collection, one of the finest in the world.)

The annual picnic in Don and Edith's back yard went off without an agenda or formal program. Its charm lay in its almost total lack of structure. We all spent the delightful day getting to know, and renewing acquaintances, with fellow book collectors, book dealers and librarians. Feasting on the glories of Allen's gourmet kitchen pales into near insignificance in the almost spiritual atmosphere generated by a gathering of book people. Don, a one time Army cook, knew how to put together the bill-of-fare: Hamburgers, hot dogs, barbecued ribs, baked beans, roast sausage, salads, cakes, cookies, and more, all prepared under the expert eye of the robust ex-GI cook and his knowledgeable, hard-working wife.

The late Van Allen Bradley, an Antiquarian bookseller of note, Literary Editor of the Chicago Daily News, author of *"The Gold In Your Attic"* books and *"The Book Collector's Handbook Of Values"*, came to Don's picnic regularly. I have the Fourth Edition of Van's book inscribed to Don, as follows:

"For Don Allen, -

Chicago Book Fair pioneer!
Dealer in rare and fine books!
Entrepreneur of Bookman's picnic!
Proprietor of fabulous book barns!
Finder of Michigan rarities!
Husband of fabulous Edith!
Friend of long ago and a gentleman I
sincerely miss -

Van Allen Bradley
Scottsdale (Arizona)
6/28/82

We visited the Bradleys at their home in Barrington, Illinois prior to their move to Scottsdale, Arizona. His impending move prompted our visit. Van needed to lighten up his book inventory and my, wanting to help him, sparked the trip. It took a half a day of picking and bargaining, but I was able to fill a station wagon with his books before we headed back to Niles, Michigan. Our station wagon, jammed with books, barely had room to carry my new nickname, but we managed to make room for it as well. Due to my reckless buying habits and the large quantities of good books I carried away, Van dubbed me, "The wild man from Michigan".

In those days I didn't look at a bookcase full of books saying, "Well, I'll look them over and pick out what I can use." More often than not, looking at the accumulation, I said, "How much for the lot?"

I adopted as my own my mentor's first law of bookselling, "If 'ya ain't got 'um 'ya can't sell 'um." Creating other laws as well, Don followed them in his business. We composed some laws together as our discussions went on concerning pricing theory and other aspects of bookselling. Following the first one, all of these became "Allen's laws." Some of them are as follows: "If a book sells, it is priced too low." or "When a book remains unsold for a year, raise its price. Anyone waiting for a markdown will buy it right now before the price goes even higher." Also, "If a customer wants a particular title, but leaves it on the shelf saying he will buy it later, remove the book from the shelf and hide it." The customer will evidence great disappointment when he returns to find the book gone. According to

188

Allen, the master merchandiser, this will teach the customer - "The proper time to purchase an out-of-print book is when you see it." (Another law.) A sub-law to this one is to raise the price of the book when you take it out of hiding. Again, the customer will glom onto the book before the price continues to escalate.

I haven't adopted all of Don's laws, but there is one that I implement religiously. A used-book dealer should buy books from the "entire spectrum," as Don phrased it. Don't limit yourself, he said, to paying only fifty cents for books at the Goodwill Store, AAUW sales or yard sales. I can still hear Don hammering home my lesson. "If books are priced in big dollars at a dealer's shop, or if you have to mortgage the out-house to buy a desirable private library, go ahead and do it, as long as you can turn a profit." He continued, "dealers who pay little or nothing for their books soon have an inventory that reflects this fact." I continue to follow this law, one of Don's better ones, a part of my bookseller's credo now after practicing it for over twenty-five years.

There are several more "Allen's laws" that bear repeating: Patronize your competition. Buying books from a competing dealer in your area accomplishes two things. The books you get strengthen your stock. Removing them from your competitor's shelves weakens his stock-in-trade accordingly.

When buying household accumulations another law sometimes kicks in. The law provides that the book dealer ask the seller how much he wants for his books. If the asking price is ridiculous and there is no chance of getting together, the dealer says to the seller, "I hope you get it," and then as unobtrusively as possible he walks out. In most cases the seller has no idea what to ask for his books and he says as much. In this case, if he tells you your offer is too low, you remind him that you asked him what he wanted. Then you say, "If my offer is too low I'll ask you again, how much do you want?"

After years of buying house lots and private libraries I find that generally, in practice, this law is not particularly desirable. Getting back to square one in these situations accomplishes nothing except maybe creating an embarrassing situation for the seller. The chances are good that the book dealer will leave the premises with his money in his pocket instead of books in the van.

There seem to be exceptions to everything. If the seller has made a big production about how valuable his books are, it may be next to impossible not to ask him to state his price. When the seller belabors the subject by bragging about how his drinking buddy told him his books would be worth a fortune in Chicago, or his cousin saying he is sitting on a small Fort Knox, the temptation to ask his price becomes overwhelming. I have never figured out what magic comes into play when passing the city limits sign of "Chicago." Hearing that a collection will command many more dollars in the windy city is not unique; I hear it quite often. The truth is that because of the overwhelming supply of books available to Chicago dealers, the price they pay could very well be lower than out here where the population, and thus the supply of books, is relatively more sparse.

I won't belabor Don's, "Ask the customer what he wants" law any further except to say that I almost never use it. My practice has been to make a fair offer which is invariably accepted. In my over twenty-five years of book buying my offers are almost never rejected. My philosophy when buying is buy to buy again; I never leave a premises unless the seller is happy with the deal. If Don were here today, we could incorporate these two ideas into his book of laws.

One day, going with Don to a house to buy books, we found a rather non-descript lot not worth a penny more than seventy-five dollars. Don put on his wary look when the seller said, "My neighbor says these books are worth at least $500." I padded after my bearded friend as he headed for the door by saying, "Sell them to him." Shocked at the time, I have said the same thing a couple of times during my book buying career.

Many times I heard Don's end of a telephone conversation with a prospective seller. The part of the conversation audible to me goes something like this, "Don't second guess me. Don't assume I wouldn't want this or that. Don't throw anything that's made out of paper away." Obviously talking to someone cleaning out the old homestead, his instructions continued, "I want to see all books, pamphlets, magazines, newspapers, letters, pictures, postcards, and anything else that's made of paper."

Don's instructions seemed quite plain to me. In spite of his clear guidance, Don often told me, and I have since experienced the same, that when we arrive at the house to look at what's for sale it's like the seller never heard our injunction. What I continue to hear coming from the mouth of those without ears goes something like this, "Oh yeah, ya know, there was so much stuff we had a hell of fire out in back. Boxes and boxes of Uncle Jim's stuff especially." Becoming a little exasperated, I ask what the eager flames consumed. The torment continue, "Well, Uncle Jim didn't stand in too well with the family, he was sorta' different, an odd duck really. He lost a leg in World War One and because he couldn't play ball and hunt and fish he sat a lot and wrote stuff about his experiences in the trenches in France. All of that junk and gobs of his letters made a pretty bright blaze along with his old Boy Scout books that nobody wants." The horror continues, "Uncle Jim was really a strange one. He collected everything. Lots of this crap about cars, tractors, and bundles of old stuff about his hometown went up in flames and we were glad to see it go 'cause no one in the family really liked ol' one-legged Jim."

The prospective seller continues, "Well, anyway, we did as you said on the 'phone. All of the books are here. Boy here's a set of Shakespeare's stuff that has to be worth a lot of money; Shakespeare ya know. Look, there's ten books here, only two are missing. This Collier's Encyclopedia should bring at least $200. Of course we wouldn't expect you to pay that much. You have to make a profit. We wouldn't ask for more than $180 from you, a fair wholesale, right? And you get to make a few bucks." On and on he goes as I slowly edge toward the door. The seller further extols the virtues of the encyclopedia. "The books smell a little funny and they're covered with some white stuff but that shows they're old ya know. The insides are as good as new."

Like mine, Don's hair was thin to non-existent. He pulled it out dealing with the likes of Uncle Jim's nephew. His beard was healthy from tugging it in response to listening to such stupid revelations. I continue to pull mine too for the same reason.

Doris and I made many trips with Don and Edith Allen to Chicago and Evanston, Illinois, Kalamazoo and Grand Rapids, Michigan to attend sales at book shops and libraries. Tourist parks and roadside rest stops all over Southwestern Michigan and Northern Indiana are familiar spots where we stopped to dig into our picnic baskets. The good food and company make these days stand out in our memory as very special times. Most of the time the weather cooperated and all went well, but one trip coming back from Evanston with an overloaded station wagon in an ice storm will live in our memories. Horrendous.

This jolly foursome traveling to many American Association of University Women (AAUW) sales discovered that these affairs were not for the frail. Not only are they contests of physical strength, but they are prize rings where those with the knowledge of books are the champions. Being the first to get to the books on display is still the name of the game. The ultimate goal was, and still is, to sneak into the book area prior to the official start of the sale. Crawling under tables to get at boxed books, and elbowing the competition is standard misbehavior.

After I opened my own book shop the roles gradually changed between Don and me, from teacher and student to friendly competitors as we continued to attend these affairs together. At a Kalamazoo AAUW sale, Don managed to intentionally entangle me in the rope that surrounded the book area, thus giving himself a couple seconds' head start as I untangled myself. To Don's dying day this episode became our favorite inside joke.

Don's two major "Thou shalt nots" were not given the status of the other Allen laws, but they approached religious status in his mind. He never under-priced a book in his shop and he never left a good book behind on a sale table at a book sale. An under-priced book, he thought, reflected adversely on his professionalism. A good book overlooked in the tumult of a sale would likewise cast a shadow over the master bookman's ability.

When I first opened my own shop many shelves in the work area began to fill up with un-priced books because I couldn't readily arrive at a selling price. Following my teacher's guidance I became overly apprehensive about putting an erroneous price on a book. Certainly I couldn't under-price an item because Don would come along and buy it. Not wanting to see my professionalism fractured by over pricing a book, I didn't price many of them at all so un-priced books accumulated. Swallowing my pride after awhile, I priced them all and have continued to come up with prices that seem sensible even though I have to, on occasion, do some intelligent guessing. Contrary to my mentor's idea, my theory is that I can't possibly know everything. So someone finds a sleeper (under-priced) on my shelves - I feel they are apt to come back again hoping to find another. Being in low regard by my customers, because of my ignorance in these cases, may be hard on my self-esteem, but it is good for business. Maybe I am a business person first and a bookman second. Perhaps Don, on the other hand, was a bookman first. In the bookselling game it takes all kinds and all kinds are accommodated.

One of my prize possessions is a two volume theological work dated 1673, bound in vellum. The books are in mint condition. This three-hundred year old publication looks like it came out of the bindery yesterday. I picked this treasure off a sale table in Evanston paying only fifteen dollars.

Because Don let me tag along on these trips, and because book selling provided his livelihood, not mine, I deferred to him, following behind him as we perused the sales tables. In other words, Don got to see the books first. As mentioned before, Don took great pride in never leaving anything good behind him. I was the gleaner, left with the leavings so to speak.

After the flurry ended and the sale was over, it was our practice to quietly inspect each other's purchases. Knowing his penchant for never leaving a treasure behind, it was difficult for me to tell my teacher I had picked up the two volume set, mentioned above, after he had passed it by. He offered to buy the set for thirty dollars but I opted not to double my money and elected to keep the little volumes. I told him I wanted to keep the set forever so they would continue to remind me that even masters are fallible. The books are a symbol of an early book buying victory too. I still have them. Today they would fetch $350 minimum.

Don's Edith tells the story about their trip to England, "Upon returning to the states, Edith relates, "he had a small quarto volume in his suit jacket pocket. He continued to advise me that that little tome would pay for the trip. It did." This is a typical Don Allenism.

Don Allen's lifestyle in Three Oaks, Michigan gave him time to indulge his life-long thirst for knowledge. After a stint in the army as a cook, Don's early work life consisted of being a watch maker, dealer in rare gem-stones, and selling roofing jobs for the Sherriff-Goslin Company and later playing weigh-master at a weigh-station on Highway 12, near New Buffalo, Michigan. This latter occupation was giving Don ample time to read on the job but the highly structured existence dampened his free spirit so he unceremoniously quit, enabling him to do his own thing on a full time basis. At this time, with six children and a good wife to support, he started his new career by planting a huge garden and, because they appealed to him, he began to buy and sell antiques and paper ephemera. In time the posters, prints, and other such material took a back seat to books. A general book stock with a strong bent toward Americana began to grow, as did Don's knowledge of the used-book trade.

Charles Everett, a New York book-seller, in his memoirs, *The Adventures Of A Treasure Hunter*, writes the best definition of Americana I have ever seen: *"Americana means to me anything showing how and why people came here and how they lived after they got here. In bookseller's catalogues it generally covers printed material alone, but I see no reason for any such limitation."* Everett's biographical work is one of my favorite books. A New York book dealer specializing in Americana, he puts together a work that stimulates me and recharges my batteries when my ampere needle is registering badly on the minus side.

The Allen's seventy-five dollars a month farm house built on the outskirts of Three Oaks, Michigan, belonged to an heir to the Warren Featherbone fortune. Featherbone, originally made from turkey quills, was used in corsets, an indispensable female garment, similar to a coat of mail and worn by all ladies prior to the revolution in styles of the 1920's. The Warrens once owned and operated a huge factory in the village. Many worthy projects, including the Allen family, benefited from their largess. The Featherbone heir wanted their old farm occupied by responsible people, thus the favorable terms for the Allens. The Allens also had the use of a large barn and an outbuilding, once a milk house. Unheated, the milk house was well-built, weather-tight, and clean with a nice smooth cement floor. The old barn, as drafty as the milk house was tight, also served Don's purpose in the book world he put together.

Both structures housed Don's stock-in-trade with the books of lesser value being relegated to the barn. Slowly-sifting chaff from the haymow above continued to give the books below a generous covering of antique hay seeds. A phenomenon peculiar only to Don Allen's place posed no problem if the browser blew on the top edge of each tome before fanning the pages. Persistent perusal of these shelves in the barn could be rewarding. Treasures hid among the spider webs, chaff, and dust. The best books though rested on shelves in the house with the very best in glass doored cabinets surrounding the master's cluttered desk in his office. Like the people in *The Silver Chalice*, the more noble ones sat, "above the salt"; the peasants abided a drafty existence "below the salt". Don's books were stored using the same system, the old barn being "below the salt."

Book catalogues generated the major share of Don's business. These sales aids, authored by Don and typed and mimeographed by Edith, were put together on the cheap, but they are outstanding works of scholarship. Don would describe to perfection the books he offered for sale in these catalogues. His brief descriptions were designed so the prospective buyer could visualize the book, allowing him to order it with confidence. In many cases catalogue entries require a great deal of research. A good cataloguer, and Don was one, is also a research scholar.

I can still hear Don exhorting me, "Ralph, if you ever expect to become a bookman lay that book aside. Read dealers' catalogues." I have read my share of book dealers' catalogues, but the ability that Don enjoyed of visualizing a book while reading its description in a catalogue still escapes me.

Book sales out of the barn and shop building, brisk in the summer months, became pretty slim in the wintertime. Garden work prevented Don from preparing book catalogues in the summer. The balance in his lifestyle worked like a teeter-totter in the Allen's' economic life as well; perfectly. Catalogue sales kept the Allen economic ship afloat when the winter winds sifted snow through the

cracks in the old barn and cooled the little shop so an Eskimo would
have shunned the place. Browsing in the frigid shop one early spring
evening until almost numb, I was rescued by Maria, one of the
Allen's' daughters. Actually ordering me into the house, she plied me
with hot coffee reviving me sufficiently so I could buy the books my
stiff fingers had removed from the shelves.

Accumulating books on a single subject and hiding them away
gave Don great pleasure. This practice became one of Don's favorite
little tricks. Maybe at a sale he acquired several books on a specific
subject such as early western travels, Indian captivities, penology,
Michigan, or perhaps books about black musicians. Hiding these
away and not offering them for sale until, after adding to the
accumulation, he had enough on one subject to fill an entire
catalogue. Some of Don's most successful efforts are those single
subject catalogues. Don developed other tricks of the trade as he
went on.

He told me that the casual browser, when going through a book-
shop, only looks at the shelves at eye level and those just above and
below the level of their eyes. Believing this to be true, and I too now
agree that it is, he taught me to use the phenomenon to advantage.
Don "stirred" his book shop stock each spring before his regular
customers came back to browse. Moving the books on the bottom
shelf to the top shelf and vice-versa and mixing up the other shelves
thereby giving the entire shop a new look. Without adding new
stock, he made the shop appear as though he was adding hundreds
of new volumes. After all, most of his customers had never seen
most of his books. His stacks being eight shelves high, most
browsers were seeing only four shelves at best. All regular
customers, returning mostly from the Chicago area, complimented
Don on all of the new stock he had acquired during the winter. The
truth was that in some of these years not one new book was added
to the shelves in the little white shop.

To hear my Guru tell it, a highly restricted secret place existed
where he spirited away book treasures. This place was in addition
to the barn, the little shop, and the shelves downstairs in the house.
Don kept, he continued to say, the absolute treasures squirreled
away "upstairs." Frequently when someone mentioned the title of

some rarity or other I can still hear Don rather nonchalantly saying, "Yeah, I believe there's a copy upstairs." Specifically, I recall him saying this when I asked him if he had ever seen the three-volume set of the government documents of the Admiral Perry Exposition opening of Japan with color pictures of nude Japanese girls bathing. I can't say he didn't have this special cache "upstairs" because I and no one else outside of Don's immediate family ever got to go above the ground floor of the dwelling. Don made it impossible to ascertain the veracity of his claims. The principal of such a caper is sound. A book stock can be doubled in value in an auditor's mind by saying, "Yeah, I've got a copy of that in the warehouse." (Locked.) The bookman can also say, when his customer mentions some unavailable item, "Oh, yes, I have lots of stuff like that in the house." (Off limits.)

Don's wife had a rule that Don adhered to without fail or complaint. The dictate was that there would be no books on their bed or on the kitchen table. As it is with most book people all space is fair game and so it was at the Allen diggings, except Edith's off-limits areas.

He teased his kids saying that when they left home he would fill their rooms with books. When daughter Janice came home from Chicago one weekend, her Mom said to her, "Why don't you put your overnight case in the downstairs bathroom?"

As she went flying up the stairs, Janice excitedly exclaimed, "He didn't, he didn't" Coming slowly down the stairs after viewing her room she mumbled, "He did."

One of the bibles of the Americana specialist is the *Bibliography of Usiana* by Wright Howes. The first edition of this important reference work is dated 1954. The full title of the book as shown on the title page of the 1962 revised edition is as follows: *"'U.S. Iana' (1660-1950) a selective bibliography in which are described 11,620 uncommon and significant books relating to the continental portion of the United States."* I can still hear my school-master nagging me to read *Howes*. I'm sure he spent a significant amount of his time memorizing this sturdily-bound brown book. He was exhorting me to do likewise. Looking at a book he had never seen before, he would tell me that it is a "Howes item." (Listed in the

Howes Bibliography.) Always impressed when he did this, I could never figure out how he knew. Now, after the passage of many years, I, too, can do the same thing and I have never even read *Howes* from cover to cover. Knowing that something is listed in *Howes* is something a bookman just gets to know. Maybe it's a little like my doctor who says he can merely look at me when I show up for my annual physical and can tell that I'm in good health. He doesn't have to take me completely apart to ascertain my general well-being. A bookman, likewise, doesn't have to look up every American history book he sees to determine if it is listed in *Howes*. The knowledge goes with the turf. The doctor and the book man just instinctively know.

Perusing my shelves when my shop first opened, pointing out my errors in pricing, provided my instructor with another avenue down which he made me travel on the road to bookmanship. Calling me on my mistakes in under-pricing books that held no interest for him was one thing. When he bought my under-priced stuff his teaching methods hurt. It seems my prices were always too timid, never too high.

I can recall his pulling a book off the shelf and exploding about it, with his expletives deleted, as follows: "I've tried to teach you by telling you, but that seems to be ineffective, so now I'm going to make you pay. Maybe you'll learn that way. I'm going to buy this book you've priced at $7.50. Damn it, Ralph, it's a *Howes* item and should be priced at $25." My education with Don as professor had never seemed to carry a direct cost, but now it began to cost in a material way.

In the late summer a large garden began to contribute to the Allen family income. Don's thirst for knowledge was prodigious and his ability to slake this craving was more than equal to the task. Seemingly he could master any field of knowledge - and did repeatedly. Applying himself to gardening, he became an accomplished practical horticulturist. Don could relate more about each vegetable in his garden and the varmints and insects that fed on it than would be found in any one book.

The major cash specialty of Don's huge truck garden was cantaloupe or muskmelons of various types. Each morning, in season, the book-man turned husband-man trotted a wheel-barrow full of the luscious fruit to the curb in front of his house. By nightfall several loads found their way to dining tables all over Southwestern Michigan and in a day or two his satisfied customers came back for more Don's melons were habit-forming.

Along with the folding money from the melons,, which was divided among the children, the garden patch was contributing an endless stream of vegetables for the Allen family dining table. The flourishing corn field was legendary, but Don didn't pick the big fat ears until the magic moment. It became a rule in the Allen household that corn for the table would not be picked until the water in the corn kettle was boiling. Eating corn on the cob this fresh, with salt and butter is to experience the apex of culinary enjoyment. Having enjoyed this delight, I could not for years bear to purchase corn from a super-market knowing that it was several days away from the corn stalk.

Selling garden produce was as uncharacteristic for a used-book dealer as publishing. Our versatile Mr. Allen did a bit of that as well. In 1974 he re-published a book aptly entitled, *Remarks On The Disorders Of Literary Men. Or An Inquiry Into The Means Of Preventing The Evils Usually Incident To Sedentary And Studious Habits.* Don's selection of this work was quite apropo. The little ninety two page book reprinted in an edition of three-hundred copies by the ISRAELITE HOUSE OF DAVID at Benton Harbor, Michigan was well received by Don's friends, all of whom were more or less literary men and women, who suffered from eye-strain and a dearth of bodily exertions. This little tome, rather scarce today, carries a rather handsome price. Don would be proud.

When Don's business was at its peak, he experienced little competition from other used-book dealers either in buying or selling. The quality and diversity of the books Don acquired thrills me to this day. Acquiring good libraries and accumulations, difficult today, was commonplace for Don Allen. I don't recall where he got them but one time he acquired about seven-thousand books on the Catholic religion. A master of applied psychology and personal manipulation, Don knew the proper approach when he wanted to unload a literary property such as the Catholic lot on me. I bit every time until I learned to ignore him when he just barely mentioned, in passing, that he had sort of decided he might just possibly part with this or that. Anyway he thought he might think about selling this unusual (useless) collection of Catholic books. I wrote him a check for one-thousand dollars before he changed his mind and the huge lot became mine. This all turned out very well. Forced to come up with ways to peddle this stuff, I developed some interesting merchandising methods. All a part of my education, this is known as learning by doing. My mentor was a firm believer in making me "do."

If he could turn a buck while I was "doing" - well, that was his way of getting compensated for teaching me in the first place.

Unable to get rid of the entire mountain of Catholic religious lore, mentioned above I did sell enough to get my money back and turn a tidy profit; all before I had my own book shop. I felt good seeing my instructor visibly moved and pleased with his student's progress.

I had no place to store what remained of these dry tomes. Don had pawned them off on me because he needed the space they occupied in his barn; what to do? The haymow was empty except for the little space taken up by a small amount of old dry hay whose seeds continued to drop on the books below. In one of our many very informal unrecorded transactions, Don "leased" the haymow to me. No money changed hands, but I did pay his kids five bucks to move the several tons of Catholic books upstairs. Everyone concerned in this transaction was happy. The books got moved out of Don's way, the kids earned their five dollars, and I was from time to time able to sell a few of this vast trove, but I didn't diminish it much. This new storage space had one additional advantage. Stored now, on the same level as the chaff, the books didn't get their light dusting with the stuff.

All was well for now, but eventually, though I didn't lose sleep over it, I knew that the time was coming when Don would want the space I was using. In time a new home would have to be found for those damned Catholic books (to use my wife's terminology). Don's big fire solved the problem.

On October 15, 1975, a quiet fall evening, we were at home in

Niles, Michigan, minding our own business, when the telephone, ringing impolitely, broke into our privacy. It was Don Allen announcing, in what I thought was a rather calm tone of voice, "Ralph, I thought you should know that the barn is burning." After ascertaining that my teacher was not joking, Doris and I took off for Three Oaks disregarding speed limits set by a legislator who never considered what a barn of burning books would do to a bookman's deportment. Crouching behind the steering wheel of an automobile, flying down the road, the bright glow in the western sky as we approached Three Oaks caused my right foot to rest even more heavily on an already overly-depressed accelerator. Religion has never been hotter. I saw what had to be flaming Catholic books flying through the air like rockets on little space ships ascending to heaven. Many of my Catholic books were written in Latin. Was I seeing Roman candles? The super heat being generated below by extra-dry paper, straw, and burning books was generating a rocket-like heat and force that sent my literary property skyward.

I stood by Don in the crowded barnyard watching it all burn up. The local firemen merely joined in the watching; nothing could be done. As the fire ebbed and the hot literary inventory finally reduced itself to glowing embers, Don and I repaired to the front porch of the big white house where some thoughtful soul kept bringing us tall glasses of iced tea. Sitting and sipping, one part of me felt relief. My storage problem had solved itself but what do I say to my best friend who, in the past three hours, lost half of his assets? Directing my half-serious remarks to Don I said, "You can have the Catholic books, my insurance won't cover the loss."

Don chuckled and said, "Nah, you keep them I don't have penny one of insurance either."

Before we left the front porch that night, in his mind, Don had put together an outline of his next business venture. He would, he was telling me, begin to phase out his book business. The fire consuming over half his inventory and his major storage space had made it necessary to shift gears drastically. He needed a business requiring less space for storing inventory. He would, he said, begin accumulating sheet music and in time he would be a specialist in music's paper ephemera. Acquiring the knowledge he needed to become a specialist in music was "can do" for Don. His mind could sponge up anything. This part posed no problem; he only needed time. And time proved that Don's idea born amid the ashes that night was sound. Seeing Don and Edith Allen creating a thriving mail order business out of nothing is still a thrilling prospect to contemplate. Working together they did it. For a short time they were even operating a little, very attractive, music shop in New Buffalo. Full of sheet music, it catered to the summer crowd from Chicago.

Requiring lots of study and establishing a modus operandi for the music venture kept the Allens even closer to their own fireside, secluded from so-called polite society. What constituted desirable material, where would he find it and how would it be merchandised, had to be worked out. A start was made toward accomplishing these aims and solving the problems of the new enterprise before the red embers of the barn fire had turned ashen gray.

On the porch that fateful night Don was not thinking about obtaining a government grant or a small business loan. Asking for help from no one, and using his own cerebral powers, he began to think. Starting at once with an idea, Don began developing his notion and over time it grew into a thriving business. By the time untimely death was knocking at Don's door, he was still acquiring an enviable inventory of sheet music and a music reference library in private hands.second to none.

His music venture was growing and it became successful enough to replace the book business completely. Then Don's health began to unravel. He was diabetic and the condition of his heart left a lot to be desired. His ailments got progressively worse as the years rolled by. His main source of treatment, the Veterans' Hospital in Chicago, was hard to get to in the winter-time. Trips to that facility put unwanted demands on the family's resources and his failing strength.

On his first visit to the Veterans' Hospital in Chicago, Don, while waiting in the lobby, suffered a massive heart attack. Certainly it's not good fortune to have a heart attack, but it is typical Allen luck to have one where he was having his. What better place for a major medical catastrophe than right in a major medical facility?

Don was near death in the hospital's emergency room. He was having an out-of-body experience while the doctors were desperately trying to save him. Afterward he told me he hovered above his own body watching the doctors working on him. Aware the guy the doctors were trying to revive was on his way out, Don was experiencing an interesting spectacle viewing his own demise. He said he was an unconcerned bystander, a completely objective observer not involved in the struggle going on below.

Don didn't die during this heart attack episode, but the medics didn't give him much hope for a long and happy existence this side of the ether realm. The doctors kept telling him to get his affairs in order. He could, they said, look forward to very little additional time to frequent his familiar haunts. Counting on a year or two at best, Don tackled the task at hand.

My friend didn't lie down and wait for the grim reaper. He continued his work. Simultaneously with building his music business, unloading his book inventory continued.

The grass didn't grow under Don's feet. Making preparations against the day when the VA doctors' prognostications would come to pass was the order of his and Edith's days. They bent their not inconsiderable efforts against the day they were told was quite imminent. Selling his extensive collection of House of David material and a Christmas book and ephemera collection he had put together through the years, Don had enough cash to buy his own house. He intended to pass on knowing Edith would be well housed. Most of the kids by this time were on their own.

I was buying thousands of dollars worth of Don's books, running up an "accounts payable" that might have been down-right scary except that the terms we agreed upon for payment were more than liberal. By this time my book shop was a going concern. I agreed to discharge my debt not to Don but to his wife, Edith, over time, when he died. In effect Don was buying an annuity for Edith with "Ralph A. Casperson Books" the guarantor.

Everyone, including Don, thought his departure was close at hand. Don, though, as is probably typical of him, confounded the experts by refusing to die. His heart continued to fail, along with his strength, but by curtailing his activities he was enjoying a near normal lifestyle. The garden was abandoned when they moved into their new house and Don and Edith managed a short walk uptown each day to the coffee shop where they mingled with the villagers, a new adventure for them.

By the time the Allens had moved to their new place, all of the kids but one had flown the coop and were on their own. Don and Edith, almost as free of live-in family as on their wedding day, were able to pare their expenses against the day when Edith would have to go it alone. The new location boasted a large room for Don's office where he kept his music reference library. Here he still enjoyed holding court and it is where he prepared his music lists and catalogues. Buying a small portable out-building solved the storage problem for the sheet music inventory; he no longer needed a big red barn. Don continued to make complete preparations for his departure, but he lived on and on and on.

I won't forget the hour Don and I spent together in his little book shop shortly before his book inventory was liquidated and he moved from the farmhouse. He told me then he was not long for this world. He didn't appear morbid describing how he wanted to be laid out in the casket, even to the brand of cigarettes he wanted in his shirt pocket (Pall Mall). The pocket containing the cigarettes had to share its space with his ever present mechanical pencil. His badly-beat-up, soiled, leprechaun type hat which he always wore would rest at a jaunty angle on the foot of the casket. You wouldn't catch Don dead wearing a baseball cap with a bill. He hated them as much as I do. Different even to the end, he wanted no funeral service. His appointments couldn't be implemented, however - Don refused to die.

His book inventory was liquidated. The House of David stuff and the Christmas collection had been sold. The Allens, together and comfortably settled in their smaller house, enjoyed pretty much a post-Don Allen lifestyle. The music business grew and prospered, a business Edith could run at least for a time without Don. He taught her how to do it. Several book dealers owed the Allens enough money to provide Edith with a small annuity. Don visited me in my shop and I went to see him, but it wasn't like our early days together. He was used to his role as teacher and though I could always learn from him, the teacher-pupil relationship no longer existed between us. We were finding that changed circumstances beget changed feelings. My coming up with desirable collections of sheet music and passing them on to Don reduced Edith's "annuity." Don hung on. Living on for thirteen years after the doctors kept saying he would only last about two, he surprised everyone. Living long enough for me to pay off my debt to him, we successfully dissipated his wife's annuity. I went with Don to the Veterans' Hospital on several occasions where the doctors continued to predict his early demise. He continued to foil the experts and he seemed to enjoy proving the medics wrong.

Finally, after thirteen years of declining health, medical emergencies and fatal predictions, Edith called us on August 28, 1991 to tell us Don was in a local hospital. Gangrene had set in. His life expectancy now was measured in days. False alarms had rung for the last time. This was for real. Don had used up all his chances, this was it.

I couldn't bring myself to go and see my schoolmaster. Right or wrong, I wanted to remember our times together as they once were, in his old office surrounded by rare tomes where I sat at his feet and soaked up book lore. I wanted to visualize again our trips when we worked together and competed against one another. We had great times philosophizing in the garden and in the barn. I wanted to preserve these times in my memory. When I thought of Don, I wanted to see him presiding over his picnic like a country squire entertaining the neighboring gentry. Let my memory preserve my image of my friend at his apex in the Prudential Building in Chicago where he ran the ABAA Book Fair. I did not want to forget our conversations about good food, its preparation, and where to find it. Lastly I wanted to retain the indelible recollection of our talks together in my book shop and his music room. Afraid that the sterile white of the hospital environment would somehow subvert the treasures stored in my memory bank; precious keepsakes not to be put at risk by visiting my friend at the end.

Always blessed with an adequate hoard of assets in the form of paper material and books, Don was equally cursed on the other hand by a perennial dearth of cash in hand. An over-abundance of ready cash was never a problem for my friend. During the time his illness incapacitated him, he became eligible for, and received, a disability pension. Receiving this check on the third of the month smoothed his way somewhat until the next check. In order to qualify for that month's check, the client must be alive on the last day of the month. Don entered the hospital the latter part of August. He knew as he lay on his death bed that Edith badly needed the September check. If he didn't survive until the end of August, that check had to be returned. In a coma part of the time, Don did have periods of consciousness. Toward the end of the month, regaining consciousness, he inquired about the date. This was happening repeatedly and when he knew he had made it past the end of August, he died.

On September 1, 1991 he passed on at 7:25 in the morning. Don beat the deadline by seven hours. The disability check was safe. Don Allen, my mentor, kindly teacher, and good friend, had discharged his last duty.

On October 6, 1991, a cold, wet, morning filled with a dark Michigan drizzle the Allen family gathered, fulfilling Don's last wish, to spread his ashes over his favorite mushroom hunting grounds. This was a beautiful spot overlooking the Galien River. As the cars, a caravan of care, neared the woods the family was not the least bit surprised to see a beautiful bright rainbow suddenly appear extending from the west to the east side of the forest area. Not one drop of rain fell on the trees. The ground was dry.

As Edith carefully spread the ashes son Brad read a letter of love to the assembled family. A letter that his Dad had written and given him to be read on this occasion. As the last car left the woods, the rainbow faded away and the rain began again.

"Eccentricity has always abounded when and where strength of character has abounded; and the amount of eccentricity in a society has been proportional to the amount of genius, mental vigor, and moral courage is contained." John Stuart Mill.

THE OBITUARY

During D.C. Allen's last years the grim reaper was constantly peering over his shoulder. With this harvest seemingly quite eminent it is natural that he would be discussing the prospect with his friends. I have written about his talking to me concerning how he would be decked out in his casket.

Jim Rose and Don, during this period were lamenting the drabness and sameness of the obituaries appearing in the *Antiquarian Bookman* magazine. Literary works this dull did not appeal to Allen. He, therefore, asked his friend Jim to try his hand at dashing off a farewell message with some originality and spice. Jim obliged.

The following spoof piece, though addressed to the proprietor of the A.B. was never sent.

James L. Rose and his wife, Eimi, own and operate a very fine book shop in downtown Niles, Michigan.

O.W. FINE, BOOKSELLER
P.O. Box 666
LOFTY HEIGHTS, MI 49120

Dear Jake:

I write to add my own small splash to the flood of letters pouring in from around the world to pay tribute to the memory of the late D.C. Allen.

In a world where contempt for one's inferiors all to often accompanies success, D.C. never forgot his own beginnings. No neophyte was ever too small or too new to trade for his attention. His question never was, "Who?," but "How much?"

He always had time to spare for the affluent buyer, and the less knowledgeable the buyer, the more willing D.C. was to teach him. Many a trouser he saved from imminent destruction by removing in the nick of time coin that might otherwise burnt holes in pockets. Tailors loathed him.

His aphorisms relating to the trade have stuck with me all these years.:

"If you don't sell a book, it may be priced too low."

"If you do sell a book, it was certainly priced too low."
"If you ain't got it you can't sell it."
"Stir your stock."
"How much for the lot?"

D.C. had--more than most--an eye for the unusual. So adept was he that he could find something unusual about even the most common piece of print. It was he who perfected the art of establishing impeccable and remunerative provenance for old wine-stains, graffiti, scuff-marks, ink-blots and dog-ears, turning otherwise tired copies of unexceptional works into highly desirable collector's items. Aficionados will recall the catalogue in which he offered a copy of Agricultural Bulletin #371 (*"Canning Peaches"*) stained throughout by juice from the first peaches harvested in Indian Territory by Samson Winfield, the inventor of the adjustable toothpick, who married the only woman spurned by Brigham Young.

Another of his strengths was a singular knack he had for picking a previously neglected subject area, buying assiduously albeit quietly in that field until he had assembled a substantial collection, and then offering it as a major component of a catalogue, if not the entire catalogue. His inventiveness in this respect sometimes astounded even him. Perhaps his supreme achievement in this line--and a monument by which we might all choose to remember him--was his 532-page Catalogue #237:*An Unparalleled Collection of Books, Pamphlets, Broadsides, Music, Photographs and other Ephemera, None of It Related to the First Introduction of the Velocipede into the Continental United States West of the Mississippi.*

If--amid such strengths--he had any discernible weaknesses, they were but the unavoidable defects of this virtues. He loved--perhaps too much--ribaldry, carbohydrates, and accounts receivable. It was this combination of predilections that led to his untimely demise.

His receipt one day, without warning, of a check in full payment of a debt 27 years past due would have been amply shocking to a system as delicately balanced as his. But the check was made of marzipan, chocolate, caramel, toffee, and god alone knows what else, and it was decorated in all of the margins with whimsically executed scenes illustrating some of the more vivacious passages of

Boccaccio's *Decameron*. He couldn't decide to cash it, eat it, or frame it and sell it. He died instantly from a surfeit of ambivalence.

We shall, of course, go on. But the world of antiquarian books will never be the same again.
Sincerely,

O.W. Fine

BOOKHUNTERS IN THE BOOKSHOP

*The following essay was written by James L. Rose when he was a book scout. It appeared in our **BIBLIO** publication number 6, February 1982.*

Behold the bookhunter primed for his quest: his wallet in his pocket, a gleam in his eye, and adrenalin flowing like tapwater. It is a territory to explore, with gold to be found. Should we wonder that his pulse quickens as he steps through the door?

Where others see trash, he sees treasure--not only because tastes differ, but because he uses his imagination to see the treasure in the trash

The bookhunter makes connections. He sees a book and asks what it represents or how it might be useful. A grubby phamplet published in Kalamazoo on the curative powers of celery might be simply a bizarre oddity to some, but the bookhunter connects it with the history of health fads and the industrial development of Kalamazoo, and it suddenly becomes a significant piece of a larger design.

And the bookhunter (a curious chap) finds treasures others miss because he does not look only in obvious places for the obvious titles on the eye-level shelves.

Most booksellers organize their shops in categories. But the bookhunter knows that books do not always fit neatly into our preconceived compartments. Does *Lincoln's Doctor's Dog* go under dogs, medicine, or presidents? Looking at the contents of a religious biography the bookhunter may find a chapter on the Battle of Bull

Run and another on pioneer life in Indiana. Besides, booksellers make mistakes, which is why our bookhunter may also find in the religion section a fine first edition of *God's Little Acre*, or, in the music section, a history of New Harmony. If they're there he'll find them--because he <u>looks</u>.

The bookhunter knows that titles do not always tell clearly what the book is about. Authors and editors sometimes seem bent on making the title as vague or dull as possible. *What I Have Learned* sounds singularly unpromising. But the curious bookhunter opens the book to discover that it is the memoir of Civil War experiences and adventures in the early West. *A Fire Was Lighted* could be almost anything. Looking within, our bookhhunter finds a biography of Hawthorn's daughter Rose who became a nun. He sees a volume entitled *Century Magazine Vol. 26*. He looks inside and discovers an eyewitness account of John Brown's raid at Harper's Ferry, a study of Thomas Bewick's students, four articles by Henry James, Edward Eggleston's narrative of Indian War in the colonies, and a report on hunting the musk-ox.

If some titles are dull, others are illegible, and some do not even appear on the backstrip. Only the curious bookhunter will reach for the untitled spine and find a copy of *Remarks on the Disorders of Literary Men.* (limited to 300 copies). Only he will pull out the slim phamplet and find Schmidt's *Turtles of the Chicago Area* or the *Emigrant's Guide to Michigan* (1849) or Benezet's *Notes on the Slave Trade* (1783).

He knows that because eye-level shelves are easiest to see, they are the most looked-at and the most plundered in the shop. For relatively untapped goods, the curious bookhunter literally looks high and low.

And his curious eye does not stop at title and subject. He knows that everything about a book may hold interest: the binding, the paper, the watermark, the printer, the author, the style, the date or place or method of printing, the print itself, the designer, the illustrator or the illustrations, the limitation notice in front and back, and the treatment of the edges.

He even scrutinizes things others dismiss as defects: The annotations scribbled in the margins by General Custer, Rudolph

Valentine's bookplate, Clarence Darrow's signature on the fly, the old bookseller's stamp, the Civil War letter used for a bookmark, the pasted in library rules from 1840, or the stamped notice on the back cover that this book was "Stolen from the Palmer House."

Besides imagination and curiosity, our bookhunter has courage: the courage of his own convictions and the courage to persevere.

He looks long, carefully, and often. The more shops he visits, the more books he looks at. And the more books he looks at, the better he knows what is common and what is scarce, what is well-done and what is mediocre. He gains perspective and a keener sense of market value. Best of all, the more he looks the more he finds.

He not only visits many shops; when he finds a lively one he visits it often. He knows that a lively bookshop changes continually: this month's stock is not the same as last month's or the next's. And a bookhunter (sly fellow) also knows that when a bookseller learns the buying interests of a regular reliable customer, he may--without being asked--hold back choice items from his shelves until the customer has had a chance at first refusal.

The courageous bookhunter also puts his money behind his own convictions--even when they do not coincide with fashion or established reputation. Illustrations by Rackham are _in_, those by AB Frost are not. If a bookhunter likes Rackham better than Frost and can afford it, he will buy Rackham. But he believes that buying Rackham simply because one _thinks he should_ is raging bibliomasochism. Elbert Hubbard's books are widely scorned by knowledgeable folk, but it's not their money the bookhunter is spending. So he looks for himself, and if he likes what he sees, he cares little what someone else thinks of his selection.

Besides, books out of fashion or in poor repute tend to be cheap. The bookhunter knows that the price of a book does not necessarily reflect its worth, only its market value--which is a product of supply and _demand_. When he moves to an area of low demand he's in a buyer's market.

And if the bookhunter can't afford what he likes, he surveys his interests and the bookshop shelves to see what else he likes that he can afford. After all, everything printed is a human artifact, and as such may contain some sort of interest.

So our bookhunter does not ignore those books for which there is presently meager demand: cartoonists, books on political parties, American humorists, religious controversies, the Spanish-American or Crimean or Sino-Russian wars, essayists, milestones in the history of education, anthologies containing first book appearances of important works, books on slime-mold or surveying, detective fiction, the temperance movement, the labor movement, the history of American theater, the effect of technology on building styles or on foundation garments, anarchists, the crusades, the whiskey rebellion, the Ursulines, modern children's books, American composers, single-book authors, temporarily out-of-fashion novelists like Galsworthy and Grayson or poets like Robinson and Bynner, or books bound in anything except cloth, paper and leather, or foreign language books published in America, or any early text-books except McGuffey's, or . . . He knows that the list of subjects is endless, and that among them is one to fit his interests and his budget.

And perhaps the hunt is not entirely self-serving. After all, he asks, what is to become of neglected books if no one preserves them? Surely no one should dutifully collect what he doesn't like. But if he doesn't collect something he might like, simply because he thought it beneath him or never thought of it at all, it may not only be his loss but the world's. The bookhunter knows that books may be destroyed more surely by neglect than by design.

So here's to the bookhunter who brings through the bookshop door a modicum of cash, to be sure, but backed with the more durable capital of imagination, curiosity, and courage. He is his own benefactor first, the proprietor's next, and ultimately, with luck, everybody's.

THE BOOK BUYER'S FUNCTION

When he buys books from an original source, the bookseller, turned book buyer, serves two purposes. An original source is an individual, a library sale, auction, or estate sale, as opposed to a purchase from another dealer or a book scout. The buyer exchanges money, which the seller can use, for items that are of no use to the seller Secondly, the buyer also, in the course of the transaction, imparts useful information that the seller needs in order for-him to intelligently dispose of items he holds.

The seller has fallen heir to an accumulation of books and, because the estate needs to be settled, the books must be disposed of. They can be exchanged for money, carted to the landfill, donated to Goodwill Industries, or maybe some of all of these. The primary aim is to get rid of Uncle Henry's books and paper material so his house can be sold. Maybe this stuff is worthless and maybe it's priceless. The heirs just don't know.

In the cases where the money realized for the accumulation is secondary to its disposal, the book buyer is lucky. When the heirs lose sight of their problem (emptying out the house) the book buyer has a problem, but that is the subject for another essay.

So the heirs can't give away or throw away their uncle's stuff because they don't know its value. Also for some reason they can't bring themselves to throw books away. Even if the books are worthless, they can't summon up courage enough to dump them. Here is where the book buying bookseller's two fold purpose in buying books comes into play.

This can best be illustrated by relating a recent happening at our book shop. Betty Brendan arrived at the shop with a trunk load of books that were her grandmother's. Betty rescued these books before her grandmother's house was put up for sale. Betty Brendan is as ignorant about books as I am about computers. Her grandmother was a reader who belonged to several book clubs. She knew nothing about book values either; she just liked to read books. Grandma's accumulation consisted of books she had read in years gone by. Grandma's book reading genes died with her. Betty, her grand-daughter, read her last complete book, because it was compulsory, in high school. She has not laid a finger on another book for forty years.

Even the one thing that Betty Brendan knew about books was wrong. She knew that a book should never be thrown away; she was really stuck with this notion. Betty was a little terrified by the responsibility she had incurred by having gained possession of her grandmother's tomes. "Maybe," she thought, "I have a small treasure in the trunk of the car. What if I have a First Edition worth millions?"

So Betty had two problems. What is her inheritance worth? Secondly, how does she turn it into money? Here, in solving these two problems, is where the bookman goes to work.

After taking each book out of its moldy box and looking them over carefully, I see that all except one are Book Club editions from the 1950's. That's bad news enough from a monetary standpoint, but to compound the agony, all but one reeked of mildew. Only one book has any value. It's a mint copy, in a dust jacket protected in a plastic bag, of Chief Pokagon's *"Queen of the Woods."* The book is a reprint edition by Hardscrabble Press, and it is inscribed to Betty's grandmother from her brother, *"Happy Birthday, Emma, from your brother Ephram."* Ephram knew that Emma read, books but apparently her interest didn't include books about Indians. The book had never been opened past the inscription on the first free end paper.

I told Betty I would give her fifteen dollars for the Pokagon book but that the others were prime candidates for the landfill; she should not burden the local thrift shop with this stuff; it had to be junked.

My offer for, *"Queen of the Woods,"* was accepted but Betty was crestfallen. She said, "And to think I have driven fifty miles for practically nothing."

I explained to her that the trip was not made in vain. "Prior to our meeting," I told her, "you knew nothing about these books." I explained that she could do nothing with them until she had exposed them to the eyes of a professional. She <u>had</u> to make the trip. "Now you know that you don't have to be concerned with these books any longer. You have also learned, I hope, that throwing them into a hole in the ground is not a breach of the Ten Commandents." "Mrs. Brendan," I continued, "you had to make this trip to solve your problem."

Two things were accomplished in my dealing with this woman. She got an appraisal that cost her nothing and she got a fair wholesale price for the only book in the lot that had any value. Anytime a knowledgeable book person buys books from an individual he accomplishes these two things. On occasion there may be no books in the trunk that have any value. In that case the seller may be disappointed, but his time has not been wasted.

ON THROWING BOOKS AWAY

Most folks find it next to impossible to screw up the courage they think they need to enable them to toss unwanted books in the dumpster. For some reason lodged in the dark recesses of an otherwise logical mind, his relatives can't bear to cart Grandpa's worthless books to the landfill. They will gleefully burn priceless one-of-a-kind letters, maps, pamphlets and other paper ephemera, but they are unable to trash common book club books from the 1950's. Disposing of this junk is impossible for them even if it is mildewed and saturated with coal soot and has been declared worthless by a reputable dealer. A hole in the ground is the appropriate final resting place but some can't summon the strength to put them there.

"Look," they sometimes say, "you take them for nothing. You can find someone who can use them."

To this request my response is, "No, no one wants this stuff and I won't throw them away for you because my garbage people are threatening to put me on a commercial dump rate now. Because you refuse to face reality, I refuse to compound my already serious refuse problem. These books are your problem. I've told you how to solve it. Now, go ahead, grit your molars together, screw up your courage, and do it." This sermon seldom nets me any new friends and old ones leave the shop, I'm sure, rethinking the reasons for retaining any kind of a positive relationship with that stupid bookseller who always wears a jumpsuit.

RECYCLING

Newspapers, bottles, aluminum cans, plastic, and glass jars are salvaged nowadays and are recycled when their original purpose has been fulfilled. The material in these items may have many lives. When used up as newsprint for the South Bend (Indiana) Tribune, the pulp may be reincarnated as the Niles (Michigan) Daily Star. An empty Pepsi can today may become a container for Schlitz beer tomorrow.

Though not billed as such (their advertising doesn't proclaim the fact), antique dealers are also recyclers. Reclaiming one individual's trash,cleaning it up and restoring it, it becomes someone else's treasure. Much, by these people, is rescued from the landfill to find proud places in Twentieth Century homes.

The Antiquarian, or used-book dealer, is a recycler too. He buys books that have outlived their usefulness from one, puts them on his shelves, and waits for another person who can't live without them to claim them as their own. A true recycling operation. We of the used-book fraternity should be subsidized by the Environmental Protection Agency for keeping this stuff out of the landfills. After all, our various governmental agencies dish out handfuls of cash for less worthy causes.

A GENUINE BOOK-AHOLIC

My office in the book shop is often used as a confessional. One difference is that I wear a jumpsuit, not a dark robe. Some people, it seems, confide in their book dealer like they would bend the ear of their pastor or doctor. I have no way of knowing if this practice is universal, but I do know that it happens frequently in our shop

An elderly lady with terminal cancer, we'll call her Mabel, tells me that her books are the only thing that keeps her alive; her only link this side of the dark abyss. She really would prefer to die, she tells me, but she can't bear the thought of leaving her accumulated treasures.

When Mabel first came to the shop she had a sickly husband who was hanging on to life by a thin thread. While Mabel lived only for books, her Fred lived only to watch Michigan State play football. They never went anyplace together, so I never met Fred. Even if they had been in the habit of going out together, I wouldn't have met him because she only came to the shop on Saturday afternoon when Fred's heroes were bashing other school boys on the gridiron.

At my confessional one day Mabel revealed that the only thing she cared for about Fred was his Social Security check. She was frantic from worry about how she would be able to buy books when her husband passed on. This event was eminent, to hear her tell it.

Mabel continued to buy Gene Stratton-Porter and Grace Livingston Hill books. One copy of a title was not enough to satisfy her, however. She had all of Porter's nature books, and books of fiction, including many magazine appearances. The strange thing about all of this was that she bought multiple copies of all of the titles. It's not unusual, of course, for a collector to try to accumulate all of the various editions of a title along with binding and dust jacket variations, etc., but Mabel paid no attention to these things. Her continuing to stack up duplicates of the same title in the same edition kept me busy. My confessional wasn't strong enough to ascertain Mabel's motive for this madness either.

Well, as it must to all men, death came and took Fred away one winter day; luckily for him the football season had just ended so there was little reason for him to stick around anyway. Reading his obituary in the newspaper prompted me to think my commercial relationship with Mabel was at an end; no government check meant no further commerce. But such was not the case. She continued her trips to the shop but I noticed they weren't confined to Saturday afternoons anymore. The death of Fred's Social Security check had no effect what-so-ever; her stockpiling of Porter and Hill continued. I have no way of knowing where the money came from.

Over the years I have found that bibliomaniacs and book-aholics will find a way to support their habit and they can be devious about it too. (Just ask my wife why we got into the book business.) Even my confessional fails to reveal their secrets sometimes.

FIRST EDITIONS

There is a little-realized aspect about First Editions that should be mentioned. Conventional thinking about First Editions is that they are the be all and end all of book collecting. It is commonly held that the First Edition of a book is always the most desirable edition, and always the scarcest and most expensive. This is not always so. A Second Edition may be more desirable because of corrections made

and additional information added. A Second Edition may be scarcer
than the First too. Perhaps the market needed only a few more
copies thus making the Second Edition the scarce edition.

A CACHE OF PAMHLETS

In 1974, a year after our book-shop opened, my friend Don
Allen located a vast hoard of historical pamphlets in pristine
condition. These treasures, held by a midwest historical society,
were one-hundred years old. The society was offering them for sale
at the unbelievable low publication price; mere pennies in today's
values. These pamphlets were stored for one-hundred years in a dark
dry room. Sunlight had not faded and mildew had not ruined them.
The entire lot was absolutely as issued - mint. Unheard of!

The practically give-away price allowed me to buy heavily. No
one-of-a-kind here, but stacks of the same title found their way to
my shop. Whenever possible, I bought the entire supply of a title.
This allowed me to control the selling price. I had a corner on the
market on these titles.

The lot was beautiful, the only blemish being the drool marks I
couldn't help but spill as I sorted them into piles: One of each title
was offered for sale in the shop. A book scout friend took several
copies of each title for sale to various book dealers around the State
of Michigan. The third stack, the biggest, was tucked away in our
warehouse for further aging. (We still have some.)

The book scout was young, hungry, vigorous, and broke. He
sold the pamphlets to dealers all over the state. This enterprise
rewarded him so well that uncharacticsticly he began to eat regularly.
This activity kept up at a merry pace until the scout ran out of
pamphlets. His market being saturated too, he was out of business.
Then the "roof fell in."

I received a letter from an attorney who was also a part-time
book dealer. The letterhead on this letter was enough to scare one
out of half of his remaining life. The legal eagle writing this letter
had seen some of our gorgeous pamphlets. He accused me of having
the pamphlets reprinted. Misrepresenting reprints as originals, he
went on to say, is an illegal act. The book-dealer, lawyer, just

couldn't believe that anything that had been around for one-hundred years could be in such elegant condition. The counselor was justified in his supposition, but he had figuratively broken his leg jumping to conclusions

Telephoning the attorney with the broken leg, I proved that the pamphlets were far from spurious. Having bested the fellow I managed to stay out of jail and in the process I wound up with a greatly inflated ego. Deciding to "have my day in court" with my lawyer friend, I told him I had a suggestion that he might ponder. "Please consider," I said, "not writing to mere, innocent, gentle, antiquarian book men on your law firm's stationery." "Because," I continued, "it is inhibiting and may cause them to mess their underwear."

PRICE GUIDE AND BIBLIOGRAPHY

Tools of the book trade including bibliographies, price guides, and auction records are expensive. Their cost will be returned in a hurry, however, when their use prevents mistakes in pricing. These tools, over their lifetime, will return their cost many times over. Their proper use will prevent under-pricing and will also keep the dealer from looking foolish by over-pricing; at least price gouging in ignorance is prevented. A dealer who gouges on purpose will soon be found out and will suffer the consequences of his folly. The book buying public and those in the trade itself are quick to learn; their retribution is swift and devastating. In pricing it is best to 'err on the low side if 'err you must.

Recently I acquired a copy of a new Civil War book price guide. Just before getting this guide I had acquired a nice lot of about sixty books about the Civil War. I had priced the books, but knowing that the new price guide was in the mail, the books were not shelved.

In checking against the guide I found that over half of the books were priced correctly. Twenty-six books were priced too low. No errors were made on the high side. The total price of the books priced too low was $608 The corrected total price, using my $35.

guide was $1060. Because I bought the guide my inventory value increases by $452. It hurts to shell out big bucks for guides - but does it pay?

ABOUT TWO MORMON MISSIONARIES

One peaceful winter afternoon when the book shop was closed, I was in the shop doing those things a bookman must continue to do in order to keep his shop appealing to the public. Rearranging sections, wielding the dust rag, pricing new arrivals, etc., I was enjoying my work and my solitude in the quiet shop. When these appointed tasks pale, I plunk myself on the comfortable davenport with the latest book I am devouring; perfect contentment is mine during these all too infrequent times. Sometimes these super times are interrupted.

Such an interruption took place during the afternoon mentioned above. I recognize Mormon Missionaries from a mile away. Always two traveling together, they are clean-cut, smooth-shaven, with short fresh haircuts. They wear dark suits, white shirts, and neckties. The image they present is one that any parent would be proud of in their sons.

On the afternoon in question, a pair of these boys came rather shyly through the book-shop door. Of course I bade them welcome, whereupon one asked if I had any copies of *"The Book Of Mormon."* I pointed out the religion section to them and retired to the office, taking my usual perch behind a cluttered desk and resumed my work. One of the missionaries followed me into the office.

I must write here that I have nothing against the Mormon Church or its messengers. Having read a great deal about this faith and its people, I know about and respect many of the things they do. These boys dedicate a year or more of their lives to the Mormon Church. Someone who has convictions strong enough for this has my admiration. I was more than cordial and accommodating to these two boys.

One of my guests began searching for the *"Book Of Mormon"* and his partner made himself comfortable on the davenport facing my desk. Before I could resume my work he engaged me in conversation by telling me about the *"Book Of Mormon"* and his great regard for this written work.

I recalled as I listened that the Mormons claim the book, printed on golden plates, was given to their founder, Joseph Smith, by the "most high." The golden plates have never been produced but this does not seem to shake the Mormon's faith in the story. Reconing that the plates, being made of gold, would surface someplace someday, unlike the stone tablets in the Bible story about Moses, I had never inquired further.

My conversation with the boy missionary is continuing and it is decidedly one- sided. Knowing that these fellows have a mission and that I am their market, I am waiting for him to pop the question. At long last it came. "Have you," he finally asked, "read the *'Book of Mormon?'*"

At this juncture the conversation, though still one-sided, became mine and I began to answer his question. "No, " I said, "I have not read your book, but I do intend to read it."

I hastened to explain that most antiquarian book people do a lot of reading, but they enjoy the luxury of picking and choosing which edition they read. Some years ago, I told him, I had picked up a copy of Hawthorne's *"Blithedale Romance"* in first edition. I explained that I wanted to read this book, but only after it was rebound in full Moroccan leather. I put off reading this work until the binder's work was finished. Only then did I relax in my tilt-back green leather reading chair with my little bright red book. "From time to time," I told the missionary, "as I turned its pages, I smelled the binding." "As a result of this experience," I said, "I never think of, or see a book by Hawthorne, but that the smell of Moroccan leather returns."

This is but one example of waiting until the right edition of a book surfaces before having at it. "Now, as concerns the *'Book of Mormon,'*" I said, "I intend to read it too, but only off the golden plates, and this as soon as your people come up with them." Before I could finish my last sentence, I was talking to an empty davenport. "Please, if you will, let me know when this happens." I'm still waiting.

Big time book dealers of old, such as Rosenbach, Everett, Randolph, Targ, and others regale us in their autobiographies with endless tales of successful book and ephemera sales. Bought for a pittance one day and disposed of shortly after for a king's ransom seems to be the whole story to hear them tell it. Life stories such as these are filled with success stories. Exciting reading, yes, but because they tell little else about the book business these tales, though true, are not the whole story; they tend, I believe, to be misleading.

After reading several of these autobiographies one is lead to believe that my theory about acquiring inventory and allowing it to collect dust as it ages is contrary to what these old boys have done. I agree there would be little to write about if all we did was buy books and hold on to them. Scribbling about this would be like putting out a thriller about watching paint dry.

Although they don't go into raptures about it in the stories of their lives I know that Rosenbach and the others were accumulating good material as they went along; the profits from the spectacular sales allowed them to do this. After all, most books cannot be sold shortly after they are acquired. Many must be held for years.

So I say again that though they don't write about it these super successful booksellers did what I have always done. They too accumulated inventory. We know this by reading the auction catalogs prepared when these stocks were liquidated after these moguls passed on. The catalogs of these sales are real drool feasts.

Under capitalization mandates that some dealers sell any glittering acquisitions quickly in order to keep their enterprise rolling. Monthly rent and the light bill can be the deadly enemy of book stock building.

Some booksellers march to a different drummer. Mazuma, the coin of the realm, or dollars if you will, is their God, not books. Books to these folks are but articles of commerce to be turned into money as soon as possible. One fellow I know marks his books with the date of acquisition. This is not a bad practice but he does it so that when a book has been around too long it is shoved out the door;

the price is reduced or it becomes a part of a sale lot to be liquidated at any price Accumulating a stock of money, not well-rounded inventory, is the thrust here.

Some old time book dealers were interested in only selling enough books to cover their meager living expenses. Living in the dingy back room of their shops, where their culinary wants consisted of stale bread, moldy cheese, and warm beer, their only interest was reading and the accumulation of more books. They abided as few interruptions to their reading as possible. Taking their customer's money seemed like an imposition. Getting their smudged fly-specked glasses focused back on the printed page of the book they were consuming seemed to be all that interested them. These old-timers were satisfied with their lives and wouldn't have traded with the King of England. Spending their time reading and presiding over a growing book inventory was their be all and end all. They had what they wanted and were eminently satisfied.

Used by most mortals money, and its equivalents are the measuring stick of success. Bibliophiles count as successful those whose life is filled with reading, study, contemplation, and a well filled growing library, or in the case of the bibliophile in the book business, an expanding inventory of quality books. Money to these folks is not the score in the game of life. It is merely the means used to obtain the things that sustain their lifestyle and as a medium of exchange for ever more books. Vaults full of gold, large figures in bank books, stacks of greenbacks, and beautifully engraved stock certificates are all meaningless to the bibliomaniac. The score in his game of life is not Uncle Sam's dollar. Surround him with shelves of his own books and he will feel he has won the game. To each his own.

STIMULATING THE BOWELS

Constipation is not one of my problems. I'm not a doctor but I do have a sure cure for blocked innards. My wife is not a bookman but when we walk into a house where we have come to buy the library she can tell at once if the accumulation is good, bad, or indifferent. If after I look at the shelves I ask her to locate the bathroom, she knows the collection turns me on This same phenomenon works when we frequent antique shops or malls where books sometimes are offered for sale.

Knowing my failing, before we take off to look at an accumulation of books in a household or a private library, my helpmate always reminds me to "go to the bathroom." I do as she suggests but somehow I retain a reserve with which I can pay tribute to any fine book offered for sale.

When visiting great libraries like the Huntington Collection at Santa Rosa, California, or the Widner at Harvard my bowels behave very well. Neither do the Library of Congress, The Hoover Library at Stanford University, or our own Rare Book Room in the Hesbergh Library at the University of Notre Dame send me on a frantic search for a potty. In order for my large intestines to be stimulated the books I am looking at must be for sale! And they must be very desirable, and I must covet them. Some of the books that don't affect me are Reader's Digest Condensed, Book of the Month, National Geographics, and text books. Let the shelves be loaded with local history, items listed in *Howes Bibliography of Usiana*, some fine bindings in mint condition, uncommon books by collected illustrators, books containing hand-tinted botanical plates. or maybe some Civil War Regimentals and my flag goes up - the speedy search for a bathroom is on.

This penchant can be damned inconvenient when the water in the old house has been turned off. Often this is the case, particularly in the wintertime The folks who lived in the place are gone and the heirs are busily engaged in getting the place emptied out so it can be disposed of The plumbing in these places is as dead as the people whose books we came to buy. During these times Doris's urge to kill is stimulated in direct proportion to the agitation of my interior. Because the option is unthinkable she does come to my aid.

Sometimes when someone comes to the shop with a trunk load of desirable stuff the reaction is the same. Then I make a beeline for the house and Doris knows I'm on to something good, she hands me the checkbook on my way outside; all of this without any words being exchanged

I know from my observations that I am not the only person on the globe with a biblioactive rectum. I take it as a profound compliment when an individual asks to use the bathroom after a perfunctory perusal of the book shop. I know exactly what is going on. Usually it is the forerunner of beautiful music at the cash box later on. Anytime my stock excites someone to the extent they "have to go" - that's good.

It works something like this with someone who has never been to the book shop. After entering the front door and eye-balling the place briefly they exclaim, "Wow, I had no idea....." After which he or she continues to peruse the place leisurely for about ten minutes. At this point they inquire about a restroom. I send them to the house. (No room in the shop to use valuable space for a mere biffy.) Like a beautiful trout that jumped to snatch a fisherman's bait, they are hooked. The shop has done to them what it was designed to do. They are impressed. Their body language is speaking loud and clear. We have scored!

ON BANNING BOOKS

And then we have my friend Mike who has convinced himself that eventually the government will ban the printing of some books. His fear goes even further than a ban on printing. He fears that the state will actually destroy libraries and accumulations of books that contain material contrary to their concept of what is politically correct. Other independent thinkers, if pressed, might share Mike's fears. The idea is not all that far fetched given the proclivity of some in power to meddle in other people's business.

I know there are folks around who are intolerant of some of my ideas and credos. Wanting to burn my reading material would be a short step from this attitude. Considering the mentality of some we elect to warm the seats in our legislatures and appoint to staff our bureaucracy certainly adds some credence to my friend Mike's idea. Trying to legislate and regulate morality has been a way of life for these entities for years. Why not books? Governments, in the past have burned books and the censorship crowd is still hard at work. As long as two of the human species survive there will be differences of opinion. If the surviving two are you and me, you

225

know who will be wrong.

Mike has plenty of fuel to fire his belief and he has started to do something about it. I don't know if he is right or misguided, but I do admire him for acting on his belief. My friend put together a list of book titles that he considers essential and important and well worth saving for posterity. This is, he says, his bedrock list. Naturally the list includes the Greek and Roman classics but does not include much of Twentieth Century fiction, particularly that written since World War II. All such fiction wouldn't be excluded. For instance, Ayn Rand's *"Atlas Shrugged"*, because it describes the kind of world Mike is preparing himself against, would be included. Ray Bradbury's *"Farenheiht 451"*, also fiction, would certainly be conspicuously present as well. I would add Albert J. Nock's *"Our Enemy The State"* to Mike's list without question.

In order not to exceed 6000 Mike must be exceedingly selective. When I think about Mike's project and realize that the Hesbergh Library at Notre Dame has over a million volumes I wonder what he would omit or include from this inventory. Mike's task is awesome. More good books would be excluded than included. I have never seen Mike's list. When I last saw him some years ago, the list was incomplete. I'm sure I wouldn't disagree with his selections, but I know I would add one title he would not include, that being Ralph A. Casperson's *"A Northern Boyhood."* This title is not on a par with the classic philosophers. It is, however, a true-to-life picture of growing up in the early years of the Twentieth Century. Source material? Worth Preserving? Some people think so.

Many of the titles that will appear on Mike's list may as well be banned because they are unavailable today. These titles are out of print because it is not economically feasible to keep them in stock. There is little interest in some important works, so new book stores cannot afford them space on their shelves. When publishing houses were small they were run by the bookmen who founded them. These people were bookmen first and businessmen second. Thusly many books were kept in print because they were important though possibly unprofitable. Nowadays with the decline of classical education demand for many titles, once thought to be essential, has diminished. Publishers today are businessmen and perhaps not book people at all. They must keep their eye on the lower right hand corner of the profit and loss statement.

The point I am trying to make here is that Mike's inventory of books may in time be important, not because some super authority may ban certain titles. These important titles will be unavailable due to economic factors alone. Mike and the Antiquarian Bookseller will have to rescue and preserve these works.

Necessarily to a large extent Mike must rely on the used-book dealer to complete his project. His library of essential books will have to be assembled off the dusty shelves in antiquarian shops. Mike has charged himself with an enviable task.

Some years ago my friend Mike seemed to vanish so it is not possible to report on his progress. Perhaps he has gone underground with his library waiting for the ban to take effect. If I could see him I would let him know that the ban is in effect in a more subtle way than what he envisioned. To support my claim I invite you to read the best seller list each week. Enough said?

THE ODDBALL BOOK PERSON

Why does the world of books so often attract those who, to put it moderately, stray from the conventional in behavior, grooming, habits, lifestyles, and dress? Perhaps I am looking for answers from the wrong end of the question. Does bookselling, or an all un-encompassing love affair with books perchance cause a perfectly normal conventional person to change into somebody who people point to with raised eyebrows.

This change happened to me when I left the corporate world and devoted every waking hour to books. When I left the world of the regular paycheck and entered the realm of uncertain economic remuneration, people would say, "There goes that fellow who has a used-book store on Buchanan Road. I've never seen him wear anything but a jumpsuit." The remarks continue, "His name is Caasper something or other. The other day I even saw him reading one of his books in the doctor's office.......weird."

Not to be left out the second auditor switches off her brain and enters the ongoing game of gossip with, "He writes articles about the

Olden Times for the paper. Someone told me he wasted four years writing a whole book about his life as a kid, as if anyone would care. What would a guy with a beard like him have to write about?"

The other friend replies, "Ya, I know his wife. She's good looking and very nice. I wonder how she got hold of the likes of him?"

The whispering continues, "People say he quit a good job with the gas company so he would have more time to sell used books. How can they possibly make it doing that. I'll bet her family has money. Certainly his wouldn't have any."

The other partner had a few more ill-chosen remarks before they departed badly bent under their load of misconceptions about yet another bookman they actually knew nothing about. Before they went their separate ways a few more remarks were exchanged. "I haven't heard him, but they say he gives talks to various groups around Niles and South Bend. My brother says he even talked to the Rotary Club, of all things. What he has to say can't amount to much 'cause they say he doesn't charge anything for his talks."

The slander ends with this remark, "Ann Tomlinson knows his wife and she tells me he almost never watches television unless it's something historical or such rot. What a dumbbell!"

"These are the square pegs who would not fit into round holes. They went backwards when everyone else went forward, and they went forward when everyone stood still. They said nay when others said aye, and they saw black when others saw white. Despite suffering, economic and spiritual, they refused to be garmented in a straight jacket of conformity. This and no other achievment - and it is enough. For when our society no longer has a voice that will rise to decent and disagree and persist in unorthodoxy, then and only then, will man have lost his last battle and his last chance."

Irving Wallace - *"The Square Pegs"* 1957

THE IGNORANT BOOK-SELLER

Bob Redfield owns a small used-book store. He is not a book-man by any stretch of the imagination, but what he lacks in this regard he makes up by having adopted the habits and colors of a man of books. If the language afforded us only one word to describe Bob that word would be "odd." When the saying, "A little knowledge is a dangerous thing," was composed, the author had to have a person like Bob in mind. The reason he is in the book business escapes me. He is much better suited to be working in a car wash. He has an opinion on all subjects, knows practically nothing about everything and really doesn't know one book from another.

When a friend of mine decided to become a book scout and came to me for advice, I loaned him the necessary cash and gave him directions to Bob Redfield's shop, telling him to make it his first stop. After very successfully raiding Bob's shop, my friend did so well with the underpriced books he purchased there that he was in time launched him into his own book business.

Bob Redfield has one habit I envy and would like to emulate, but have not as yet done it. When a party frequents his shop spending several hours fingering and reading his inventory without making a purchase, Bob has a stock phrase for them as they glide toward the door to leave. "Next time," he shouts in a voice that would be envied by a carnival barker, "go to the library!"

SOME BOOK PEOPLE ARE DIFFERENT

For obvious reasons some of the people I am writing about in this chapter will carry fictitious names.

When I told George Johnson I was going to write about him and was going to use a name other than his own he protested. "Look, Ralph," he snorted, "I'm not ashamed about who I am or how I act, go ahead and use my correct name." So I am doing just that, the only exception in this section.

George is a printer, is well read, is largely self-educated, and lives in the world of the printed word in books, pamphlets, and broadsides. He sports a full beard and long hair and though I see a lot of him, I have only seen him more or less dressed up on two occasions. His wife managed to get him into a sports coat when they attended our book signing. (*A Northern Boyhood*). A special act of the legislature, I have heard, put him into formal attire for his son's wedding. These uncomfortable duds were doffed shortly after the ceremony. George does not believe that clothes make the man. He amply disproves the adage. A Confederate Gray uniform with the gold stars of a Colonel in the Rebel Army is George's chosen garb when on some weekends he affords himself the luxury of liberty from his cluttered print shop. The crossed sabers on the lapel of this splendid outfit indicate that his branch of service is the calvary. Indeed, George patterns himself after the fabled Southern Raider, Colonel Mosby, of those feared Mosby's Raiders.

George is convinced, without any dissent from this writer, that our politicians have made a mockery of the Constitution. It is now, he says, but a scrap of paper largely ignored by our courts, its contents completely unknown by people we are electing to run our government.

My good friend is no respecter of persons. When an FBI agent recently called on him about a paper that had rolled off his presses, George invited the man into his premises and promptly recited pertinent portions of our Constitution to him. He is proud to give these recitations not only to officers of the law - local, county, or federal, but to anyone he can get to listen. Mostly, though when his words emanate from one of our most sacred documents, they fall on barren ground. Like sowing seeds in wet concrete George's sermons rarely take root.

The first flag of the Confederacy, the Stars and Bars and the Snake Flag (Don't tread on me) of the American Revolution fly from a staff at this print shop. George's library would be the envy of The Heritage Foundation or a Constitutional scholar, if there is such a thing nowadays.

Here is a man who has created a printing business, filling a niche, out of material scrapped by others. He pays his bills, takes care of his family, and pays his taxes to a government that he knows is too big and too intrusive. It hurts George to support an entity that performs contrary to the intentions of our Founding Fathers, but he does it anyway. When you ask him why, he replies with a grin, "Because they have the guns, damn it."

George does not conform. He chews tobacco. (If he conformed he'd chew snuff, the smokeless tobacco of choice by the mainstream.) He believes in the intent of those who wrote the Constitution. He is a student of our founding documents and is well-versed in the works of the modern day philosophers who support the ideas of limited government. He is a student of the bible and can recite long passages bearing on Hebrew law from the Old Testament.

One would think that George would be looked up to in his community, that his thoughts would be in the mainstream of American thinking. Sadly, such is not the case. George is looked upon as someone who differs radically from the mainstream. George Johnson is my very good friend, and his own man.

Jay Lunt, another bookish friend, read enough to prove to his own satisfaction that the Federal Income Tax is illegal. Jay has a library on Political Science and Economic Philosophy that would rival the best in the country. Now on the shelves of his library, many of the books once rested on the stacks in Casperson's book shop. Jay had purposely avoided filing Federal Income Tax forms for a number of years. The Feds neglected to apprehend or prosecute him for his dereliction. He then threatened to bring an action against the Internal Revenue Service because they were failing to uphold their oath, that being to enforce the law. Jay's saga is a book length tale. For my purposes here, suffice it to say that Jay spent several years in the Federal hoosegow. He, too, is another of my friends who refuses to be like everyone else.

A steady stream of people passes through our bookshop. Many are normal people who conform to modern society. Some fight what society has become. Others as outlined above are strictly non-conformists. All are book lovers. I wish there was time to unwrap them all to find out what really lies beneath the outside wrapper.

Students looking for books that are not in the school library frequently come to the book shop to further implement their quest. We try to be of assistance in this search but quite often we don't have the book in question. A search of our shelves and the warehouse fails to turn up a copy

Our anger is mixed with disgust when a harried student or parent shows up looking for a title needed to fulfill an assignment when the book is not available in the school library. I can't imagine an instructor assigning a title without first checking to see if it is available in the institution's library. Usually in these cases the frantic student is facing an assignment deadline and the book is not available, Frustration reigns supreme.

Teachers who unthinkingly assign obscure titles without first checking to see if they are available should be taken on a treasure hunt in a deep dark cistern. I wish the negligent teachers could see the expression of hopelessness on their students faces when I tell them that I have never heard of the tome in question and their chances of finding it are about as good as finding a sod hut on Manhattan Island.

I do believe that when a student has need to search for a title in a book-shop, the student should do the errand, not his or her parent. Sometimes there is a question about a book's subject matter that would be of help in locating the volume. The student could provide this information. The parent cannot. Then too, getting the material together toward the successful completion of an assignment is part of the learning process. The search therefore should be done by the student.

Conducting these searches in a used-book shop teaches the student about a used-book shop, intelligence that can have inestimable value in later life. Often there are more titles available in a good shop full of used books than will ever be found in stores that vend only new books. The student will learn about new shops. He should become acquainted with used-book shops as well.

THE WAREHOUSE

The stock of a used-book shop should not reflect current buys. When glittering private libraries or fine household accumulations flow into the shop they make for an inviting inventory and the bookseller's income, if plotted on a graph, would show a very satisfying spike. Inversely, when the dry buying periods come along, and they always do, the stock of the book shop suffers.

After much thought I developed a plan which, if implemented, will erase the spikes. This plan acts as a leveler. The stock will look good all of the time, not favorable one week and sickly a month later. The idea is to price newly acquired books and hold them in a warehouse. As books are sold out of the shop they are replaced from this warehouse stock.

Using this method of restocking will level out the stream of good stuff going onto the open shelves. The buying fortunes of the bookseller, good or bad, wouldn't be reflected in the book shop stock at all. The stock would have the same mix of super books and mediocre books all of the time.

It gives me pleasure to think about this plan. It all boils down to having two book shops, one a little smaller (warehouse) than the main shop. This warehouse will have the same labeled sections as in the shop itself. For instance, if there is a railroad section in the shop there would also be a railroad section in the holding area.

Doris could see my preoccupation when I was hatching this plan in my head. The plan was firmly implanted in my mind but I was short of half the space I needed to implement it. I didn't have a warehouse. So engrossed mentally with my plan, I was distracted from my surroundings. So preoccupied was I that I neglected to don my spaghetti bib one night at dinner, resulting in a mess of bright red sauce dribbling down the front of my freshly laundered jumpsuit.

As is always her wont, Doris posed her standard question, "What's the matter? You seem to be in another world lately."

Knowing that the time had finally arrived I spilled the beans with the "chief implementor" around here. I said, "You see, I have this idea that will lead to a used-book selling revolution, but I need a warehouse."

Having ascertained that we could pay for another building, our third, Doris put on her engineering hat and a warehouse materialized on space previously occupied by junk and squirrels. To me, the mechanical moron, this was sheer magic. Doris, like Aladdin and his shining lamp, had done it again.

The warehouse was built during the summer. The place was filled with nice wooden shelving in the fall. After all of this work was done, Doris got out of the way, turned the place over to me, and my fun began. I spent many hours that winter making my new toy into a mirror-image of the main bookshop. First a list of all the subject sections in the shop was made. Then each section and aisle in the warehouse was given a letter and number to be used in a subject locator file. Labels for all the shelves and sections were made, etc., etc., which all translated into a very satisfying winter season.

By spring my holding area had been created. Our real estate taxes went up but my plan worked! Everything starts with a dream, but dreams never grow into bricks and mortar without a knowledgeable implementor on the staff.

PICKING MY BRAIN

She called herself Liz Cramer and told me that I could call her Liz. Before I had finished my business with her, I could have come up with more appropriate and descriptive things to call her.

Liz lived near the big lake in Berrien County, Michigan about fifteen miles from the bookshop. She called me on the 'phone one evening and before three minutes had elapsed I knew I had one more individual who wanted to know all there is to know about bookmanship in not over twenty minutes.

It turned out that Ms. Cramer had an assortment of books, accumulated by her late mother, which she wanted to do "something" about. The "something" was a bit murky. In a half hour 'phone conversation I attempted to field her questions ranging from what is a first edition, to how to determine if a book is priceless. This talk was not unique. She wanted to know the titles of the two books I had read to learn the book business and the one with all the prices in it.

Telling Ms. Cramer that there are many price guides, auction records, and books about books, and that becoming a knowledgeable book person was not a goal accomplished in a day or two, I had the feeling my words of wisdom were falling on concrete.

This intelligence didn't have much effect on my adversary. Usually I'm quite convincing, but I got the impression I was failing big-time with Liz.

After awhile I was able to ascertain that she wanted to sell her accumulation of books. She would bring me the books all right, but she also wanted to be let in on the magic she was sure I was keeping from her. She was convinced that I could impart information to her that would serve her in good stead when she stumbled upon used books in the future. Liz was satisfied that each book I looked at spoke to me, telling me what it was worth. She gave the impression that she believed I could tell her what there was about a book that prompted me to want it.

At last my new found friend (?) arrived at the shop with her car trunk full of a motley mildewed collection of book club editions. Ninety-eight percent of the lot would have insulted the local landfill, but I was able to rescue a hand full that I could use. Picking them out, putting them in my cart, and my offer being accepted, I thought I was finished.

This Cramer lady had other ideas. She poked around in the cart among the books I had just bought and paid for. Picking up a "Everyman's Library" copy of the Roman poet Ovid, she held it before me and asked, "Why is this little book so special? What is there about it that makes it desirable? Why do you want it?"

My quiet reply, though muted, delivered the same result as a bombshell. After hearing what I said Liz, frowning, quickly assumed a defeated continence and, beating a hasty retreat, drove off. In answer to her query about the little green Everyman's book, I said, "I selected that book because I have a customer, a Seventh-Day Adventist minister, who collects 'Everyman's Library' books."

INTERIOR DECORATORS

On occasion Antiquarian book dealers are asked to put together a collection of books by the foot to be used for decoration in a house, office, restaurant, or other space inhabited by those who have no particular interest in books. In these cases the buyer wants books, just books. The contents of the book is of no consequence. Maybe the color of the book is important and maybe the request is for leather bindings, but what the author wrote makes no difference. Be the request for twelve feet of books or three red and three blue books, all of these orders are welcome because we are in the book-selling business.

One time a man called asking, "did we have leather-bound books." I answered his query in the affirmative and he then wanted to know if we had a large stock of these items. I told him that size is relative and he should come and take a look. Only by doing this could he ascertain the size of our stock. Later, upon visiting the shop, he agreed we had more than enough bindings to fill his needs. He wanted to decorate his office.

Giving me a criteria other than footage made my job easy. He had budgeted $3000 for the project. "Can you fill the bill?", he asked. I assured the man that I could indeed fill his need but that I wanted to deliver the books so I could place them on the shelves myself. My customer thought that my request was strange and unnecessary. Certainly, he said, anyone could put books on shelves --- a simple matter.

After explaining that there is a right and a wrong way to shelve books for esthetic effect, the man agreed to let me do it. Shelve the books incorrectly, I explained, and your office will look like a tired flea market stall. Correct placement will create the effect of a gentleman's well-ordered library.

With this sale concluded all I had to do was "regrow" my fine-binding stock which was done quite quickly. Such a task would be more difficult today, Old leather in fine condition is hiding today and does not surface as readily as it did a few years ago.

The first time I worked with a decorator was difficult for me. I had not gotten used to people who just wanted books on their shelves to look at. Reading the books held no interest. The contents of the volumes is immaterial to the interior decorator.

One time, in my green days, a decorator called needing sixty feet of books to fill the shelves in an old mansion she was decorating for a young gentleman. Sixty feet of empty shelving is a book accumulator's dream. This big gaping, yawning space terrified the decorator -- a problem.

I told my prospective customer that she will need six hundred books to fill the space. using a rule of thumb average of ten books per foot. It seemed the lady dropped the telephone when she heard these figures. Regaining her composure, it was my turn to be shocked when she asked if I could come up with this quantity and said that the subject matter was of no consequence.

My prospective customer seemed to evidence some disgust following my inquiry concerning the subject matter of the wanted books. I had never worked with a decorator before and it was becoming apparent that my caller was having her premier experience with a book lover. Our train, very near to derailment, completely jumped the track when the exasperated-sounding decorator said, "Look, the man who is having the mansion restored has no interest in books, but the shelves are glaringly there and leaving them unfilled makes the place look like an ancient grandma without her dentures."

Meekly, I said, "Do you mean to tell me you are willing to spend $100 just to fill those shelves?"

By this time our encounter is becoming a little adversarial when she said, "We are willing to spend whatever it takes to fill those shelves. Do you have six hundred books?" She continued, slowing down a little, by saying (rather plaintively, I thought), "Mr. Casperson, I need six hundred books today and will come and pick them up at three o'clock this afternoon."

Hurriedly I said, "I will box up the books and will have them stacked on the screened patio behind the house. They will be ready by three o'clock. Just leave the check under the rug. I won't be there." As this conversation ended, I had the feeling that I had had enough contact with people who held my life blood in such low esteem.

Lots of buying errors were made in those early years, so I had no trouble finding six hundred mistakes.

A person who looks at books as so much brick and cement, or pretty wall paper, is a person I have no interest in meeting. Leaving the premises after piling the boxes on the patio, we returned at six o'clock to find the boxes gone. The check was under the rug.

M.T.

Places of advanced learning are places I have not frequented on a formal basis. As a consequence I don't, like those who went to college, have any letters following my name. Though not formal, any education I have is self-acquired and ongoing, gleaned with the help of countless authors. Having earned the right in the Army of signing my name with "Captain" preceding it, I have earned no suffix.

When I took time to dwell on it years ago, my lack of academic credentials bothered me to some extent. What to do? A large chunk of my life had slipped away. Now it was too late to sit in the classroom to try to earn those lofty letters. The classroom is a place I can't hack now anyway. During World War II, in the process of gaining the right to use "Captain" with my name, I lost a great deal of my hearing. Extended time spent in the proximity of exploding machine gun bullets and other ordinance is not good for tender ear-drums. My disability exempts me from jury duty - a plus. But it also prevents me from wearing a mortar-board. that is, if I have to earn it by straining to hear what the professor in a classroom has to tell me. In this guise, the ivy covered walls of the halls of academia are closed to me forever.

Thinking about this one quiet afternoon, when the shop was closed, I decided to do something about coming up with those missing letters. The impossibility of attaining the missing tabs was clear to me. I realized, though, that I didn't win the prefix to my name by giving up. If I could get the "Captain" for the first part, then I would let nothing stand in my way to acquire those big letters for the after-end as well.

So...I began to ask myself some questions. What course of study would one pursue to prepare himself for "Antiquarian

Bookmanship?" No formal courses are offered, as far as I knew then, to prepare a person to operate in this field. Okay, then, what should a body study to prepare for a career in the used-book field? What do you have to know? You aspire to fill a building with books in every field of human knowledge. A book-store with a general stock is your aim. One person, I thought, can't possible know everything there is to know about all these disciplines from Anatomy to Zoology, and everything in between. Plus, it is essential to have a good working knowledge of the physical book itself, along with at least a little business know-how (buy low, sell high for a starter).

Our budding bibliophile needs to know about books from fishing to physics, art to karate, architecture to H.G. Wells. He has to know something about fine literature written in England, America, Germany, and every other region of the world along with the history of Idaho. Our bookman should be conversant with atomic physics, various religions, popular fiction, and philosophy. Being able to talk about art, mathematics, antiques, fine bindings, hunting, the American Civil War, and even pornography, he must know a little about hundreds of subjects.

Finally I arrived at the answer. A Liberal Arts course and years of independent reading, and study in every subject under the sun would be the proper course to follow on the road to Bookmanship. The more trivia and general and obscure knowledge our bookman can cram into his head, the better his preparation will be.

As the shadows lengthened that afternoon I began to realize that I had been preparing myself for Bookmanship all of my life without really being aware of it at all. Being interested in almost everything, and reading widely in just about every subject, has been my life. I had pursued the requisite course of study for sixty years, not merely four.

Post haste, without waiting for a university to do it for me, that very afternoon I conferred an academic degree upon myself. I would have a Master's Degree in Trivia. I knew at least a little about many things. I would now proudly sign my name, "Captain R. Casperson, MT."

BIOGRAPHY

Everyone has a life story, but unfortunately that tale remains untold until written. Then it becomes a biography, or if written by the one who lived it, an autobiography. Because biographies abound and there are many in used-book stores, this book wouldn't be complete without my mentioning them.

A question posed quite frequently in the book shop is, "Where are the biographies?" This is often followed by, "Are all of the biographies and autobiographies in the same place?" These generally should not all be shelved in the same section.

To support the above, let me state that all biographies are the same only in that the people being written about were born, lived, and died. There the similarity ceases. The differences in biographies are much more numerous that the similarities. What the subject people did with their lives should determine where the book is shelved.

In our shop we have no one biography section. There are many sections that contain biographies. The literary biography section contains records of lives of writers and poets. Graphic artists have their own section, as do theologians, American historical figures, US presidents, and people who have made their mark in commerce and industry.

If we don't have enough biographies to form a respectable section, these books find their way into subject sections where the person spent his life: World Wars, Musicians, Stage Players, Actors, Aviators, etc.

For the purpose of organizing a used book store, it is my opinion that biography, as a category, is meaningless. To coin a word, how the biographees spent their lives is what counts.

PAPER-BACKS

Some of the uninitiated visiting the shop for the first time ask, "Where are the paper-backs?'

As they enter the front door, a casual look would reveal any number of soft-cover books shelved among their hard-backed brothers. My answer to the inquiry concerning the location of the paper-backs used to be, "All over the place, just look about you."

The rejoinder to my answer was, "Ya, I see, but I mean the paper-backs." After awhile I was able to translate their words into contemporary usage. Translated, this question really means, "Where are the Romance novels, Mysteries, Westerns, Science Fiction, etc.?"

The word paper-back shouldn't denote subject matter within the book but how a book is constructed. Does the book have a hard or soft cover? After all, treatises on Atomic Physics and Anatomy are sometimes bound in paper, as are Agatha Christie's thrilling mystery stories.

If the paper-back question were the only language peculiarity we who deal with the modern public had to deal with, we could count ourselves fortunate. Sometimes I feel like telling folks that I am fluent in English and speak a little Italian and Norwegian, but would appreciate, if they wish to communicate with me that they, "Open your mouth, enunciate properly with reasonable force - in English, please."

AGE & VALUE

The general public harbors the mistaken notion that an old book is a valuable book. This idea, I believe, stems from the antique trade where the age of an artifact is important in establishing its value. In book evaluation age is but one of a number of criteria that comes into play. Because this misconception is so ingrained and widespread in the mind of the public, it is important that it be refuted. Because of its importance, I have mentioned it in other chapters of this book. In this case repetition is no vice.

The uninitiated listen in disbelief when I belabor the subject. "An old book is a valuable book" seems to be a part of some sort of universal credo. Talks with other dealers reveal that they, too, battle this same problem.

Age is only relative anyway. A book printed in 1940 is old to someone born in 1965, or later. To me a work doesn't begin to have a white beard until it is at least 100 years old. It is necessary to constantly stress the other factors that come into play in a book evaluation: topography, paper, binding, edition, author, condition, to name some. In the end, value all boils down to supply and demand.

It is difficult to impress the foregoing facts on a person who has an "old" book to sell. As a last resort I have come up with a ploy that tends to settle the argument. When a seller is bending my ear and twisting my arm about the value of his book, based on age alone, I play my ace. Reaching casually to a shelf of old books near my desk, I select a tome printed in the last quarter of the Eighteenth Century. I hand the book, a nondescript nothing, dated 1776 and priced at four dollars, to my adversary. The person with the "old" book has little more to say after I say to him, "Please note the date and the price."

IGNORING "VALUABLE" BOOKS

On some occasions when I am invited into a house to buy a private library or household accumulation, the seller has a pre-conceived notion about the value of some of the books. Usually the books I've come to look at are part of an estate and the heir has no interest in, or knowledge of, books. In spite of his ignorance, or maybe because of it, he has segregated out a small pile of books for my special consideration. I am told that these books are very old and therefore very valuable. It is almost a rule in the book business that this kind of opinion is wrong.

The scenario goes something like this: Once in the house you are ushered into the basement, garage, or spare room where the books are stored. They are stacked in piles, boxes, or if you're lucky they are still on bookshelves. (I hate to bend over.) Sometimes there is a small stack of books off to one side. The seller directs your attention to this small pile. Usually these books are old and tattered (beaten up) or they have been written by a well-known author. The seller then tells you that he has been informed that these books are "valuable, 'cause you can see they are very old." An incomplete set of Shakespeare is the centerpiece of this pile of junk. It would be consigned to the wastebasket if it had the effrontery to sneak into our shop. A Book-Of-The-Month Club Hemingway title, sans the dust jacket, along with a chewed up copy of *Treasure Island* completes the pile of "special books" that the seller's neighbor, who helps out at the local library and is a book expert, has adjudicated as worth a small fortune. You are told that this self-styled expert says that the Shakespeare is very rare and the Hemmingway is a first edition.

Even if there is something in this special hoard that is of slight interest to me, which is hardly ever the case, I completely ignore the gems. I don't buy any of them.

After I have bought and paid for what I want from the rest of the books and I am ready to leave, I'm invariably asked why I'm not interested in the "better books." I either brush off the inquiry with a non-committal remark and make my departure, or if I feel adventurous, I say something like this, "Because of their value, as appraised by your neighbor, I would suggest that you sell them to him. After all, he knows their value. I don't have that kind of money."

UNWANTED TREASURES

An accumulation of *The National Geographic Magazine* is an item that people call about most often when they have things to sell. It is a wasted call because I don't buy them. It's a shame that such a desirable item is so unwanted. When I was a kid, I was told that it is against federal law to destroy a *National Geographic Magazine.* Maybe it is - is that why there are so many around?

HONESTY IS THE ONLY OPTION

In the month of March, some years ago, we were buying books in the back room of a Chicago bookshop. Noon hour came and the proprietor went out to lunch. My wife, Doris, and I continued to go through the shelves in the shop's store room. I asked Doris to make up a set of *Sanberg's Lincoln.* The search continued until I heard Doris squeal from across the large cluttered room. She held volume one of *The Prairie Years* in her hand. It was open and had money laid in between the pages. There were paper bills in large denominations and several checks dated July of the previous year. When I handed the book to the proprietor, upon his return from lunch, he told us the story.

The previous summer he had hired some temporary help. The shop is located in a relatively high crime area and it was subject to holdups. Because of this unhappy fact, the new cashier was instructed to hide the surplus cash in volume one of a boxed set of *Sandberg's Lincoln* in the back room. The new cashier put the money in volume one all right, but it was the wrong one.

THEY GROW UP

We have had our shop long enough so that the babies that parents brought into the shop years ago are now teenagers. Recently I told one cute teenage girl that I remembered her mother changing her diapers on the office couch. My remark went over like I should have expected it to - leaden.

DON'T TOUCH THAT SIGN

One day we had to take our sign down to have it repainted. My ego got a good trip when a regular customer burst into the shop and exclaimed, "Oh, thank God you're here! The sign is gone and I thought you went out of business. I just love this place and I couldn't stand it if you weren't here." Nice listening.

WHAT TO SAVE

A fellow book dealer who earlier in life had been an antique dealer, and I were spending an enjoyable afternoon talking books. In time the conversation turned to aging and value. We were talking about what to save and preserve today that would be valuable tomorrow. We talked about the things we had discarded or which we could have collected years ago that are collectibles today. Things that came to mind were bottles, watches, military artifacts, Disney items, Lionel trains, books, comic books, and iron toys. The list is endless.

No conclusions were reached concerning what we should be squirreling away right now. We couldn't focus on anything so we decided that the thing to do was to buy a ten acre lot, put it all under roof, and save everything.

PRICING THEORY

One afternoon I was in the shop with Don Allen. We were having a lengthy talk about book pricing theory. This went on for quite awhile. Near the end of the talk we tried to put our theories in one cogent sentence. Finally Don came up with it. He said, "I would sum it all up this way. If a book sells, it is priced too low."

SOLVING A PROBLEM

A couple of years ago a woman visited the shop and told me unhappily that her house was cluttered with thousands of books. She seemed to be somewhat distressed about the mess in which she had to live. She only wanted to know if I would be interested in buying the books when the time came. I couldn't figure out why she didn't dispose of them right now if they were such a source of unhappiness. She left the shop telling me that she would contact me "when the time comes."

Several months went by. One day the once morose unhappy woman returned to the shop. Her face was wreathed in smiles. First she wanted to know if I remembered that she might have books for sale. I answered in the affirmative. She said, "you can come and get all the damn books; he died yesterday." On the day of the funeral I relieved her of her husband's treasures. I hope she is happy now in her empty house.

REBINDING

We have all heard the expression, "Oh, I wouldn't have that book rebound. Rebinding reduces the value." This is a case of comparing apples and eggs. Certainly a book not in its original binding is not worth as much as a book in fine condition, as issued. When a book has deteriorated to the extent that rebinding is necessary, that rebound book is certainly worth more than it was in its disbound condition. Let's get our comparisons straight.

WRITERS IN THE BOOKSHOP

One book is in print today because of a conversation in the bookshop and another is now being written for the same reason.

Robert Jackson, author of *Kriege. A Prisoner of War,* had the manuscript for his book in hand along with a number of rejection slips from publishers. He knew that I had authored a book and was seeking my advice. After reading his manuscript, I told him that because of his background in merchandising he should self-publish *Kriege.* Bob did this and his book is in its third edition and is still selling well.

One Sunday afternoon near Christmas in 1995 I was visiting in the shop with Bill and Sally Lewis of Constantine, Michigan and Darlene (Mrs. Robert) Jackson, my neighbor and friend. Bill Lewis, knowing that I scribble on occasion, asked me to write a biography of General Frank Baldwin, a military figure, who lived in Constantine, in the Nineteenth Century. I told Bill that I was working on several of my own books, so doing his bidding was out of the question. "But," I said, pointing to Darlene, "your author is sitting right there." Bill and Darlene began to talk about the project and now the biography is being written.

This is one of the things that a used-book shop is all about. A place for kindred spirits to meet. A place where good books beget more books. In my opinion we have too many places in our society where money and merchandise change hands without any intercourse between those doing and exchanging. Our bookshop is an oasis in an otherwise cultural desert. Stop by sometime and pass the time of day with us. If you stay awhile and let the place seep into your consciousness, you may agree that our bookshop is a metaphor of life.

Now that this book is finished I can safely have my say about editors without fear that they will scramble ashore and leave me all alone on the stormy seas of authorship. No pun intended here, but you can bet that one of my editors will be after me to clean up that last sentence. They all strive to keep me on the straight and narrow but maybe after reading this critique, I will be left to guide my ship alone. Like most authors I have a love/hate relationship with my editors. First of all, I hate them because I need them. Secondly, like Gilbert Chesterton, how can a writer love someone who delights in "killing his children?" Conversely, I love them because they provide the safety net between my rough manuscript and the publishable copy. The security they provide allows my thoughts to run wild paying little attention to correct composition. Even when I do pay attention to correct usage, and I still err, may God love them, they fix it all up bright and shiny and grammatically correct.

Now I'll relate what happened when I tore open, with gleeful anticipation, a package from my editor containing a chapter of my first book. My facial color turned a deep rosy red and slowly I was consumed with rage as I read her critique of what I submitted to her as faultless prose. To think that anyone had the effrontery to require changes in my superb scribbling infuriated me. I tossed the manuscript to a far corner of my desk in disgust.

My temperature moderated somewhat in a few days so I read the editor's inflammatory remarks again. This time I paid particular attention to her demands and realized just what she wanted me to do to correct the mess. She wasn't at all nice about it either. Do you think she asked that this and that be done? No, she demanded changes and rewrites with underlining, exclamation points, and lots of red ink.

This second reading left me with an entirely different emotion. The anger was gone. Now I felt helpless, disillusioned, and defeated. I just couldn't do what this vile person commanded. There is, I thought, a limit to what I can do. My editor's bright red script told me that I had reached the end. I could do nothing. Completely beaten, I shoved the manuscript to the other corner of the desk. At this point there would have been no book if I had had a handy brightly burning fireplace.

A good night's rest cleared the murk from my brain. Slowly pulling the monstrosity to the center of the desk, I decided to look at it one more time. The chapter had become just that ---a monster. It loomed large and scary, dark and obnoxious.

Reading that inhibiting red ink for the third time engendered yet another emotion. Maybe this time my Viking genes and "never give up" Nordic heritage came to the fore. I'll never know. What I do know is that I was experiencing a kind of slow, deep anger. But unlike the fury after the first reading, and hopelessness after the second, this time the frustration was absent. Determination, pushed to the fore by my submerged wrath, dominated my feelings. I finished reading the editorial notes for the third time. My fist hit the desk with a resounding wallop and I screamed, "I'll show you, God damn it!"

Much later, upon relating this incident to my editor she said, "Good, Ralph, you reacted like I hoped you would. If the young students in my writing class would respond like that I would be one happy teacher."

In my opinion, all writers need editors. A pair of eyes, other than those of their immediate family, should go over all writing on its way to publication. These eyes should be those belonging to a person well-versed in the English language -- grammar, punctuation, composition, and correct usage. A language technician is needed for this important job.

I get a little exasperated with some writers I know who claim they don't need editorial assistance. After all, writers like Ernest Hemingway and Ringgold Lardner had editors. I'm sure all of our brilliant writers had that second pair of eyes poring over their manuscripts and maybe a third and fourth pair as well.

So, as I continue to write, my butchering editors continue to spill their red ink and my blood on my manuscripts. But I pose this question, "Where are my editors when I'm staring at that blank piece of paper?"

During the many years our book shop has been in existence Doris, and I have acquired many friends, people we first met in the shop. We like to feel that all of our customers are friends, but a number have become super-close to us through mutual interests and experiences.

Some of these friendships have generated an ongoing exchange of letters. The limited space and the scope of this book does not permit the publication of all of these files, but a few are included to dramatize what can materialize from the kind of book enterprise we have created.

The following is by "Punkie", the lady who baby-sits the shop on those rare occasions when Doris and I can escape for a few days. She also spoils me by putting books on the shelves after I have priced them. This does deprive me of some much-needed exercise, but I'm used to it now and would have it no other way. Sometimes when she needs a change of pace she becomes an expert with the dust cloth and our shelves exhibit a happier countenance after she has rearranged them.

My family is inclined to collecting; the pack rat syndrome abounds within my genes. Aunt Bertha accumulated Notre Dame memorabilia, butterfly jewelry and sundry items connected with Gen. Douglas MacArthur. Grandma collected poetry and thread. Porcelain dolls are a passion of my sister and she has forced this aspiration upon my mother. At various times my father collected cameras and miniature machine guns. Brother Jim married a gal who loves hoarding knick knacks as much as he. And so when I lacked "a collection" of my own, think my kin were suspicious and may even have thought of genetic testing to make sure I was truly related.

A room full of books should qualify as a bona fide collection but books are as natural in my family as food in the cupboards. So I have been considering items that I could assemble and proudly display. Peel-off labels from bananas, no. Erasers, no; Gynell, my daughter, collected those. Military epaulettes, no. Ship anchors, toe nail clippers, masks used in bank robberies, no, no, no, no. Nothing seemed right until I was given a "going-away" gift in July. I didn't go away, Doris and Ralph Casperson did. So I'm puzzled why I got the gift. But, nonetheless, I received the "makings" for a collection.

There upon the book-store desk was a stack of used bookmarks with a note that read: "A going-away gift." Thus began my genuine collection: bookmarks from the Caspersons. I don't want just any bookmark. What fun would it be to go to a store and stock up on all their markers? No character, no variety, no entertainment.

Ah, but if they come from used books, they are bound to reach back into time and originate from every corner of the globe. This I say with confidence as Ralph obtains only high class and diverse literature.

Looking through the first handful I was given, there is a Santa marker from Waldenbooks, a Metropolitan Museum of Art "Pear Tree" marker, an Ames Bookstore (Whittier, California) advertisement, A Lutheran Hour prayer, a HUGS poem, a mineral water ad written in French, a German postcard of the "Bookworm" and a USA bumper sticker.

My next acquisition I found in a stack of books with this note from Ralph attached: "For the putter awayer, so you don't get lost in a book and we will never again find you." This unique marker is a hand crocheted cross in variegated light green thread. My dear Aunt Margaret, rest her soul, crocheted ones just like this, so as I add to my collection, I will envision her sitting in her favorite overstuffed chair, fingers flying, making those delicate book markers.

Today I spied a neat pile of objects that looked like they might be fodder for my unusual accumulation. Brazenly I asked for the stack of bookmarks and was given yet another load. Slowly I turned over each one and

The following is excerpted from a letter from a dear friend and author who recently turned off her computer and faded away into the mists. She and her letters will be missed.

"That picture of Ralph is a delight. Of course cameras turn toward him. I was a newspaper reporter-photographer a number of different years and times ago working for the New York Herald Tribune. I was one of the first female reporters to carry a camera. I would have gone INSTANTER to Ralph if he were there for any story. He's different and GREAT; he has personality oozing out his ears; he's intelligent and looks it. He's good copy, and you know it on sight. You would be too, Doris, except you retire behind him and do the building and control the environment to show him off."

In the next portion of the same letter she refers to the large condominium complex recently completed next to our home and shop in a wooded area that once was the dwelling place for birds, deer, woodchucks, rabbits, and field mice. Bees stole nectar from the wild flowers there. I can still taste the wild blackberries we once picked in that place. For memory's sake we are hoarding pints of jam made from the berries in the raspberry thicket. It's now gone, under blacktop and manicured sod. Only fond memories remain. I continue with my friend's letter:

"Even if condo owners are certified to have a supply of bucks they're not certified to be able to read or write. They probably won't harass or steal from you; but I shouldn't expect them to beat a pathway to the bookshop. Maybe

one or two interesting characters will show up, but don't hold your breath.
Love you dearly, and miss you very much. Come to the mountains when you get tired of the condos. Bring the BOOKSHOP."

The following letter was received from a friend after one of my essays, bemoaning the use of the language, appeared in one of the local papers.

"I was interested in your comment about the lack of reading of books in today's society. Two of my grandchildren in Indiana read practically nothing. (Their grammar is awful!) My grand-daughter in Ohio reads all the time, and I give her mother full credit for starting her to enjoy books at an early age.
My grandson in Niles gets good grades but is bored to death in school. He told me that they were studying ROMEO AND JULIET in English. Come to find out they were shown the movie of the play, which Alex thought was 'corny'.
A good article, my friend. I wish we could get more people concerned."

And from another letter received after another of my essays about language was published. My correspondent here is "in education".

"The incident you wrote about, unfortunately, rings all too true to me.... Repeated over and over all over the country.... We routinely get drop-outs who can't read or write. ...several hundreds of graduates (high school) every year who come to us, or are sent to us, by employers because their grades are so low that they can't find or keep regular employment or function adequately in society. You are absolutely right about standards and values of the parents too. Even among the well-educated parents there

*are often not the fostering and nurturing of print literacy
that children need to inoculate them with the 'reading
bug'".*

I am especially proud of the following excerpt. It comes from
James J. Kilpatrick, author of *"The Writer's Art"* and other books.
He is a syndicated columnist. His letter is in response to several
essays I sent him. These particular writings don't appear in this
book.

*"I thought the story of "Bill and Betty" was beautifully
done -- a straight-forward piece of writing, made all the
more effective by the absence of stylistic trimmings. I also
read with admiration your piece on the Great Depression.
I was born in Oklahoma in 1920, so I count myself a
survivor also."*

The following three letters, two of mine and one of hers, were
exchanged with a book shop friend. In the course of a lengthy
conversation one afternoon in the book shop I introduced her to
David Grayson, one of my favorite authors. Grayson is a
pseudonym used by the muckracker Ray Stannard Baker when he
wrote books of a light nature. Writing these books provided
relaxation for him. There are nine titles. Some are *"Adventures in
Friendship", "Adventures in Contentment", "Great Possessions",
"Adventures in Understanding", and "The Friendly Road"*.
. I made a deal with my new friend during our conversation to the
effect that if she would buy three David Grayson books, I would
refund her money if she didn't thoroughly enjoy them. Needless to
say she didn't bring the books back. Her reading them sparked the
following three letters, an exercise in pure fantasy.
December 13, 1990
Dear Alice,
*I called David Tuesday night to talk about a manuscript he
had left with me. He wasn't at home so I chatted with Mrs.
Grayson and she was slightly pissed. Said David had taken
up with a good lookin' chick who lived in a cabin in the*

woods and that's probably where he was she thought.

Then I got your card, "I spent the evening with David Grayson", and that explained where he was and Mrs. G's suspicions were right on the money. Because you are my friend I think I should tell you that Mrs. G. is overly possessive of David bordering on deep jealousy. She's a nice gal but where David and other women are concerned she can be a bitch and she's handy with firearms.

Yours for a long life. . . . .
Ralph

20 December 1990
Dear Ralph,
You are, of course, quite right. I should always include the date on correspondence. I was in such a rush the night that I wrote the note I'm amazed that I was able to write at all!!
*You see, Ralph, your warning came too late. I did just as you said. "Drop everything and read David Grayson **today"** I absolutely adored his writing and so called to thank him. Well, he was most gracious and said that he would like to meet me and especially since I was a friend of yours. I invited him for tea that very afternoon. He arrived promptly at 4 pm and we had a lovely tea in front of the fire. Those little English sandwiches, cakes, scones and all. He told stories and I asked questions and, oh, it was a wonderful time!*
It had gotten quite dark out when we heard a terrific racket down at the bottom of the hill. It seems that Mrs. Grayson had driven right through the gate, overpowered Alan, the Caretaker, and was on her way to my house. Evidently David is wildly frightened of her because he turned white as a ghost and ran out of the house and disappeared into the woods. She drove up, screamed at me that she would send for the car and spun out. That was it. I was puzzled on how she knew that he was gone. I learned from the man who came for the car that this happens quite

254

frequently with the Graysons and it's always the same scenario.

So, Ralph, thanks for the excitement but please give more thought to the authors that you recommend to me.

PS On my evening walk I scared up a ruffled grouse over on Trillium Hill.

Your book friend,
Alice

December 25, 1990
Dear Alice,

Because the area where you reside is so remote and is far removed from civilization I am sure you are unable to receive the weekly news sheet, so it is incumbent on me to bring you up to date as concerns the Graysons. After all, I do feel responsible; being as how I recommended him and all.

Well, David is in the hospital and Mrs. G. is in the county jail on an open charge (aggravated assault and battery if he lives, first degree murder if he goes on to the writer's paradise). I have seen him and feel that Mrs. G. is safe from the latter charge, but I can assure you that David will not <u>sit</u> at your fireplace or any other place for quite some time. Not comfortably that is. When Mrs. G. chased David through the woods she cradled a 12 gauge shotgun in her ample arms, loaded with 00 buckshot, nine pellets per shell. When she got within range she let fly and David received five of the pellets in his posterior. The other four pellets went astray taking out the last of an endangered Michigan fern so where she failed to make David extinct she succeeded with the fern and the DNR has a warrant out for her. I guess they don't know that she has already been incarcerated.

At any rate, in case you are worried, don't be 'cause when Mrs. G. gets over one of these violent spells she always forgets what brought it on in the first place.

I walk three days a week, two miles a day., at the Loftus Center at Notre Dame. Will keep an eye peeled for ruffled grouse the next time I go around the track.

Happy hunting,
Ralph

Following is a letter from a book shop customer and friend. Two words that become synonymous in our shop.

Dear Ralph,
An automobile, like pets, children, and even spouses, has to be trained. All our vehicles were disciplined so that they automatically turned into every Dairy Queen. The doctor frowned on all the fat in ice cream and chocolate so our car had to be "de-programmed." No easy task, I might add.
An alternative to Dairy Queen, became "fat-free" trips to Ralph Casperson's Book Shop. Our little compact auto took to the retraining program with ease and now as we cruise along the Niles-Buchanan Road, she flips on the turn signal and swings into the book shop driveway without us even guiding her. When Ralph installed the fence and we approached his establishment from the west the first few times, our car had to make some fast adjustments to the left. But Wally (that's our car's name, she's a girl) has adjusted to the friendly barricade and the small village of condos on the other side.
A good vehicle will even sense days of the week. Ours knows when it's Wed., Sat. and Sun. - the days the shop is open. We haven't trained our auto to go to a specific parking spot at Ralph's but we never park in Doris's place. She's the gal who's always coming and going & occasionally brings Ralph a plate of food.
Patiently Wally waits as we pay our respects to the bookseller. The bookseller probably wishes we'd pay more attention to the books than the conversation we always seem to develop. But there is some consolation, others partake of Ralph's good humor, book knowledge and his comfy couch. In fact, quite a few folks mosey down to the

256

*"throne room." Sometimes as we laugh and talk, I suspect
his little Trolls are taking notes on all the banter. Material
for his next book.*

*With or without a book, we stroll up to our car, happy at
having spent a few minutes amongst the rare book
treasures and with a special person and friend.*

*Wally knows her way home, she's well instructed. She only
goes to all the important places.*

Jessica Nelson, a first year college student, is highly
accomplished for a person as young as she is. She was home-
schooled and is a pianist, an avid reader, a writer, a diarist, and a
budding illustrator. Academic pursuits are only a part of her
activities. She skis and skates and as we get to know her better I'm
sure we will uncover other activities at which she excels.

Currently Jessica is the receptionist at the local YMCA where
your author does his two miles a day walking on the indoor track.
This is where I met her. Doris and I were casting about for an artist
to illustrate the cover of this book. Because Jessica is personable
and easy to talk to, we found out that she could probably provide the
art work we needed. Doris and I have given Jessica her first
commission as an illustrator. We couldn't use her pictures, but will
always treasure them.

One morning when I walked into the Y for my daily session on
the track Jessica handed me the following, a copy of her journal
covering her first trip to our book store. She came to see the shop to
get ideas for the book cover illustration.

Dec. 19, 1996

*Last night I opened the door to Mr. Casperson's book
store. A long center corridor led the way through narrow
aisles, with tons of books filling tall shelves. I wandered
along slowly staring at the many titles and covers. I pulled
down one book and read the back cover.*

*At the end of the passageway, in a small room containing
a little desk and a sizable davenport, all surrounded by
more book-filled shelves, sat Mr. Casperson reading a*

newspaper. He looked up at me through his dark-rimmed glasses. His jolly round face broke into a smile. This being the Christmas season, with Mr. C's snow-white beard I was reminded of Santa. He put his newspaper down and stood to greet me. His eyes seemed to twinkle as he said hello. This room, his office, seemed to be lined with finely bound books. Seeing many leather bound spines as I looked around in awe.

"Take your time and look around," he said, smiling.

I thanked him and began to read the labels on the shelves' small handwritten signs. Finding the section on writing, one of my major interests, I let my hand wander from book to book. I pulled this one and that one off the shelves.

The cowbell on the front door clanked as Mrs. Casperson came into the shop. I wanted to see her but she proceeded briskly on to Mr. C. I knew she had sketches and ideas for the book cover with her.

A thin bald man was quietly perusing the shelves. Mrs. C. spoke to him. Then turning in my direction and seeing me she smiled.

She showed me her sketches of what they wanted on the cover of the book. She and I decided it would look best in watercolor. She pulled some books off the shelves and we inspected their covers trying to get an idea of what would look good on theirs. After this Mrs. C left the shop but told me to come up to see her at the house before I left.

A copy of "Watership Down," the story of a rabbit, jumped off the shelf and into my hands. I loved the title and wanted to read it.

I sat on an antique piano stool near Mr. C's cluttered desk. Then he uttered some unbelievable magic words when he said, "I'm going to let you have special borrowing privileges. You may take home any book you want to read. And," he continued, "you may have for your very own any book in the writing section that you think will help you in your writing."

Sitting on the stool looking at the book I held, I could only

*smile. Strange. How do I say thank you to such an offer?
I feel like I've been handed freedom to be a writer, to be a
child of a mentor, to be allowed to grow. I've been handed
a dream.*

The following entry is from Jessica's journal dated Dec. 19,
1996, a day after her visit to the shop. This happening took place at
the reception counter at the YMCA.

*Mr. Casperson, wearing a blue hat that reminded me of
something a railroad engineer would wear, bounded
through the Y's front door and up to the counter. He
plunked a plastic bag down in front of me. As his eyes
squinted into a smile he said, "I've got to help you build
your library. Here are some books for you. Have you read
these?"*
*I stared in delight at the stack of books. "Gulliver's
Travels," "The Grapes of Wrath," "Treasure Island,"
"Ivanhoe," "Frankenstein," "Kidnapped," "The Pearl,"
"The Red Pony," and a large dictionary. I wish I had days
and days stuck in the house just to read and read and
read.*
*Looking at these literary treasures, I asked, "How do I
accept these?"*
*Mr. Casperson laughed and said, "You just take them. If
you're going to be a writer you've got to be a reader."*
*Mr. C. turned away from the desk and headed for the field-
house track, but he came back and said something that I
will always remember and I hope in my day I can emulate
what Mr. C is doing and what he said. "I am extending a
helping hand to you because through my life folks have
helped and encouraged me. I can't thank those people now
because they are gone. But you see, Jessica, my way of
thanking them is by helping you."*

"Doris computing - she is the FINAL WORD."

THE FINAL WORD

How many times has a wife wished that she could just one time have **THE FINAL WORD?** This happened frequently to me, but now that I have the opportunity, I seem to be speechless - yes, dear friends, Doris is speechless - but not for long.

Our first book, *A NORTHERN BOYHOOD*, was transcribed from Ralph's scribbling and printed on a word processor. What a challenge for both of us, but with the help and advice of many friends, especially our understanding printer, George Johnson and his wife Velma, the finished product was 'wrapped' up and was seemingly well received.

Many of you evidenced interest in the book which takes Ralph on his journey into the U.S. Army and his adventures there. Well, you still have that one to look forward to. After the word processor was put to rest and I graduated to a computer, we decided that this book, ***BIBLIO - THE INTIMATE CONFESSIONS OF A USED-BOOK DEALER,*** would be a bit easier for me to 'get my feet wet' on in getting used to the new machine.

I didn't shed as many tears just redoing these **BIBLIOS** and essays as the next one will take transcribing Ralph's scribbles of new text - but I will truly enjoy that challenge too. In fact, I'm going to use my **FINAL WORD** and insist that a sample of his scribbles be included here.

So, on with it. Ralph asked for a **FINAL WORD**, not a complete essay, so I have once again humored him. This has really been a fun manuscript to complete and he, and we both, hope that you have enjoyed the facts and fiction therein.

Stay tuned. - Unless my wonderful computer helpers begin to ignore me, you will, before too long, get yet another book - about Ralph's Army experiences.

This shows a sample of Ralph's handwriting when he is in a hurry.

The following is Doris' transcription of part of the above:

"Doris has asked in the preceding chapter that I write a few words so you all can see what she has to put up with as she translates my stuff. . . . .
. . . . .so now Doris has her sample and I am naked before my reading public."

BIBLIOGRAPHY

Alexandri

Ball, Ian - Pitcairn: Children of Mutiny

Beagehole J. C.- The Life Of Captain James Cook

Bradley, Van Allen - Gold In Your Attic, More Gold In Your Attic,
        Collector's Handbook Of Values

Brehm, Victoria

Casperson, Ralph A. - A Northern Boyhood

Curwood, James Oliver

Danielson, Bengt - Love In The South Seas

Defoe, Daniel - Robinson Crusoe

Elder, Donald - Ring Lardner

Everitt, Charles - The Adventures of a Treasure Hunter

Garland, Hamlin, Son Of The Middle Border

Grayson, David - Adventures in Friendship, Adventures in Content-
        ment, Great Possessions, Adventures In Understanding,
        The Friendly Road

Hall, James Norman, My Island Home

Hawthorne, Nathaniel - The Blithdale Romance

Henty

Heyerdahl, Thor - Fatua-Hiva, Aku Aku, Kon-Tiki, American
        Indians in the Pacific

Hill, Grace Livingston

Hoges, Robert - The Fatal Shore

Holmes, Mary J.

Howes, Wright - Bibliography of Usiana

Jackson, Darlene - Biography of Gen. Frank Baldwin

Jackson, Robert - Kriege

Kyne, Peter B.

Massie, Larry B.

Mitchener, James - Hawaii

Nock, Albert J. - Our Enemy The State

Nordhoff, Charles and James Norman Hall - Mutiny On The
        Bounty, Men Against The Sea, Pitcairn's Island, Botany
        Bay

Norgrove, Ross - Blueprint For Paradise

Pokagon, Simon - Queen Of The Woods
Rand, Ayn - Atlas Shrugged
Remarks on the Disorders of Literary Men
Rosenbach, A. S. W. - The Unpublished Memoirs, A Bookhunter's
        Holiday
Sandberg, Carl - Lincoln
Smith, H. Allen - Two Thirds Of A Coconut Tree
Stratton-Porter, Jean
Swiss Family Robinson
The Book Of Mormon
Unset, Sigrud
Wallace, Irving - The Square Pegs

INDEX